2050 – Tomorrow's Tourism

ASPECTS OF TOURISM

Series Editors: Chris Cooper *(Oxford Brookes University, UK)*, C. Michael Hall *(University of Canterbury, New Zealand)* and Dallen J. Timothy *(Arizona State University, USA)*

Aspects of Tourism is an innovative, multifaceted series, which comprises authoritative reference handbooks on global tourism regions, research volumes, texts and monographs. It is designed to provide readers with the latest thinking on tourism worldwide and push back the frontiers of tourism knowledge. The volumes are authoritative, readable and user-friendly, providing accessible sources for further research. Books in the series are commissioned to probe the relationship between tourism and cognate subject areas such as strategy, development, retailing, sport and environmental studies.

Full details of all the books in this series and of all our other publications can be found on http://www.channelviewpublications.com, or by writing to Channel View Publications, St Nicholas House, 31–34 High Street, Bristol BS1 2AW, UK.

2050 – Tomorrow's Tourism

Ian Yeoman

with Tan Li Yu Rebecca, Michelle Mars
and Mariska Wouters

CHANNEL VIEW PUBLICATIONS
Bristol • Buffalo • Toronto

To Vikki, the best raspberry top in the world

Library of Congress Cataloging in Publication Data
Yeoman, Ian.
2050 – Tomorrow's Tourism/Ian Yeoman, with Rebecca Li Yu...[et al.].
Aspects of Tourism: 55
Includes bibliographical references and index.
1. Tourism--Forecasting. I. Yu, Rebecca Li. II. Title.
G155.A1Y46 2012
338.4'791–dc23 2012009340

British Library Cataloguing in Publication Data
A catalogue entry for this book is available from the British Library.

ISBN-13: 978-1-84541-302-6 (hbk)
ISBN-13: 978-1-84541-301-9 (pbk)

Channel View Publications
UK: St Nicholas House, 31–34 High Street, Bristol BS1 2AW, UK.
USA: UTP, 2250 Military Road, Tonawanda, NY 14150, USA.
Canada: UTP, 5201 Dufferin Street, North York, Ontario M3H 5T8, Canada.

Typeset by Techset Composition Ltd., Salisbury, UK.
Printed and bound in Great Britain by Short Run Press Ltd.

Contents

Authors

Dr Ian Yeoman is eligibility the world's only professional crystal ball gazer or futurologist specializing in travel and tourism. Ian learned his trade as the scenario planner for Visit Scotland, where he established the process of futures thinking within the organisation using a variety of techniques including economic modelling, trends analysis and scenario construction. In July 2008, Ian was appointed an Associate Professor of Tourism Management at Victoria University of Wellington, New Zealand.

Ian has published extensively within the field of tourism futures, with articles published in leading academic journals such as Tourism Management, Journal of Travel Research and Journal of Vacation Marketing on a variety of topics from climate change to the future of energy and consumer trends, all within the context of travel and tourism. He is a popular speaker at conferences and was described by the UK Sunday Times as the country's leading contemporary futurologist. Ian is the holder of a number of honorary positions, including Visiting Professor at the European Tourism Futures Institute at Stenden University of Applied Sciences, Netherlands and Visiting Research Fellow at Sheffield Hallam University, England. Ian has undertaken consultancy projects for the UN World Tourism Organisation and is sought out by many organisations for advice about the future. Ian is presently undertaking research for the Ministry of Science and Innovation examining the future of tourism in New Zealand in 2050 (see www.tourism2050.com). Publications include "Tomorrow's Tourists: Scenarios and Trends" (www.tomorrowstourist.com) which looks at where the tourist will go on holiday in 2030 and what they will do. Other new titles include "Tourism and Demography" (Goodfellows 2010), "Revenue Management" (Palgrave 2010). When not doing the above, you will find him tramping, watching movies, cooking, supporting his native football team (Sunderland AFC) and adopted one (Wellington Phoenix).

With........

Tan Li Yu Rebecca is a Management Associate with Sentosa Development Corporation, Singapore and a Bachelor of Tourism Management (Honours) graduate of Victoria University of Wellington. She has been a research assistant to Dr Ian Yeoman in contribution for this book.

Dr Michelle Mars is the Research Manager for Medical Technology Association of Australia. She has published across a wide range of topics and disciplinary areas. Her areas of expertise are gender and sexuality, and disability.

Mariska Wouters currently works for Local Government New Zealand as a senior policy analyst in the area of local body governance. Her interests are tourism, conservation, and community development.

Acknowledgements

Chapter 4, *Tomorrow's Tourist: Fluid and Simple Identities* is republished with the permission of the *Journal of Globalisation Studies* Vol. 1, No. 2, pp. 118–127.

Chapter 9, *California and Metropolis Los Angeles 2050: Changing Landscapes, Cities and Climate Change* is an extended version of a book chapter which appeared in Schott, C. (2010) *Tourism and the Implications of Climate Change: Issues and Action*. Emerald Group, Bingley and reproduced with permission.

Chapter 7: Amsterdam 2050: Sex, Robots and the End of Human Trafficking. The scenario appears in Yeoman, I (2012) Robots, Men and Sex Tourism. *Futures*. Vol. 44, Issue 4, May. pp. 365–371.

Chapter 11: Shanghai: The Future of Hotels. Scenario appears in Imagine staying in a Shanghai hotel bedroom in 2050. Tan, R and Yeomen, I (2012) Research in Hospitality Management Vol. 1. No. 2. pp. 85–95.

Every reasonable effort has been made to locate, contact and acknowledge copyright owners. Any errors will be rectified in future editions.

I would like to thank the Faculty of Commerce and Administration at Victoria University of Wellington for providing a range of small research grants for the publication of this book.

I would also like to thank Tricia Lapham for painstakingly proof reading this manuscript over and over again.

Foreword 1

The Future

In 2009, the European Tourism Futures Institute was founded with its base at Stenden University of Applied Science in the Netherlands. The founders were inspired by Dr Ian Yeoman's work as a pioneer scenario planner thinking about the future of tourism. The relevance both for the industry and for education is growing. Future thinking in future labs and developing scenarios in unusual settings with different stakeholders as a way of non-linear thinking are welcome tools in tourism and also act as inspiring methods to create innovative new ideas for tourism development.

Picturing tourism destinations in 2050 as scenarios helps the tourism educators, policy makers and the tourism business to think in a structured way about the future and at the same time stimulate creative solutions and new ideas. Scenarios are like paintings and just like good quality paintings, good scenarios are based on well-thought ideas and drivers that have relevance and serve as a base for daily routine.

Following on from Ian Yeoman's *Tomorrow's Tourist* (2008) book that focused on the drivers and trends that shape tourism demand and destinations to 2030, this book takes a longer view by taking a more quantum leap into the future in order to envisage technological change, new wealth and resources. It serves as a painting that will inspire tourism educators and especially tourism students and everybody working in the tourism industry to look to the future.

Dr Falco de Klerk Wolters
Head of School Leisure and Tourism
Stenden University of Applied Sciences,
Leeuwarden
The Netherlands

Foreword 2

Travelism and Life in 2050

It is a tour de force, where a touch of science fiction is woven through serious academic research, with alternate scenarios to test his hypothesis.

Above all, it is fun to read, as Ian wanders irreverently around a world dominated by billions of Asian travellers from hundreds of megacities and where third-age tourists are still working routinely. He takes a tongue-in-cheek view of the coalescence of consumer choice and destination service through seamless shared technology which interfaces naturally with human thought.

His brilliant description of the re-invention of Amsterdam's famous night life by the use of android sex workers reads like a combination of Harold Robbins, Mr Spock and Dr Phil. But it carries a serious message about creatively confronting today's deep-rooted social challenges around sex tourism. His careful description of Korean tourists from a somewhat homogenised future, celebrating a return to today's simple life with a traditional Kimchi meal overseen by a 135-year-old chef is entirely believable, as is his analysis of Singapore's incredibly planned focus on the lucrative meetings and medical market segments.

There are a couple of places where the analysis falls a little short. First, the assumption that New Zealand would need any support to remain dominant in world class rugby ignores the lessons of history; but he nicely recovers by using this as a base for rightly covering the massive impact of sport, entertainment, telecommunications and travel. Second, his coverage of the response to climate change could put more emphasis on the fact that over the next 40 years a combination of necessary regulation, massive capital injections and dramatic technology innovations will solve those parts of the problem which humans can fix. And the unfixable will be part of our planet's future with or without humankind, as natural disasters in the previous year have again demonstrated the immense power of nature.

This book is a valuable guide for today's policy makers and practitioners; it is essential reading for students who are tomorrow's leaders and is indeed a great insight for anyone interested in life in our grandchildren's world.

Last, on a personal note, I wish he had thought of his inspirational idea of a UNWTO (United Nations World Tourism Organization) award for the best massage parlour before my retirement from the organisation.

Professor Geoffrey Lipman
Director, Greenearth.travel

Foreword 3

Looking to the Future

Knowing what will happen tomorrow has always fascinated humankind. However, predictions require not only a systemic approach but imagination and the ability to think outside of the box.

Tourism, one of the most important global economic activities today, is only a recent phenomenon. Decades of constant global growth of the tourism sector have been rarely interrupted and these have remained temporary set backs. The growth of the tourism sector is expected to continue in the decades ahead. It implies that tourism is not only an activity for an increasing number of people but also influencing an increasing number of lives, positively and negatively.

The United Nation's World Population report projected for 2300 a world population of slightly below 9 billion people – after peaking in 2075 at 9.2 billion – not much different from the figure projected for 2050. Seeing this against the experience of recent years with a population growth like never before in history, what will tourism look like by then?

Professor Ian Yeoman contributes to this question with a rich and thought-provoking analysis of tourism in the year 2050. Looking at the many interesting facets and the different scenarios unveiled is especially important from a sustainability point of view, as they help us to be better prepared, more responsible and inspire us today to find the most suitable answers for the challenges the tourism sector is facing.

Dr Dirk Glaesser
Chief – Risk and Crisis Management,
UN World Tourism Organisation, Spain

Introduction

1   An Introduction to the Future

Introduction: My Predicament

> *My first futures book,* Tomorrow's Tourist *(Yeoman, 2008) upon reflection was very linear. A series of predictions about where the tourist will go on holiday in 2030 and what they will do. Although well written and well received it was lacking something. That was a realisation that the world was changing more rapidly than I thought, so as a consequence I decided my second book would be more creative, illustrate a quantum leap into the future in order to provide a more realistic analysis of what is coming beyond a rational perspective. Hence* 2050 – Tomorrow's Tourism *is more of a real blue skies thinking book about the future of tourism.*
>
> Ian Yeoman

What Future? Scarcity of Resources or a Society of Plenty

Whether economic growth can be sustained in a finite natural world is one of the earliest and most enduring questions in economic literature. In a world where 25 million tourists (Yeoman, 2008) took an international holiday in 1950 and 100 years later it is forecasted to grow to 4.7 billion. Is such a forecast sustainable? As Krautkraemer (2005) points out, the past two centuries have seen unprecedented growth in human population and economic wellbeing for a good portion of the world. This growth has been fed by equally unprecedented natural resource consumption and environmental impacts, including conversion of large portions of the natural world to human use, prompting recurring concern about whether the world's natural resource base is capable of sustaining such growth. To some degree, this concern is supported by simple mathematics: exponential physical growth in a finite world eventually generates absurd results. For example, any positive population growth rate eventually has the population completely covering the face of the Earth and expanding rapidly into space; any positive growth rate for petroleum consumption eventually results in annual production that is greater than the mass of the Earth. As a result, economists propose a scarcity of resources where the world just runs out of space, oil, food and water.

However, it must be remembered that it was Thomas Malthus who wrote *An Essay on the Principle of Population* (Malthus & Gilbert, 2008), published from 1798 to 1826, observing that sooner or later population is checked by famine and disease. He wrote in opposition to the popular view in 18th-century Europe that saw society as improving and in principle as perfectible. He was wrong. Why? While exponential growth can be expected to lead to increasing resource scarcity, human creativity can ameliorate increased scarcity. Humans have been quite adept at finding solutions to the problem of scarce natural resources: finding more abundant substitutes for various natural resources, exploration for and discovery of new reserves, recovery and recycling of materials, and perhaps most importantly, the development of new technologies that economise on scarce natural resources or that allow the use of resources that were previously uneconomical. So, can humankind in an innovative world create a society of plenty rather than one with a scarcity of resources? This is the key question; can humankind adapt to the forthcoming drivers of ageing populations, peak oil or climate change and what does this all mean for tourism?

The purpose of this book is to illustrate the future but not provide an exact future. The chapters in this book do make you think, you might not agree with them but you will find them illuminating and thought provoking, sometimes scary and humorous, other times 'oh really' or 'I never realised that'.

Futures Studies: A Quantum Leap of Science Fiction

Although thinking about the future has always been a part of human culture (e.g. soothsayers, prophets and later 'utopians') it has only been in the past four to five decades that it has produced the academic research field known as futures studies. Futures studies is a plural term rather than the singular 'future' studies to counter the notion of *only one future*, the latter having both conceptual limitations and political implications. This pluralisation of futures opens up the territory for envisioning and creating *alternative* and *preferred futures*. While it is commonly thought that futures studies are an attempt to *predict the future* based on extrapolation from present-day trends, futures studies historically shows that there has been a shift from what Inayatullah (2002) calls single-point forecasting – as precise prediction – to scenario planning, that embraces not only one outcome but several, and then further to foresight and backcasting to map out complex, layered causal powers involved in social processes and outcomes. According to Strand

(1999), forecasting in terms of predictions is seen as a naive scientific activity among futures scholars today. In line with Blackman (1994) he further declares that futures studies is to make more informed decisions and choices when trying to manage the processes of change, rather than an engine for making predictions.

Bergman *et al.* (2010) present a useful typology of futures studies within four paradigms of thought; namely prediction, prognosis, utopia and science fiction. Predictions usually have scientific ambitions and are more precise than in the other outcomes, as they indicate mechanisms and tendencies behind the events and states. Prognoses are characterised by not being rooted in an explanation; they do not make explanatory claims about future events and states. They do, however, raise claims that the forecast really will occur. A common form of prognosis is to extrapolate empirical, usually statistical, trends. They can be very sophisticated, but the basis is that the development will continue to follow the direction that data point out. Utopias (or dystopias) are put forward without pretensions of being true and neither do they show why things are going to be the way they are said to be. The word utopia, or outopia, means 'no place' which seems to us to be a good term for forecasts that neither want to tell truths nor point out causes that are put forward without pretensions of being true. Neither do they show why things are going to be the way they are said to be. It is another thing that authors of utopias often want to offer critical truths about the society in which they live, and perhaps also indicate mechanisms behind a social development that they want to give warnings about. We call the combination of not making truth claims and indicating mechanisms behind the descriptions science fiction.

What has led Bergman *et al.* (2010) to the term is a common definition, that stresses that the literature makes explanatory claims: science fiction involves systematically altering technological, social or biological conditions and then attempting to understand the possible consequences. Science fiction writer Robert Heinlein *et al.* define science fiction as:

> realistic speculation about possible future events, based solidly on adequate knowledge of the real world, past and present, and on a thorough understanding of the nature and significance of the scientific method. (Heinlein *et al.*, 1959: 1908)

More generally, science fiction is a broad genre of fiction that often involves speculations based on current or future science or technology. Science fiction is found in books, art, television, films, games, theatre and other media. Science fiction differs from fantasy in that, within the context of the story, its imaginary elements are largely possible within scientifically established or scientifically postulated laws of nature (though *some* elements in a story might still be pure imaginative speculation). Settings may include the future or alternative time lines, and stories may depict new or speculative scientific principles, such as time travel or new technologies. As British Telecom futurist Lesley Gavin said:

> The future, as defined by science fiction movies, is already shaping our daily existence, according to BT's first female futurologist, Lesley Gavin. Speaking at today's Smart City Futures conference in Salford, greater Manchester, Gavin told the audience that there were cyborgs currently living among us.
>
> 'We are becoming more used to cyborgs in our lives. There's already over 3m in the world today, and there are probably some in the audience. People with pacemakers for example.' As well as pointing out people who are to some degree a synthesis of organism and technology, she went on to illustrate her talk with the everyday use of robots such as Leonardo, which looks like a toy along the lines of a Gremlin, but has been manufactured to help autistic children communicate.
>
> The films Blade Runner, Judge Dredd and Solyent Green may seem unlikely places to search for solutions to the issues of world overpopulation and shortage of natural resources but Gavin believes the current development of cities shows trends 'along the same sort of lines as Hollywood'.
>
> Giving an example of a couple playing Wii Tennis in the living room she pointed out that even the basis on which we build houses might need to be re-thought alongside the big issues of food production where hydroponic towers and gardening on urban roof spaces are already starting to become a reality.
>
> 'Cities are only as limited as our imagination,' she concluded. (Gavin, 2009)

The further into the future we illustrate it, that is, 2050 rather than 2025, the more uncertain that future is, and given the pace of change in the world, especially considering technological change, it seems appropriate to adopt a science fiction interpretation about the future of tourism. It was Steven Spielberg who consulted with a number of futurologists (those who discuss and talk about the future) when trying to frame the film *Minority Report*, as Healy illustrates:

> The film respects this basic point about social change, and this is the main reason its vision of the future is compelling. Spielberg's distillation of the futurologists' predictions results in a world that mixes the familiar and the new in a convincing way. John Anderton (Tom Cruise) works in an antiseptic Department of PreCrime that is all perspex and chrome,

but the city outside still has ratty back alleys, dumpsters and construction work. He drives a high-tech Lexus, recently assembled on a make-
to-order production line, out to his ex-wife's 20th-century wood-frame
house by the lake. It's convincing.

Two other features of Anderton's world stand out. The first is that retinal scanning is everywhere. It's used at work. People casually glance at
the scanner as they enter their office building. It's a tool of law enforcement. In a brilliant sequence, a team of electronic 'spiders' search for
Anderton in a low-income apartment building. The building's residents
hate the spiders but know exactly how to react to them. And most of all,
retinal ID is used to pay for what you buy and (much worse) have products personally pitched at you by smart billboards wherever you go.
(Healy, 2002)

As Healy notes, many of the predictions illustrated in *Minority Report*
are happening now; therefore if one wants to move beyond rationality,
suspend beliefs and think outside the box, a quantum leap is required,
hence in this book science fiction is used as the paradigm for futures
thinking.

Scenario Planning

One of the ways to express futures studies is by using scenarios or scenario planning. In the postmodern era, which is characterised by uncertainty and contingency, increasingly we see scenario thinking and planning
used in the public and private sectors for business and government decision
making. Facilitating strategic conversations of diverse stake holders and
embracing the complexity of their multiple perspectives, scenario planning
promotes a broader perspective of the landscape, free thinking and promoting action. Lindgren and Bandhold (2009) provide a number of rationales for
the success of the scenario planning method. First, by reducing complexity
to a finite number of divergent options, scenario planning provides a
complexity-reducing framework. Second, by availing team players to a collectively understood structure for thinking outside known parameters the
scenario framework offers a means to communicate more efficiently. Third,
the human brain relates easily to stories; the narrative thinking used in
scenario thinking matches the way the brain works, thus expanding the
brain's capacity to process information. Finally, by forcing your mind to
think in qualitatively different directions you can train your brain to think
the unthinkable.

Effective scenarios must have meaning and relevance to the key players. They must be plausible to stakeholders and enable them to imagine

themselves in the situations outlined. At the same time the scenarios must challenge the minds of these same members, they must be novel and innovative and need to move outside the framework of business as usual. In this book, scenarios (stories) are used to express what the future could be in the form of a narrative. Then those stories are explained through a number of drivers that shape that story. For example in Chapter 11, 'Shanghai 2050: The Future of Hotels', nine drivers are used, including new personal technologies and return on investment. The drivers illustrate or signpost how change could occur followed by a discussion on the implications of the scenario. It must be remembered when viewing the scenarios, they are not forecasts of the future but illustrations of how the future could be. The scenarios illustrate how a combination of drivers, which are fundamentally qualitative, could unfold. The scenarios presented in this book evoke thinking and debate, in which readers can draw their own conclusions. For a comprehensive guide on how to construct scenarios visit www.tomorrowstourist.com.

Chapter Outlines

Before I wrote this book, I had to think about how to structure it. In the beginning I just started to write, the words flowed, some chapters were written, thoughts developed and then suddenly I realised: the book was starting to be shaped around three central themes about the future, namely the driving forces of wealth, resources and technology as identified in Figure 1.1. It was one of those eureka moments.

First of all, wealth is the key determinant of tourism, as according to the UNWTO (2010) tourism demand depends strongly on the economic conditions in major generating markets. When economies grow, levels of disposable income also rise. A relatively large part of discretionary income is spent on tourism, in particular in the case of emerging economies. In reverse,

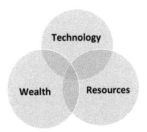

Figure 1.1 Driving forces of change

a tightening of the economic situation will often result in a decrease or trading down of tourism spending.

It is clear from a number of studies (Stancil & Dadush, 2010; Yeoman, 2008) that the world economic order is shifting with the economies of Mexico, Brazil, Russia, India and China (MBRIC) dominating this shift. Today, the G20 countries represent approximately over 85% of global GDP, 80% of world trade and 66% of the world population. The economy of the G20 is expected to grow at an average annual rate of 3.5%, rising from $38.3 trillion in 2009 to $160.0 trillion in 2050 in real dollar terms. However, over 60% of this $121 trillion dollar expansion will come from the MBRIC countries. This fundamental shift represents how the MBRIC countries will increasingly become more important as outbound travel increases from these countries.

Second, tourism distribution channels are changing now with the demise of the travel agent compared to the direct channel of the internet. Most adults have a mobile phone (and lots of children do as well) and the fixed line telephone seems to be thing of the past. It is observed that Generation X and Y do not wear watches as a mobile phone will suffice. Today, a flip point has been reached in the use of the mobile phone as Google's Claire Hatton said:

> 30% of hotel bookings in the cities of Tokyo and Seoul are on the day of arrival through the mobile phone and this trend can only grow. Today's typical tourist is pointing their mobile phone at a hotel, using augmented reality platforms to view information and then make reservations via www.expedia.com. (Hatton, 2009)

This flip point, a point where a trend becomes important, is irreversible and is now mainstream, illustrating how technology is changing, how consumers use information and how this impacts on tourism. Looking to 2050, will robots acquire human intelligence, illustrate emotions and think in an illogical manner? You may find that answer in this book.

Finally, what about the future of resources? In some countries social order has already begun to break down in the face of soaring food prices and spreading hunger. Could this be the portended collapse of global civilisation? Until recently it did not seem possible, but our failure to deal with the environmental trends that are undermining the world food economy – most importantly falling water tables, eroding soils and rising temperatures – forces the conclusion that such a collapse is possible. What if the world ran out of oil? We are at the point of peak oil or thereabouts according to Becken (2008), in which the maximum rate of global petroleum extraction is reached, after which the rate of production enters terminal decline. On the other hand, the world is increasingly paying attention as choice through competition and accessibility because of the low-cost carrier, what has emerged is the concept of fluid identity. However, as wealth decreases that identity becomes simpler, a new thriftiness and desire for simplicity emerges. This desire for simplicity is driven by inflationary pressures and falling levels of disposable incomes, squeezing the middle-class consumer. As the economies of wealth slow down, whatever the reason, new patterns of tourism consumption emerge, whether it is the desire for domestic rather than international travel or what some call the staycation.

Technology

In Chapter 5, 'Edinburgh 2050: Technological Revolution' we encounter the possibility that we will control computers via tiny brain sensors and, like magicians, move objects around with the power of our minds. Artificial intelligence will be dispersed throughout the environment, and internet-enabled contact lenses will allow us to access the world's information base or conjure up any image we desire in the blink of an eye. This chapter identifies 10 drivers that will shape and revolutionise how tourists interact with technology, whether it is brain computer interfaces or haptic technologies. Chapter 6, 'Singapore 2050: Medicine, Science and the Meetings Industry' demonstrates how complexity and the pace of discovery is changing the world of science, technology and medicine, to the extent that simple human mortals cannot keep pace with this change, and as a consequence the meetings industry has been a beneficiary. The pace and complexity of change in the medical arena, the largest sector of the meeting's industry for the last decade, means that meetings are occurring more frequently in an effort to try to keep abreast of the complexity of change. Increasingly innovation is shifting eastwards as government and industry investment in science and technology grows; for example, Singapore's creation of a knowledge cluster in the pharmaceutical and biotech industry. Capitalising on this investment, the Singapore Tourist Board has created a meeting strategy to attract medical and science conferencing. This chapter looks at the future of the medical meetings industry in Singapore driven by the complexity of scientific change. Chapter 7, 'Amsterdam 2050: Sex, Robots and the End of Human Trafficking' suggests that the future of sex tourism in Amsterdam needs an innovative solution and the use of androids as sex workers is that futuristic solution. The present situation of human trafficking, sexually transmitted infections, pressure from the local community and the threat to the destination brand means change is inevitable. The chapter is based upon a story of The Yub-Yum club, a sex club for business travellers where entry costs €10,000 for an all inclusive service in which patrons are 'serviced' by android sex workers; as a result, HIV and human trafficking is no longer a problem. The chapter discusses how such a scenario could come about, the impact and our relationship with technology.

Rugby Union, the number one sport in New Zealand and the All Blacks is the country's leading brand. Chapter 8 'New Zealand 2050: The Future of Professional Sport and Sporting Events' postulates that by 2050 demographic change will result in an ageing population and a smaller cohort of young students entering the sport. Looking to the future, how does New Zealand Rugby maintain its position as the sport of choice for participation, spectators and broadcast audiences? How do the All Blacks maintain their enviable historical winning records? Maybe, technology and science will revolutionise and enhance the game. This chapter provides a futuristic presentation of what rugby in New Zealand will look like in 2050 focusing on the professional game, sport science, interactive technologies, stadium and home experiences.

Resources

Chapter 9, '2050 California and Metropolis Los Angeles: Changing Landscapes, Cities and Climate Change' draws together the drivers of climate change, peak oil, rising sea levels and the continued scarcity of resources against a background of urbanisation. Research suggests that Los Angeles will have a climate that will be unbearable to future tourists and the rural landscape of California will undergo radical reshaping. Does this mean Los Angeles will be akin to the science fiction film *Logan's Run*, in which a reversal of fortunes occurs where ecotourism is an exclusive experience for the mega rich and tourism for the middle classes is restricted to an urban environment and controlled mass tourism excursions? Imagine a world in 2050, where the world is overcrowded and food production systems have failed. In order to feed this world, mass produced synthetic food is the norm. In Chapter 10 'Seoul 2050: The Future of Food Tourism' draws inspiration from the film *Soylent Green*, but is set in Seoul where 100 million people live mostly in housing that is dilapidated and overcrowded, and the homeless fill the street and line the fire escapes and stairways of the buildings. In this chapter, Kenny Jeong-Keun Oh and 'Liu', live in a gated community apartment complex. The community is self-sufficient in some foodstuffs due to a vertical farming system. For those that have money, real food and the cultural history of ancestors are luxury experiences. Kenny has booked an overnight stay in a traditional Korean guesthouse owned by the Yoo family in the city. This is a place where the elite of society can escape, live like their ancestors did and learn how to make Kimchi guided by Park Yoo, a 135-year-old chef. So, what does the above mean for the future of food tourism? A world where real food is the new authentic luxury? The chapter highlights a number of important drivers including food inflation, the advancement of science and the role of food in society.

Chapter 11, 'Shanghai 2050: The Future of Hotels' emphasises a future world of contemporary design, sustainability and technological innovations as the foundation of the hotel industry through highlighting the growing pains of Shanghai where pollution, competition for urban land and decreasing availability of clean water will impact on the quality and price of accommodation in the city. The chapter draws heavily on innovative solutions to the future, such as claytronics, or programmable matter. The concept of claytronics combines nanoscale robotics and computer science to integrate sight, sound and feel into original ideas, allowing users to interact with the idea physically in three-dimensional form. The applications of claytronics would be the reconfiguration of everything, so just imagine the future hotel bed that could change its degree of comfort from a hard to a soft mattress without too much effort, the possibilities are endless. Or, the room attendant as we know today may become redundant in the future. New innovations such as cleaning robots act as labour substitutes as they provide faster and smarter ways to get jobs done. The final chapter, Chapter 12, '2050: The Future of Transport', postulates that with increasing pressure caused by the surge in demand for transportation of people and products, will alternative fuels and green economy initiatives develop to the point that transportation will continue to underpin the expansion in tourism? Is investment in transport infrastructure money wisely spent? Or will oil be the flip point in a sclerosis of travel? Is there an alternative to oil? Futurist literature discusses bullet trains, hypersonic travel, fourth-generation biofuels and even teleportation. This chapter looks at the critical issues pertaining to transport and tourism, examining what transport might be in 2050. So, in the words of Captain Kirk, 'Beam me up Scotty.'

Conclusion: Utility Value

If you are interested in the future, this book is for you. Its main purpose is to inform you of the possibilities of change, what is coming next, to stir your imagination, or to enable you to take knowledge and build your own scenarios. This book does not tell you the exact future, but possibilities of alternatives in order to help you make sense of the future thus reducing uncertainty and clarifying how and when change could occur, this is its utility value. By adopting a perspective of wealth, technology and resources. A series of worlds, pictures and stories about tourism in the year 2050. Many of these scenarios are happening now but some belong to the realms of science fiction. It is up to 'you' to ask yourself the question 'What if this "did" occur?' There are many features not included in this book, especially about 'how one would behave in the future', that is, will the world be cooperative or be antagonistic towards climate change? This, will probably be the focus for my next book. In the meantime, for further details about the book, the author's blog, a guide to scenario planning and useful (or useless) information about the future visit www.tomorrowstourist.com.

Wealth

2 World Economic Order: The Tourism Economy in 2050

Learning points

- The global financial crisis has accelerated the shift of the economic balance of power from West to the South and East with consumers in emerging markets witnessing relatively rapid growth in personal spending power as their economies expand.
- The key economic drivers which will shape the transformation from West to South and East are labour force growth, capital stock, technology progress and exchange rate appreciation.
- By 2050, 60% of the world economic growth will come from Mexico, Brazil, Russia, India, Indonesia and China (MBRIIC).
- In 1950, 25 million people took an international holiday representing 1 in 1000 of the world's population. One hundred years later, 4.7 billion people will take an international holiday representing nearly 1 in 2 of the world's population.

Introduction

The world's economic balance of power is shifting rapidly, accelerated by the global financial crisis. According to Stancil and Dadush (2010), China remains on a path to overtake the United States as the world's largest economic power within a generation, and India will join both as a global leader by mid-century. Traditional Western powers will remain the wealthiest nations in terms of per capita income, but will be overtaken as the predominant world economies by much poorer countries. Prior to the Global Financial Crisis, the world's balance of economic power, as measured by real gross domestic product (GDP), was gradually shifting to the South and the East. In the coming years, the most successful developing countries, especially but not only those in Asia, will converge even more rapidly towards their advanced counterparts. Is the future a financial contagion in which a series of small shocks spread across Europe, America and the world leading to global meltdown? With travel traditionally being strongly correlated to GDP and the ageing of the population in Western countries in the long term, there will be a fall in GDP per capita. This will have a major impact on the outbound travel from Western countries such as Germany and France, which in the past has fuelled the growth of world tourism. Driving this new economic growth are the new middle classes, whose desire for lifestyle and tourism is a representation of globalisation. To some (Large & Meier, 2009) these new consumers will lead to the end of the world, due to vehicular traffic, expanding meat consumption or rising energy levels. To others, they are the hope and opportunity. This chapter explores the underlying drivers of economic growth and tourism scenarios for 2050.

Drivers of World Economic Growth

If economics is a key driver of the world tourism, what are the key drivers of the world economy and economic growth? Stancil and Dadush (2010) identify the key drivers as:

- Labour force growth.
- Capital stock.
- Technological progress and productivity.
- Exchange rate appreciation.

Labour force growth

By 2050, the labour market will grow rapidly and nearly exclusively in developing countries. These countries will see economic benefit from population growth in the working population age range, while in advanced economies labour source will contradict. Today the world population stands at 7 billion (Bloom, 2011) and will reach 9.2 billion in 2050 (UN, 2009), a large rise from the 2.5 billion in 1950. Concurrently, the global labour force is expected to expand by nearly 1.3 billion. Developing regions will see their workforces expand by 1.5 billion people – more than the total current population of developed regions – while the labour force in developed areas will shrink by over 100 million workers. Developing Africa and Asia will contribute the most to the increase, adding 1.4 billion workers to the global labour force. In contrast, Europe's working age population will decline by more than 110 million. The dependency ratio, or the number of people not in the labour force compared to those who are, will dramatically increase in developed regions, with the UN predicting that the working-age population in these areas will fall sharply from 62.8% of the total population in 2009 to 52.0% in 2050. The same measure will also decline in developing regions but only modestly, from 61.1 to 59.5. Thus, population and labour force growth will contribute to global economic growth, but all of the increase will occur in developing countries, shifting economic weight in their favour.

Capital stock

According to Stancil and Dadush:

Physical capital stocks will continue to accumulate as incomes rise and savings rates cover depreciation and allow for new investments. However, as the marginal contribution of capital to output declines, the incentive to invest will be reduced. In industrialized countries, savings as a share of GDP will likely decline as populations age and dependency ratio increases (Stancil & Dadush, 2010. 3)

For developing countries where capital-to-output ratios are much lower, stocks will rise substantially as the working population increases. An exception to this is China, despite a shrinking population investment is expected to remain high. Developed countries invest approximately 20% of GDP in fixed capital formation each year whereas developing countries invest significantly more, between 30% and 40%. Japan provides a useful case study, as its investment in capital stock can be traced through the different stages of development. Japan's yearly investment rate peaked at 36% when its economy was growing rapidly and moderated towards 20% in recent years. To 2050, China and India are expected to have the highest average investment rates at 33–34% per year while the United Kingdom and Germany are projected to invest at the lowest rate at 17–18% per year.

Technological progress and productivity

Investment in technology will restructure industries from labour- to capital-intensive, which requires degree-educated workers resulting in an increased middle-class society as described in a World Bank (2009) report on technology and development:

Part of the strong projected performance for developing countries derives from stronger labour force growth, but much can be attributed to technological progress. (World Bank, 2009: 62)

The potential for technological catch-up is greater when productivity and per capita income are low, therefore convergence of the poorest countries will potentially be the most rapid. Catch-up rates will depend on each country's ability to adopt and adapt to technology which is influenced by a number of factors including: function of openness, educational attainment, communication and transportation infrastructure, governance and business and investment environment. Thus, Russia, China and Mexico are better prepared for rapid adaptation of foreign technologies due to high levels of educational attainment and supportive infrastructure, whereas India exhibits the lowest level of education attainment and the worst business climate for innovation, according to the World Bank (2009).

Exchange rate appreciation

As productivity in developing countries increases relative to that in developed countries, wages will increase and the price of non-tradables relative to tradables will rise in developing countries, as predicted by the Balassa–Samuelson effect (Balassa, 1964). Additionally, rapid growth in emerging markets will make them more attractive for investments, increasing capital inflows to these countries. These trends will put upward pressure on exchange rates, causing real exchange rates to appreciate in developing countries. A stronger currency implies improved terms of trade and cheaper imports, which both boosts the purchasing power of consumers and lowers the cost of imported inputs, relative to the cost of labour. Higher exchange rates can also spur innovation and productivity improvement, since domestic producers must now compete with cheaper imports.

Risk: Global Economic Disorder

Is the world about to end? Some would think so, given the present economic crisis, sovereign debt in Greece, Italy, Spain, Portugal and the United States, which all leads to a next great depression. If the present economic disorder disputes cannot be resolved peacefully, at what point would Germany abandon the Euro? *The Economist* (2012) magazine suggested four scenarios for the near future. The first scenario, *Muddling Through* is the most optimistic and least likely due to inadequate political action on both sides of the Atlantic, where the sovereign debt crisis in Europe is stabilised; developed economies resume 2–3% annual growth and develop realistic plans to reduce government debt over the medium term. The second scenario, *Inflate Debt Away* is based upon ever larger doses of quantitative easing by central banks but where a surge in commodity prices pushes inflation higher. The third scenario, *Chaotic Default in Greece* involves failure to prop up the region's banks or protect Italy and Spain from collateral damage, resulting in a sharp drop in European GDP and ripple effects in the rest of the rich world. The final scenario, *Japanese Style Stagnation*, is due to inadequate political action on both sides of the Atlantic resulting in more frequent recessions being likely, followed by sluggish growth. This final scenario has resonance as turbulent financial markets are driven down in a negative spiral, as confidence in banks and stock markets disappear. Interest rates continue to rise despite national bank interventions. The national government interventions do not work as planned, and the banks' loss of capital leads to a renewed tightening of financial capital. The general willingness to take risks declines markedly. Businesses close and unemployment rises significantly. This leads to increasing protectionism, which only exacerbates the problem. Housing prices continue their decline and governments are forced to intervene. They begin to buy housing and rent it out. Governments continue large-scale capital injections into the banking system, which becomes predominately nationalised. All in all, a world of global economic disorder and not a lot of hope for tourism.

A New World Order

The weight of global economic activity is already shifting substantially from Western developed countries towards emerging economies in Asia and Latin America. From Table 2.1, this trend is expected to accelerate. The

Table 2.1 G20 GDP forecasted growth

G20 country	Average annual GDP growth	Real GDP in 2050 at 2005 US$ prices
China	5.6	46,265
USA	2.1	38,646
India	5.9	15,384
Japan	1.1	6,216
Brazil	4.1	6,020
Mexico	4.3	5,709
United Kingdom	2.1	4,997
Germany	1.4	4,535
France	2.1	4,528
Russia	3.3	4,297
Turkey	4.4	3,536
Canada	2.6	3,154
Indonesia	4.8	2,975
Korea	2.5	2,818
Italy	1.3	2,580
Saudi Arabia	4.8	2,419
Australia	2.9	2,257
South Africa	4.3	1,919
Argentina	4.1	1,267

Source: Stancil and Dadush (2010)

economy of the G20 countries is expected to grow at an average annual rate of 3.5%, rising from $38.3 trillion in 2009 to $160.0 trillion in 2050 in real dollar terms. The G20 represents over 85% of global GDP, 80% of world trade and 66% of the world population. Over 60% of this $121 trillion dollar expansion will come from six countries: Mexico, Brazil, Russia, India, Indonesia and China (MBRIIC). US dollar GDP in these six economies will grow at an average rate of 6% per year; their share of G20 GDP will rise from 19.6% in 2009 to 50.6% in 2050. In contrast, GDP in the G7 will grow by less than 2.1% annually, and their share of G20 GDP will decline from 72.3% to 40.5%.

Currently, the G7 (France, Germany, Italy, Japan, United Kingdom and Canada) claim more than half of G20 GDP compared to approximately one-third in the MBRIIC economies in 2050. The MBRIIC economies will be over twice as large as the G7. China, India and the United States will emerge as the world's three largest economies in 2050, with a total real US dollar GDP of 70% more than the GDP of all the other G20 countries combined. The growth of China and India's economy is expected to grow by US$60 trillion by 2050, the present size of the world economy. However, wide disparity in GDP per capita will still remain.

China will become the richest country in the world by 2032 due to an annual growth rate of 5.6% and a strong currency. According to Stancil and Dadush:

> The renminbi's real exchange rate against the dollar is predicted to appreciate by more than 1%—will drive China's U.S. dollar GDP up from $3.3 trillion in 2009 to $46.3 trillion in 2050, 20% larger than that of the United States in real dollar terms and 90% larger in PPP terms. (Stancil & Dadush, 2010: 10)

India is predicted to post the most rapid growth – 5.9% annually – of all G20 countries, though the current modest size of India's economy will prevent it from surpassing either China or the United States in real US dollar terms. India is expected to become the world's most populous nation in 2031 eventually pushing US$ GDP to $15.4 trillion in 2050, over 14 times its current level. The path to 2050 will be critical for the European Union (EU). Germany, the United Kingdom, France and Italy – currently the fourth through seventh largest economies in the world – are expected to grow by only 1.5% annually from now until 2050. Forecasters expect these four countries share of the G20 GDP to shrink from 24% in 2010 to 10% in 2050. Real GDP in Brazil and Mexico is expected to increase by over 4% per year, nearly matching the GDP of today's second-largest economy, Japan. Japan's political and economic influence is waning with a poor long-term growth rate of 1.1%, the slowest rate of all the G20 countries.

The New Consumer

Rising income (and the wealth improvement connected with it) has been the driving agent of modern society; a key indicator of societal success and responsible for the empowerment of consumers in relation to companies, brands and governments (Yeoman, 2008). Increased personal prosperity creates an emboldened consumer-citizen, a more demanding, sophisticated and informed actor with intensified expectations of, for instance, quality innovation and premium choices in every market; of efficient and ever-personalised customer service; of visible corporate commitment to tackling the environmental and ethical problems of the day. Following the emergence of the Global Financial Crisis, one might have anticipated a rebalancing of power within the consumer–company relationship as consumers in several developed markets witnessed marked declines in both spending power and in the value of key symbols of personal wealth (e.g. housing). However, contended material and psychological shock of affluence interruption has paradoxically emboldened consumers further. Consumers in emerging markets are witnessing relatively rapid growth in personal spending power as their economies expand. While parity with developed markets is still some way off (US GDP per capita in real terms, for instance, is 10 times that of China – Figure 2.1), as personal prosperity in emerging markets rises, so millions more consumers will, as has traditionally been the case in the developed West, enjoy greater discretionary spending power and a more varied

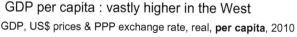
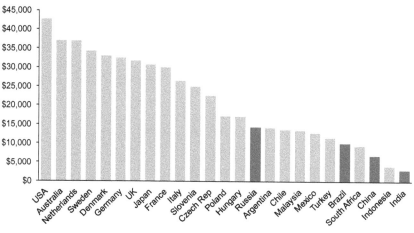

Figure 2.1 GDP per capita
(*Source:* Future Foundation)

consumption portfolio. This will hugely diversify newly enfranchised middle-class consumer demands, with brands and companies invited to creatively 'welcome' new market entrants and to ultimately sustain profitable relationships as consumers progressively climb the income ladder.

The Future Foundation (2011) notes developing market consumers have strong aspirations to accumulate and enjoy quality products, enhanced leisure and travel experiences and all manner of services previously unattainable. Populations are also more optimistic about their prospects; it is a widely held belief in countries such as Russia and India that future generations will enjoy significantly greater prosperity in their lives than citizens have enjoyed so far (Figure 2.2).

The MBRIIC countries are the most optimistic about improving prosperity for future generations when compared with Western European nations and other developed markets. From a global perspective, the middle classes are growing and new found wealth is diversifying the spending power of millions. Price sensitivity is nevertheless an embedded consumer value and is prompting many consumers to monitor their spending and finances ever more carefully. Over six in 10 of the more urban wealthy Chinese, Brazilian and Indian consumers surveyed by the Future Foundation (2011) agree that they budget carefully each month. The expansion of the global middle class is the dynamism of the age. Millions of consumers can now afford a greater level of choice in every theatre of their lives. The expanding wealth of developing markets at impressive pace will be one of the key drivers impacting on the global consumer landscape as we progress, creating new demand and market opportunities. The appetite for luxury goods, for example, is something we expect to

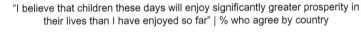

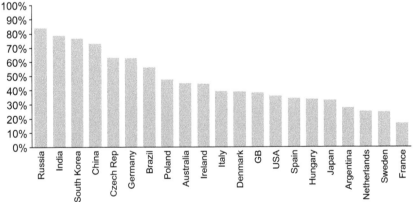

Figure 2.2 Consumer prosperity
(*Source:* Future Foundation)

continue to grow rapidly as more affluent consumers seek new levels of quality consumption. This is the big story of the future of MBRIIC consumerism. In developed economies recently affected by recession, many behaviours adopted by consumers in reaction to a period of economic turbulence continue to bear a sustained influence over spending and budgeting. Confronted with the pressures of living under a period of relative austerity, a keen focus on value-for-money will be at the front of many consumers' minds. The Future Foundation (2011) attest that price will become even more influential in shaping consumer perceptions of value and will encourage more and more consumers to use multiple methods to find the best prices.

How Does Economics Shape World Tourism?

An important advantage of tourism is the fact that it has in general, high income elasticity. This means that a relatively large part of discretionary income is likely to be spent on tourism, particularly in the case of emerging economies with burgeoning middle-class populations. Outbound travel from China, for example, increased 338% between 2000 and 2008. This trend is likely to continue. Inbound travel also increases alongside GDP with arrivals to India having increased in the same 10-year period by 93%. As industrialised countries slowly recover from the recent global recession, developing countries, with lower losses during the crisis, will accelerate out converging rapidly towards their advanced counterparts. According to the UNWTO, the relationship between the world economy and tourism is summarised as follows:

> Tourism demand depends above all on strong economic conditions in major generating markets. When economies grow, levels of disposable income will usually also rise. A relatively large part of discretionary income will typically be spent on tourism, in particular in the case of emerging economies. A tightening of the economic situation on the other hand, will often result in a decrease or trading down of tourism spending. (UNWTO, 2010)

As a consequence, Figure 2.3 shows that the growth of international tourism arrivals significantly outpaces growth of economic output as measured in GDP. In years when world economic growth exceeds 4%, the growth of tourism volume tends to be higher. When GDP growth falls below 2%, tourism growth slows down. With a GDP at 3.5%, tourism grew on average 1.3 times faster than GDP. In the period 1975–2000, tourism increased at an average rate of 4.6% per annum.

According to tourism economist Adam Sachs (2010), travel demand tends to have an income elasticity above 1.0. This means that travel growth tends to be faster than GDP growth, but correspondingly drops by more than falls

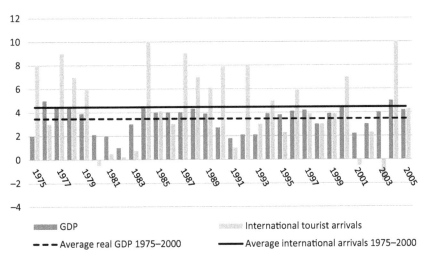

Figure 2.3 Economic growth (GDP) and International tourist arrivals
(*Source:* IMF & UNWTO)

in GDP during recessions. Adam (2010), points to this effect by noting that global international arrivals generally exceeded global GDP growth of around 4% per annum between 2004 and 2007. Conversely, recessions may be especially pronounced in some sections of the travel industry.

A New World Order: China and India

Table 2.2 reflects the rise of outbound travel from the G20 countries, with the developing economies China and India leading the way. Between 2000 and 2008, outbound travel from China and India has grown 338% and 146%, respectively. Other emerging economies such as Russia (99%), Indonesia (57%) and Turkey (87%) led the way with percentage increases whereas traditional developed economies of the United States (4%), Japan (−10%) and Germany (−2%) show evidence of stagnation and decline. So, who will be the future tourist? China and India in 2050 will be the first and third largest economy in the world, with average GDP growth rates of 5.6% and 5.9%, respectively per annum.

Between 2000 and 2008, India's outbound travel has increased by 146% to an estimated 10,868 million, totalling international tourism expenditure to US$12.1 billion in 2008. By 2020, India will account for 50 million outbound tourists, with total outbound spending projected to cross the US$28 billion mark as mentioned in Kuoni (2008). India's outbound travel market is wide and complex because of its size and variety. According to Pacific Asia Travel Association (PATA), 40% of all outbound trips by Indians are for business

Table 2.2 Outbound departures from source country (,000)

Country	2000	2001	2002	2003	2004	2005	2006	2007	2008	2000–2008 outbound increase/ decrease
Republic of Korea	5,508	6,084	7,123	7,086	8,826	10,080	11,610	13,325	11,996	118%
Argentina	4,953	4,762	3,008	3,088	3,904	3,894	3,892	4,167	4,611	–7%
Australia	3,498	3,443	3,461	3,388	4,369	4,756	4,941	5,462	5,808	69%
Brazil	3,228	2,674	2,338	3,225	3,701	4,667	4,625	4,823	4,936	53%
Canada	19,182	18,359	17,705	17,739	19,595	21,099	22,732	25,163	27,037	41%
China	10,473	12,133	16,602	20,222	28,853	31,026	34,524	40,954	45,844	338%
France	19,886	19,265	18,315	18,576	21,131	24,800	25,080	25,139	23,347	17%
Germany	74,400	76,400	73,300	74,600	72,300	77,400	71,200	70,400	73,000	–2%
India	4,416	4,564	4,940	5,351	–	7,185	8,340	9,783	10,868	146%
Indonesia	–	–	–	3,491	3,941	4,106	4,967	5,158	5,486	57%
Italy	21,993	22,421	25,126	26,817	23,349	24,796	25,697	27,734	28,284	29%
Japan	17,819	16,216	16,523	13,296	16,831	17,404	17,535	17,295	15,987	–10%
Mexico	11,079	12,075	11,948	11,044	12,494	13,305	14,002	15,083	14,450	30%
Russia	18,371	18,030	20,428	20,572	24,507	28,416	29,107	34,285	36,538	99%
Saudi Arabia	–	–	7,896	4,104	3,811	4,403	2,000	4,126	4,087	–48%
South Africa	3,834	3,733	3,794	–	–	–	4,339	4,433	4,429	16%
Turkey	5,284	4,856	5,131	5,928	7,299	8,246	8,275	8,938	9,873	87%
UK	56,837	58,281	59,377	61,424	64,194	66,494	69,536	69,450	69,011	21%
USA	61,327	59,442	58,066	56,250	61,809	63,503	63,662	64,028	63,684	4%
Spain	4,100	4,139	3,871	4,094	5,121	10,464	10,678	11,276	11,229	174%
Belgium	7,932	6,570	6,773	7,268	8,783	9,327	7,852	8,371	8,887	12%

Source: UNWTO

purposes, while 20% are for leisure, visiting friends and relatives (VFR) (Travelmole, 2007). The United Nations World Tourism Organisation and European Travel Commission (2009) identify that international leisure travellers belong to the 25–65 years age group, are well educated and belong to the upper socio-economic strata of society. The Indian market is family oriented with two-thirds of leisure travellers taking holidays with their families. The top five factors that influence destination selection for Indians are safety and security; variety of things to see and do; overall image of holiday destination; good tourist facilities and infrastructure; and the ease of obtaining visas.

China is one of the fastest-growing outbound travel markets in the world today, driven primarily by rapid urbanisation, rising disposable incomes and relaxations on overseas travel. Outbound tourism has grown by 338% since 2000 and reached 27,037 million in 2008. Despite the growth, over 70% of Chinese outbound tourism is to the Chinese Special Administrative Regions (SARs) of Hong Kong and Macao. Around half of the rest are 'border' visitors, on day trips to Russia, Vietnam and Laos for trade and/or shopping.

It is understandable that China is treated as a single, homogenous market. However, geographical and cultural differences in different operating environments can create huge variations and significantly influence demand. The following brief summary draws together a number of reports as highlighted by the UNWTO and the ETA (United Nations World Tourism Organisation and European Travel Commission, 2009) on Chinese outbound tourists as follows:

- The proportion of female-to-male travellers is relatively balanced, with a ratio of 53:47, respectively.
- Around 50% of outbound travellers are aged between 25 and 44 years old, an age segment widely considered with the best growth potential. Long-haul destinations such as Europe and Australia are more popular with Chinese tourists in the 45-plus age group, a number set to increase sharply in future.
- At least 70% of outbound travellers are travelling for leisure purposes, with a majority to North Asia and some destinations in Europe.
- The major urban centres of Beijing, Shanghai, Guangzhou and Shenzhen account for most of the outbound travel demand among Chinese tourists.
- Group travel numbers are still high (60% overall and 80% for first timers), but is falling.

What are the Prospects for World Tourism in 2050?

Forecasting, by its very nature, is a hazardous exercise. Projecting future international tourism flows has become more difficult over time, because,

Table 2.3 Best-case scenario

Arrivals	Base year (million)	Forecast (million)		Average annual growth rate (%)	Market share (%)	
	2010	2025	2050	2010–2050	2010	2050
Europe	475.3	621.1	970.2	1.8	50.7	23.3
Asia and the Pacific	204.0	488.9	2098.3	6.0	21.7	50.3
Americas	149.7	247.2	570.2	3.4	15.9	13.7
Africa	50.3	90.6	241.5	4.0	5.2	5.8
Middle East	60.9	109.7	292.4	4.0	6.4	7.0
Total	940.2	1557.5	4172.6	3.8	100.0	100.0
Arrivals	Base year (US$ billion)	Forecast (US$ billion)		Average annual growth rate (%)	Market share (%)	
	2010	2025	2050	2010–2050	2010	2050
Europe	410.9	537.0	838.8	1.8	44.2	17.6
Asia and the Pacific	203.1	522.3	2521.7	6.5	27.1	52.9
Americas	166.2	299.3	797.9	4.0	19.8	16.8
Africa	28.8	51.9	138.3	4.0	3.4	2.9
Middle East	42.0	103.5	465.8	6.2	5.5	9.8
Total	851.0	1514.0	4762.5	4.4	100.0	100.0

impromptu short-term events such as 9/11 cause a temporary disruption while long-term impacts such as climate changes causes more permanent change to tourist flows. Given that the present economic order is extremely uncertain and economists cannot agree on an end date for the Global Financial Crisis, or the depth or pace of recovery; therefore, two scenarios have been prepared based upon different economic growth rates, oil prices, climate change, transport flows and personal disposal incomes. The scenarios are called *Best Case* and *Sclerosis of the Middle Classes* (Table 2.3).

Scenario one: The best case

Over the next 40 years, market shifts are going to occur given Europe's ageing populations and the rise of middle classes of Asia, but what about oil? In this scenario, technological innovation overcomes many problems with oil and is not seen as a barrier to growth. As a consequence, international arrivals will grow by 3.8% per annum and receipts by 4.4%. Most significantly, Europe's demography paralysis means its share of international arrivals falls from 50.7% to 23.3% and receipts from 44.2.0% to 17.6% respectively. Fundamentally, in a best case scenario, the growth rate of international arrivals to Europe is only 1.8% compared with a global average of 3.8%.

The Americas' market share could be described as under-performing, reflecting different growth rates for different regions. Asia's star performance is driven by China and India with international arrivals growing at 6.0% per annum and receipts by 6.5% per annum. Asia's market share of arrivals increases from 21.7% to 50.3% by 2050, a staggering achievement. International tourism by 2050 will grow at a rate of 4.4% per annum from US$940 million in 2009 to US$4.7 trillion. This growth rate without doubt is about Asia Pacific as the future star and cash cow of world tourism (Table 2.4).

Table 2.4 Sclerosis of the middle classes

Arrivals	Base year (million)	Forecast (million)		Average annual growth rate (%)	Market share (%)	
	2010	2025	2050	2010–2050	2010	2050
Europe	475.3	551.8	707.7	1.0	50.7	39.8
Asia and the Pacific	204.0	308.7	615.7	2.8	21.7	34.6
Americas	149.7	187.2	271.6	1.5	15.9	15.3
Africa	50.3	58.4	74.9	1.0	5.2	4.2
Middle East	60.9	76.1	110.5	1.5	6.4	6.2
Total	940.2	1182.2	1780.3	1.6	100.0	100.0
Arrivals	Base year (US$ billion)	Forecast (US$ billion)		Average annual growth rate (%)	Market share (%)	
	2010	2025	2050	2010–2050	2010	2050
Europe	410.9	477.0	611.8	1.0	44.2	41.3
Asia and the Pacific	203.1	273.3	448.5	2.0	27.1	30.3
Americas	166.2	207.8	301.5	1.5	19.8	20.4
Africa	28.8	33.4	42.9	1.0	3.4	2.9
Middle East	42.0	52.5	76.2	1.5	5.5	5.1
Total	851.0	1044.1	1480.9	1.4	100.0	100.0

Scenario two: Sclerosis of the middle classes

The middle classes of the world are facing rising prices and less monies for out-of-home expenditure, all shaped by the economic disease of scarcity of resources, inflationary pressures and falling GDP in real terms. In this scenario, the world has not been able to adjust to the transformation from the end of oil, therefore making transport and travel more expensive. Inflation has had a large impact on the world economy, curtailing demand and slowing down the Asian tiger as exports have faltered. This scenario presumes political economic policies cannot trigger growth so the world falls into a sclerosis of decline through economic shocks, political instability and environmental disasters. The low-priced oil economy has ended squeezing economic growth amongst the middle classes of the world and leading to economic demise. In this scenario, a growth rate of 1.6% per annum is assumed representing 1.78 billion international arrivals and receipts growth of 1.4% per annum resulting in US$1.48 trillion. The clear impact of this scenario is that in real terms, there are fewer tourists spending less annually and therefore the growth rate for revenue does not match arrivals, suggesting over supply and lack of demand. The short-term impact of this scenario sees the end of low-cost carriers and in many destinations, long haul travel becomes more characterised by travel for the rich, exclusive and necessary. Intercontinental travel subsequently slows down, whereas interregional travel is supplemented by alternative public transport systems. In this scenario, city-based tourism with good connectivity fares better than rural destinations. Europe's market share will fall from 50.7% to 39.8% but the Asia Pacific region does not see the rapid rises as seen in the *Best Case* scenario due to slowdown in economic development. In fact Europe's compactness, an increase in interregional travel, along with a slow down in outbound travel to other world regions acts as a buffer.

Concluding Remarks

New emerging consumers

With each passing year this decade will witness the gradual expansion of the global middle class. Drawn from emerging MBRIIC countries, millions of consumers are joining the global marketplace, creating significant opportunities for every consumer-facing sector. Indeed, as discretionary incomes rise, consumers will be able to afford a greater level of choice in every aspect of their lives; from personal mobility to healthcare, from communications to new types of food and drink. However, as incomes rise, so too will expectations towards brands and companies. Meanwhile, concerns will be raised about the *polarisation* of wealth within societies (a particularly live issue in those countries where the pace of growth has been most dramatic) and the extent to which it is the state's responsibility to encourage greater redistribution of wealth. However, this new middle class will have a significant impact on resources; their intensive lifestyle thus may thwart the world's drive for a more sustainable future because of a lack of resources (the issues surrounding the future of resources is discussed in a number of chapters throughout this book). The middle classes of the future with their lifestyles and attitudes are promoters of globalisation, a highly heterogeneous group in socio-economic terms as well as in habits and preferences, including their societal role as consumers and citizens.

Prospects for world tourism

As this new middle class becomes mainstream, the tourists of China and India will dominate world tourism. Imagine a world in 2050, when Asia and the Pacific represent 49.8% of all international arrivals compared with 20.6% today or US$2.7 trillion out of a grand total of US$5 trillion in 2050. By 2050, China will be the world's largest country in terms of country wealth with India in third place. Why? According to Stancil and Dadush (2010) in purchasing power parity (PPP), the shift is dramatic, currently the G7 claims more than half of the G20 GDP compared to approximately one-third of the MBRIIC economies. In 2050, it is forecasted that the MBRIIC economies will be twice as large as the G7. In GDP terms, China and India are predicted to increase by nearly US$60 trillion, to the present size of the world's economy. At the same time, Germany, the United Kingdom, France and Italy are expected to grow by only 1.5% annually through to 2050, fundamentally because of ageing populations. In 1950, 1:1000 of the world's population took an international holiday, today it is 1:100, whereas in 2050 it will be nearly 1 in 2, unless there is economic meltdown of course.

Or is it a case of the end of the world

In the scenario, *Sclerosis of the Middle Classes*, the world is facing rising prices and less monies for out-of-home expenditure, all shaped by the economic disease of scarcity of resources, inflationary pressures and falling GDP in real terms, in which world tourism grows from US$851 billion to near US$1.5 trillion in 2050, an annual rate of growth of 1.4%. In this scenario the world could expect a breakout of trade protectionism – that will slow down the diffusion of pre-existing technologies into developing countries and reduce competitive innovation around the globe. Slower growth will also make it more difficult to deal with the fiscal constraints implied by ageing in the industrial countries and the debt build-up incurred during the current and future financial crises. In the worst-case scenario, do not think about the *Great Depression* but the *Long Depression*. The Great Depression was fuelled by the second industrial revolution and ran until the conclusion of the

American Civil War. The Panic of 1873 has been described as the first truly international crisis. The optimism that had been driving booming stock prices in central Europe had reached a fever pitch, and fears of a bubble culminated in a panic in Vienna beginning in April 1873. The long depression affected different countries at different rates, and led to a period of falling price levels and rates of economic growth significantly below the periods preceding. The depression went on through the 1880s and 1890s and led to a period of protectionism, monetary responses, labour unrest and new imperialism (all of which sound familiar).

3 Where Have All the Tourists Gone? Pensions, Demography and the Germans

Learning points

- Demography will have a significant impact on the future of tourism demand as populations age, demand for well-being products will increase as consumers attempt to extend their healthy years as will medical tourism as tourists search for cheaper procedures.
- To 2030 tourism prosperity will be shaped by baby boomers retiring with wealth, thus facilitating the growth in world travel.
- Post 2030, retirees will probably have an insufficient level of income to travel as countries such as Germany, Italy, Holland, France and the United Kingdom reform pension policy.

> *Just like Japanese in the 1990s and now in 2050, the Germans have disappeared. Once they were the travellers of the world that every country chased for the tourist dollar. Today, they are part of history as ageing populations lead to falling wealth per capita and pension reform. The boom years for world tourism were over.*
> UNWTO Secretary-General General Assembly Address,
> New York 2050

Introduction

UNWTO tourism expert Paul Flatters (2009) notes that in the next couple of decades tourism prosperity will be shaped by baby boomers retiring with wealth and facilitating the growth in world travel. However, post 2030 change will occur, the looming pension crisis and burgeoning world ageing populations means a greater divide between rich and poor and structural changes to tourism demand across the world. The United Kingdom, Germany, Italy and Japan represent over 70% of world's tourism expenditure and these are the countries with rapidly ageing populations. What if the future was about pensioner poverty? What would this mean for world tourism in 2050? Even countries such as China have a demography time bomb which is going to impact on its GDP and wealth. So, what is the future of world tourism given the certain trend of ageing populations and falling birth rates? Demography is about wealth and this is the most important trend that will shape the future. This chapter discusses the key demography trends, the forthcoming pension crisis, illustrating the structural changes that will occur in developing countries such as Germany and what this means for world tourism.

World Demography Trends

Demography is the statistical study of all populations. It can be a very general science that can be applied to any kind of dynamic population, that is, one that changes over time or space. It encompasses the study of the size, structure and distribution of populations, and spatial and/or temporal changes in them in response to birth, migration, ageing and death. In 2009, the United Nations forecasted that by 2050, 9.15 billion people would live on planet Earth compared to 2.5 billion in 1950 (see Figure 3.1). In 2011, these estimates rose to 9.31 billion, 156 million larger than that projected by the 2009 report. Most of the difference can be traced to a higher number of births projected by the *2010 Revision* and fewer numbers of deaths over the same period. The projection of fertility in the *2008 Revision* assumed that the fertility of all countries would converge towards 1.85 children per woman. However, the projection of fertility in the *2010 Revision* is carried out using probabilistic modelling that provides more accuracy via simulation of many future fertility paths for each country. Small variations in fertility could lead to major long-term differences in the size of the global population with correspondingly major impacts on food, water, housing,

	Population (millions)			Total Fertility Rate (per woman)			Life Expectancy at Birth (Years)			% of Total Population			Median Age		
	1950	2010	2050	1950	2010	2050	1950	2010	2050	1950	2010	2050	1950	2010	2050
World	2532	6896	9306	4.95	2.52	2.15	47.1	69.3	76.3	100	100	100	23.9	29.2	37.9
More Developed Countries	811	1236	1312	2.81	1.66	1.99	65.9	75.6	83.3	32	18	14	29	39.7	44.3
Less Developed Countries	1721	5660	7994	6.07	2.68	2.16	42.3	67.5	75.1	68	82	86	25.1	26.9	36.8

Figure 3.1 Key demography trends
(*Source:* UN, 2011)

environmentalism impinges on tourism. No transport means no tourism and climates affect tourism destination products such as skiing in the French Alps or sunbathing in Hawaii. Over the next 40 years, the world faces many challenges relating to the future of resources, whether it is food, oil, water or the environment, all of which will impact upon tourism. Therefore, the chapters of this book are clustered around Figure 1.1 whether it is the rising middle classes of China and India, the debate about the future of oil and aviation or emerging technologies such as claytronics used in hotel design.

Wealth

Chapter 2 'A New World Order: The Tourism Economy in 2050' addresses how the economic balance of power is shifting rapidly to developing economies of the world. China remains on a path to overtake the United States as the world's largest economic power within a generation, and India will join both as a global leader by mid-century. Traditional Western powers will remain the wealthiest nations in terms of per capita income, but will be overtaken as the predominant world economies by much poorer countries. In 2050, 4.7 billion people will take an international holiday that is, one in two of the world's population will become a tourist, compared to 1950 when 25 million people took an international holiday or a ratio of one in 1000. By 2050, we will see significant shifts in distribution patterns of world tourism. In one scenario, *The Best Case*, Europe's share of international arrivals falls from 50.7% in 2010 to 23.3% in 2050, compared to a significant shift in the Asia region with a growth from 21.7% to 50.3%. The purpose of this chapter is to examine what the world economy will look like in 2050, scenarios for the future of international arrivals and a discussion on future travellers from India and China.

Chapter 3 'Where Have all the Tourists Gone? Pensions, Demography and the Germans' states how in 2050 there will be 2.4 billion extra people on this planet, but many structures of the world's population will be fundamentally different in 2050, as a result of falling birth rates and longevity. Ageing populations and demography will be the trend that significantly shapes tourism flows and expenditure. On one hand, an ageing population means tourists will seek to extend the wellness years through well-being tourism, spirituality and medical procedures, whereas on the other hand the structural changes in pension provision from state and company to individual will reduce per capita wealth, particularly among German tourists. Chapter 4 'Tomorrow's Tourist: A Simple or Fluid Identity' examines two scenarios for the future behaviours and attitudes of the tourist. The tourist has demanded better experiences, faster service, multiple choice, social responsibility and greater satisfaction. Against this background, as the world has moved to an experience economy in which there is endless religion, values, institutions, laws, family structure, crime, trade, wealth, politics, transport, climate and tourism. Population impacts upon everything and everyone.

The world's population has grown from 600 million in 1700 to 6.89 billion in 2010 (UN, 2011). According to Cohen (2003), it took until 1927 to put 2 billion on the earth, less than 50 years to add another 2 billion (by 1974); and just 25 years to add the next 2 billion, highlighting that the world population doubled in the most recent 40 years.

From 1750 to 1950, Europe and the New World experienced the most rapid population growth of any region, while populations of Asia and Africa grew very slowly. Since 1950, rapid population growth shifted from Western countries to Africa, the Middle East and Asia. The most important demographic event in history occurred around 1965–1970.

In 1800, roughly 2% of people lived in urban centres; in 1900, 12%; in 2000, more than 47% and nearly 10% of those city dwellers lived in cities of 10 million people or larger. Between 1800 and 1900, the number of city dwellers rose more than 11-fold, from 18 million to 200 million; between 1900 and 2000, the number of city dwellers rose another 14-fold or more, from 200 million to 2.9 billion. In 1900, no cities had 10 million people or more. By 1950, one city did: New York. In 2000, 19 cities had 10 million people or more. Of those 19 cities, only four (Tokyo, Osaka, New York and Los Angeles) were in industrialised countries (Cohen, 2003).

Demographic Projections of the Next 50 Years

In 2010, the world's population was 6.9 billion with 5.7 billion (or 82% of the world's total) living in the less-developed regions (Figure 3.1). There will be 9.3 billion people in 2050 compared to 2010, an increase close to the combined populations of China and India today. Most of this growth will be absorbed by developing countries. Between now and 2050, the population of the more developed regions will remain largely unchanged moving from 1.2 billion to 1.3 billion inhabitants, but the population of the less-developed regions is projected to rise from 5.6 billion to almost 8 billion in 2050. At the same time, the population of the least-developed countries is projected to more than double, from 832 million inhabitants to 1.7 billion in 2050. Consequently, by 2050, 86% of the world's population is expected to live in the less-developed regions, including 18% in the least-developed countries, whereas only 14% will live in the more developed regions. Most of the world's population lives in a few countries. In 2010, 37% of the world's population lived in China and India. A further eight countries account for an additional 22% of the Earth's inhabitants, namely, the United States, Indonesia, Brazil, Pakistan, Bangladesh, Nigeria, the Russian Federation and Japan.

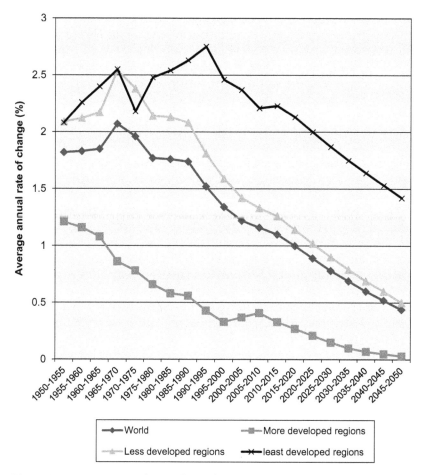

Figure 3.2 Average annual age of populations change for the world and the major development groups 1950–2000 (medium variant)
(*Source:* UN, 2011)

The primary demographic consequence of fertility decline (Figure 3.2), especially if combined with increases in life expectancy, is population ageing, a process whereby the proportion of older persons in the population increases and that of younger persons declines. In 1950, just 8% of the world's population was aged 60 years or over. By 2010, that proportion rose to 11% and it is expected to reach 22% in 2050. Globally, the number of older persons (aged 60 years or over) will increase by a factor of 2.6, passing from 759 million in 2010 to 2 billion in 2050. In contrast, the number of children (persons under age 15) is projected to decline over the next 40 years, passing from 1.85 billion in 2010 to 1.90 billion in 2050 and their share of the total population will drop from 27% in 2010 to 20.5% in 2050. The median age worldwide (half the people are older and half are younger) will rise from 29 in 2010 to 37.9 in 2500. But disparities among countries are enormous: Niger's median age now is the world's lowest at 15.5, while Japan's is highest at 44. Population ageing, which is already pervasive in developed countries, is expected to be common in the developing world of the future, and is projected to occur more rapidly in developing countries than it did in their developed counterparts.

According to the *2010 Revision* (UN, 2011), total fertility – that is, the average number of children a woman would bear if fertility rates remained unchanged during her lifetime – is 2.52 children per woman in 2005–2010 at the world level. This average masks the heterogeneity of fertility levels among countries. In 2005–2010, 73 countries, mostly developed regions, have fertility levels below 2.1 children per woman (replacement level), while less-developed regions have total fertility levels at or above 2.1 children per woman. However, fertility levels appear to be gradually converging. Most of the high and medium fertility countries in 2005–2010 are projected to have declined below a fertility level of 2.1 children per woman by 2100. According to the *2010 Revision* (UN, 2011) there is empirical evidence, that at least 21 countries with sub-replacement fertility have experienced slight increases in total fertility – after they had reached their lowest fertility level. While birth rates continue to be high in less-developed nations it is predicted that fertility will converge towards around replacement level sometime between 2010 and 2100 (United Nations Population Division, 2011).

The Future of Pensions

The countries that dominate world tourism receipts today could be less well off in 2050. Many countries such as Germany, Italy, Holland, France, Spain and the United Kingdom are reforming pension policy; therefore, pensioner's post 2050 will be economically less well off compared to previous generations and as a consequence the economic value of tourism will fall in real terms. Countries in the OECD have a large public sector with favourable pension provision compared to the private sector. With falling birth rates and rising life expectancies, the commitment from government to pay for public sector pensions and benefits is declining.

The calculations about the affordability of pension provision by governments and companies are moving the responsibility of pension provision on the individual. For example, Turner *et al.* (1998) estimated that public debt relative to GDP would increase to almost 100% in Japan and the EU, and close to 70% in the United States by 2050. Sinn (1999) projected that German tax increase would rise to 24% by 2040. Further, the trustees of the US Social Security [Social Security Administration (SSA), 2002] estimated that expenditures for public pensions as a share of taxable earnings would rise from

11% in 2002 to 23% in 2050. Similarly, Yeoman *et al.* (2011) forecast that public pension expenditure would rise from 14.5% of GDP in 2000 to 15.8% in 2032, before falling again to 14.5% in 2050.

The UN predicts globally that the percentage of people aged 60 or older will double between 2007 and 2050. By 2050, one-third of the total population in the developed countries will be 60 years or older, while in the less-developed world, one-fifth will be over 60. Of the world's major regions, Europe had the highest old-age dependency ratio (24%) in 2007, and is also expected to be the oldest region in 2050, with an old-age dependency ratio of 48% (UN, 2009). However, the UN predicts that all regions will experience dramatic increases in the dependency ratio. These increases will stem not only from a rapid increase in the number of elderly, but also from a decline in working-age populations (typically, those aged 15–64), particularly in the high-income countries. The World Bank (2007) expects the labour force in high-income countries to peak in 2010 and then begin to shrink significantly. In Japan, the working-age group has already begun to shrink, while in Europe the peak was reached in 2007–2008. In other high-income countries the peak will occur later – in around 2020 for the United States and 2015 elsewhere. There will also be a considerable slowdown in labour force growth in East Asia, including China. Less-developed countries are forecast to add nearly 1 billion workers to the world's labour force by 2025, assuming that there is no change in the labour force participation rate; however, according to Sikken *et al.* (2007), the productivity of these workers is a concern. The key challenges according to the World Economic Forum (Sikken *et al.*, 2007) are:

- Growing expectations that the private sector will come to the rescue.
- Significant pressure on pay-as-you-go public pensions and health systems.
- Lack of individual financial knowledge as a major policy concern.
- The growing prevalence of chronic diseases around the world.
- The lack of formal social security in many parts of the world.
- Underdeveloped private pension and health insurance markets.
- The double burden of infectious and chronic diseases in less developed countries.
- The diminishing role of family in old-age social security.

Countries such as China will be confronted by a significant increase in old-age social security expenditure, due to rapidly ageing populations (see Figure 3.3), increasing medical technologies costs and higher incidences of chronic diseases. As Figure 3.4 suggests, the United States, Switzerland and Holland will see significant increases in public expenditure related to ageing populations whether it is pension provision, health care or social security payments.

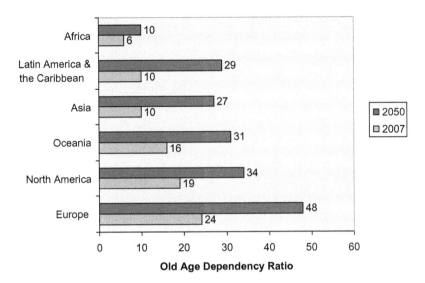

Figure 3.3 Old age dependency
(*Source:* Yeoman & Butterfield, 2011)

Looking to the future, one of the problems facing the world is the massive increase in chronic diseases such as cardiovascular and neurological complaints, which exponentially rise when people reach 65. The problem is further extrapolated with people living longer, well into their 90s. As ageing

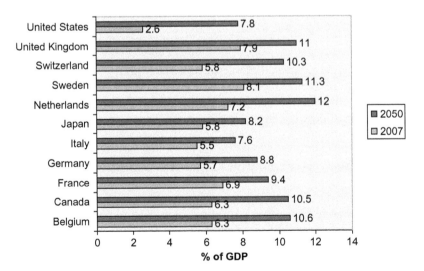

Figure 3.4 Health, long-term care: Projected in *Age Related Public Spending*
(*Source:* Yeoman & Butterfield, 2011)

raises the number of consumers relative to producers, the growth of material living standards (i.e. consumption per capita) will fall unless relative declines in the workforce are offset by increases in labour productivity and the effective supply and utilisation of labour. Decreases in labour force participation rates associated with projected demographic trends will depress the growth of GDP by as much as 1/2 to 1 percentage point per year in many of the developed countries. Therefore, projections for GDP growth rates for Italy, Germany, Spain and Japan will never be more than 1.5% and many cases negative (OECD, 2007).

At the same time, government revenues will be adversely affected as the baby boom generation moves from its high income generating years to retirement. Per capita expenditure for the elderly is high and is forecasted to dramatically grow over the forthcoming decades, especially in the areas of health and medical support. If advances in medical technology come at ever-increasing costs and if the incidence of health expenditure on the elderly continues to rise, the fiscal burden could become substantial in many countries. Countries whose revenues are tied more to consumption or value-added taxes will tend to experience less of a deterioration in revenues than those that depend more heavily on income or payroll taxes. Although most countries have improved their fiscal balances in recent years, longer-term projections suggest that budget deficits would continue to be at unsustainable levels, especially given the Global Financial Crisis (Flatters, 2009). This would create a severe drag on national saving at a time when saving will be crucial to fostering the growth of labour productivity; therefore, many countries face severe financial deficits and greater uncertainties in financing the future. A clear example of the burden of extra expenditure is highlighted by examining the national accounts of Japan (Faruque & Mühleisen, 2003; Sikken *et al.*, 2007; Yeoman & Butterfield, 2011).

Sikken *et al.* (2007) note that Japan's government debt has worsened in the last decade and is considered higher compared to other OECD countries. General government debt (excluding social security) has roughly doubled over the last decade. Given the fact that the Japanese government currently finances roughly 20% of social security benefits, an increase in pension payments and costs of health services for the elderly will impact directly on the expenditure side, while revenue prospects would be affected by the slower economic growth. Chand and Jaeger (1996) estimated the value of Japan's net pension liabilities is around 110% of GDP. Broadly consistent with these findings, the Ministry of Health and Welfare estimated that the main public pension system would need to raise contribution rates to 1.5 times their current level over the next 25 years to remain viable (Faruque & Mühleisen, 2003; Sikken *et al.*, 2007; Yeoman & Butterfield, 2011).

Reform of public pension systems is on the agenda in many countries, however as Figure 3.5 shows many countries will have problems addressing reform as in a democratic society, the over 50 age group bear significant

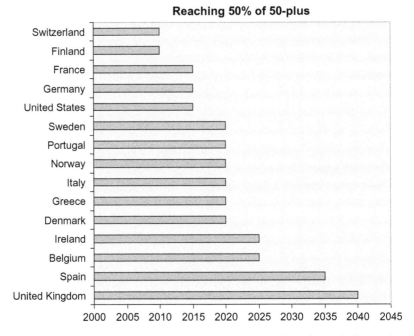

Figure 3.5 Citizens who are 50 and over as a percentage of total population – when it happens
(*Source:* Yeoman & Butterfield, 2011)

responsibility in shaping the values of society and are more active in politics and voting in elections. By 2050, the over 50s will be the majority in nearly all countries of the world. In addition, voter turnout of over 50s is relatively stronger compared to under 50s, for example, in Portugal the turnout is 41% higher in over 50s groups compared to under 50s groups. In other countries the figures are France 20%, Sweden 25%, the United Kingdom 17% and Switzerland 36%. As politicians are often focused on re-election, addressing structural welfare changes will be difficult and seen as a vote loser.

So, What Does This Mean for Tourism?

On a positive note, an ageing population will try and extend the well years ...

Figure 3.6 highlights that functional health falls gradually throughout a person's life; this reduction does not cause problems until very old age, when it ultimately leads to an individual losing independence. One of the biggest conditions associated with advanced economies is obesity, which limits life

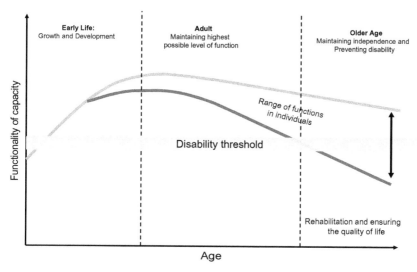

Figure 3.6 Maintaining functional capacity over the course of life
(*Source:* Yeoman & Butterfield, 2011)

expectancy and increases the risk of chronic health diseases that can dramatically increase both mortality and morbidity in remaining years. As a
consequence, in order to maintain a healthy lifestyle in old age, consumers
are searching for a means to extend healthy retirement years. This means in
general terms that:

- Demand has increased for healthier foods and for better access to a variety of physical activities as a way of combating growing anxiety problems and depression – as well as growing waistlines.
- There is an increasing interest in Eastern medicine and health-related activities such as yoga, meditation and herbal remedies. Growth in this area may
  be most closely linked to affluence because they will remain an alternative
  to the staunchly supported public health service of western societies.
- At present, women make up a significant majority of 'health' consumers,
  but a steady growth in participation by males in the market is
  anticipated.
- Disparities between the self-reporting of conditions and the actual treatment of conditions suggest a demand for non-medically prescribed remedies or treatments, particularly in areas of the greatest discrepancies
  between condition and treatment, for example, heart and circulation
  problems, as well as alcohol and drug problems.
- An increasing use of beauty aids, combined with continued growth in
  disposable income, suggests a bright future for cosmetic treatments and
  for those searching for the fountain of youth.

Wellness can be defined as a balanced state of body, spirit and mind, with fundamental elements such as self-responsibility, physical fitness, beauty care, healthy nutrition, relaxation, mental activity and environmental sensitivity. According to Mueller and Lanz-Kaufmann (2001), wellness is viewed as a way of life, which aims to create a healthy body, soul and mind through acquired knowledge and positive interventions. Health tourism is defined as any kind of travel to make oneself, or a member of one's family, healthier. Health tourism and wellness tourism are frequently used interchangeably. According to Lister (1999), healthcare and health treatments will be the world's largest industry in 2022, principally driven by an ageing population who are active rather than passive when it comes to healthcare. Lister goes on to say that tourism will become the world's second largest industry over the same period. Combined, health and tourism will represent 22% of the world GDP.

Medical travel is a fast-growing market. Sikken *et al.* (2007) estimate that gross medical tourism revenues were more than US$40 billion worldwide in 2004, and will rise to US$100 billion by 2012. It is driven largely by long waiting times for public treatment and high costs for private treatment in high-income countries. As medical cost inflation drives up insurance premiums relative to income, more people choose to decline coverage and meet their medical expenses out-of-pocket; in the United States, over 45 million people, around one in six of the population, are uninsured. The enormous price advantage of travelling overseas for treatment may reflect the quality of provision, particularly pre- and post-surgery care, but also reflects both the lower wages paid to healthcare workers in low-cost countries and cheaper prices offered there by global suppliers of medical devices and other healthcare products. Medical travel is a global phenomenon. In addition to middle- and low-income patients from high-income countries travelling to lower-income countries in search of cheaper care, high-income patients from low-income countries travel to higher-income countries in search of better care. Singapore, Thailand, India, Costa Rica and Colombia are notable examples of countries that have successfully established themselves as hubs for medical tourism, while the governments of South Korea and Taiwan are about to launch campaigns to promote medical tourism services within their countries. In 2007, 600,000 foreigners sought medical treatment in Thailand and 450,000 foreigners in India. Singapore aims to service one million medical tourists annually by 2012 (Sikkenden *et al.*, 2007).

On a more negative note, simply less wealthy tourists, especially the Germans

Post baby boomers in 2050, senior tourism could be a different proposition as many countries such as Germany, Italy, Spain and the United Kingdom reform pension policy; therefore, pensioners post 2050 will be economically less well off compared to previous generations and as a consequence the economic value of tourism will fall. In 2050, generations X and Y will probably retire with insufficient levels of income. The average worker in 2050 as shown in OECD countries (Figure 3.5) is expected to have combined public–private pension benefits that represent less that 70% of final earnings. As a consequence, increased contributions with longer careers will become mainstream and retirement will become a fluid concept. Many private sector employers have already closed defined contribution schemes to new entrants and many public sector schemes have redefined many of the benefits.

Developed countries in the OECD have a large public sector with favourable pension provision compared to the private sector, and as a consequence tourism has been one of the key beneficaries of this policy. With falling birth rates and rising life expectancies, the commitment from government to pay for public sector pensions and benefits is declining. However, the future of pensions and public pensions depends only partially on demographics; it depends on the economic trends in employment and earnings that determine a national ability to pay for pensions in the future, and it also depends on political factors that determine a country's willingness to pay (Figure 3.7).

In 2008 international tourism receipts were recorded as US$944 billion (UNWTO 2009), with the top 10 countries representing 47% of that

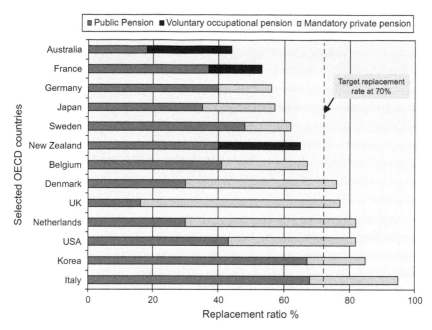

Figure 3.7 Projection of potential replacement ratio in 2050 at normal retirement age (as a % of final salary)
(*Source:* Yeoman & Butterfield, 2011)

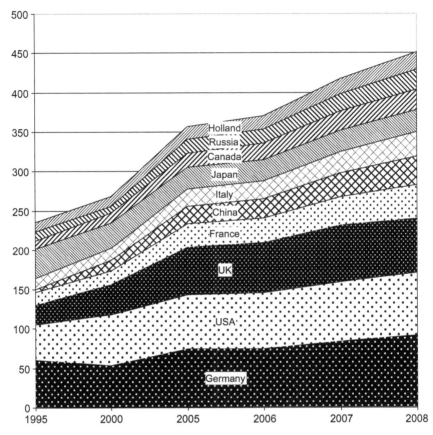

Figure 3.8 Outbound expenditure in US$ billion
(*Source:* UNWTO, 2009)

expenditure (Figure 3.8). The world's leader in outbound travel are the Germans, spending US$91.2 billion or US$1093 per capita compared to US tourists who spend US$79.7 billion or US$256 per capita. The Germans spend nearly four times as much per capita than US tourists or 40 times more per capita compared to Chinese tourists. The world's travellers are the Germans, Dutch, Spanish and Italians but these countries face rapidly ageing populations, falling wealth per capita, labour shortages and pension reform. For example, demography projections for Germany show that the number of persons aged 60 years or older will rise from 28.5% of the total population in 2000 to 35.8% in 2050. Studies by Muskat and Quack (2005) conclude in the short-to-medium term, as baby boomers retire, the benefits for tourism will be large due to secure pensions and inherited capital. A recent study by Grimm *et al.* (2009) for the German Federal Ministry of Economics and Technology concluded the impact of demography on tourism was manageable and demand will be relatively stable. But taking a more long-term perspective, ageing populations will become problematic for Germany and propensity to travel and actual travel patterns will fall due to less wealth per capita, health issues and stagnating house prices (Lohman & Danielsson, 2004). A recent study by McKinney and Co (2009) examined Germany's demographic structure and observed that it is passing through an important point; its baby boomers are approaching retirement age and this will have an increasingly negative impact on wealth per capita in coming years.

This demographic pressure comes from two sources:

- Households available to create wealth will be limited by slowing population growth and reduced household formation.
- Financial asset accumulation will slow because the falling prime saver ratio will lower average savings per household and limit the pool of money that can be allocated to acquiring financial assets.

The adult population is increasing, with the total population declining. While the total German population will begin to decline within the next two decades, the adult population (defined as people above 17) will still increase, with the group aged 55 and over growing the most at 1.3% per year. With an older population characterised by a higher household-to-population ratio than any other age group, the decline in the number of households will lag the decline in total population. Household formation will be reduced. Lower rates of household formation will constrain aggregate wealth accumulation since there will be fewer households earning income and generating savings. Financial asset accumulation will be slowed by lower savings per household. Average savings per household will be reduced going forward because there will be fewer households in their prime saving years. The prime saving ratio measures the number of households in their peak savings years (defined as the 20-year age bracket with maximum household savings) relative to the number of elderly households (who save at lower rates or dis-save) and therefore, captures the lifecycle effects caused by ageing. The ratio of German prime savers to elderly households has now passed an inflection point: the prime saver ratio will consistently decline over the next two decades, reaching 0.54 by 2024. This decline will impact the flow of savings from German households as older households save less.

Population ageing impacts wealth accumulation through lifecycle savings behaviour. Germany has a traditional 'hump-shaped' lifecycle profile. The German household lifecycle savings curve is steeply inclined, reaches a peak in the late 40s, and then rapidly slopes down in the late 50s and retirement years. With income peaking at age 54 and the savings rate hitting the highest point earlier at 41, an average German household experiences peak savings around ages 45–49. This relatively early age for peak savings magnifies the impact of an ageing population since the decline in savings occurs at an earlier age than in other countries. Therefore, as the German population ages, it will experience a 'lifecycle effect' on savings earlier than in other countries that have peak savings at later ages. While population ageing will affect German savings and GDP per capita accumulation in the next two decades, the impact may be appreciably larger after 2030 because of the impending sharp decline in population.

Concluding Remarks

The slow driver of demography

The world in 2050 will have 2.4 billion extra people, but as a result of falling birth rates and longevity the structure of the world's population will be fundamentally different. Ageing populations will be a trend that significantly shapes tourism flows and expenditure. On one hand, ageing populations mean tourists will seek to extend the wellness years through wellbeing tourism, spirituality and medical procedures. On the other hand, the structural changes in pension provision from the state and company to individual will reduce wealth per capita, particularly among German tourists. To 2030, baby boomers and senior tourists will still dominate world tourism, but as wealth accumulation falls we will see structural changes in outbound travel patterns from countries such as Germany, Italy, Spain and developed countries with rapidly ageing populations. Healthy public pension provision and final salary pension schemes in many companies have contributed towards baby boomers wealth, but this provision is changing due to uneconomic dependency ratios. Retirement will retire, becoming fluid as the retirement age increases over the forthcoming decades. Many people will not fully retire, continuing to work part time to fund their own retirement.

One thing is certain about the future, that is, birth, death and demography. As noted at the beginning of this chapter by the Secretary-General of the UNWTO, in 2050 German travellers, once the saviour of world tourism will, like the Japanese in the 1990s 'be no more'.

However, as the modern consumer ages ...

It can be expected that, as modern consumers age, their later life stages post work/family will become more and more fragmented and varied with a growth in mature education, work, travel, second careers, new leisure habits, and so forth. In the developed markets of Western Europe, the United States and Japan where demographic populations are ageing fastest (particularly as baby boomer generations reach retirement age) the concept of agelessness will soon be of concern. Emerging economies will follow the same trend as longevity continues to rise and population's age. Forecasts predict a continuing weakening of age boundaries and a less age-targeted approach to the way that brands address and service older consumers. Indeed, greater age neutrality within marketing communications across a whole range of sectors will be important.

Nevertheless, this does not mean that generational differences are set to evaporate completely. Younger consumers will continue to seek recognition for their sense of individuality and for their interpretation of the latest fashion trends while older people will crave products that make them feel and look younger. The quest for youthfulness simply does not apply to young consumers. The price elasticity of tourism means that generational wealth accumulation patterns will also impact on tourism products. Changes in demography will impact tourism in ways that are much more predictable than other factors such as sustainability and technological innovation.

4 Tomorrow's Tourist: Fluid and Simple Identities

Learning points

- Wealth will be the key driver that will shape tourist behaviour and activity by 2050.
- Fluid identity will be the privilege of more prosperous tourists as they choose from a plethora of tourism products.
- Simple identity will be the only recourse for less prosperous tourists due to a rise in mercurial consumption and the slow down of excessiveness.

Introduction: Which Identity?

Rising incomes and wealth accumulation distributed in new ways alter the balance of power in tourism. The tourist is the power base that has shifted from the institution of the travel agent through the opaqueness of online booking for holidays and travel to the individual. At the same time, the age is rich for new forms of connection and association, allowing a liberated pursuit of personal identity which is fluid and much less restricted by the influence of background or geography. The society of networks in turn has facilitated and innovated a mass of options provided by communication channels leading to a paradox of choice. In the future market place, the tourist can holiday anywhere in the world whether it is Afghanistan or Las Vegas, to the extent that the tourist can take a holiday at the North Pole, the South Pole and everywhere in between including a day trip into outer space with *Virgin Galactic* (Yeoman, 2008).

Since the 1950s, both people's propensity to travel and tourism choices have increased. In all, 25 million tourists took an international holiday in 1950 and 903 million took a holiday in 2008 (Yeoman, 2008). Why? The growth in world tourism is founded on increases in real household income per head, which doubles every 25 years in OECD countries. This increase in disposable income allows real change in social order, living standards and the desire for a quality of life, with tourism at the heart of that change. Effectively, consumers want improvement year on year, as if it was a wholly natural process such as ageing. Travel demand tends to have income elasticity above 1.0; this means that travel growth tends to be faster than increases in GDP (Sachs, 2010), therefore change in disposable income means greater and enhanced choice for tourists.

Today's tourist demands better experiences, faster service, multiple choice, social responsibility and greater satisfaction. Against this background, as the world has moved to an experience economy in which there is endless choice through competition and increased accessibility because of low-cost carriers, what has emerged is the concept of *fluid identity*. This trend is about a concept of self which is fluid and malleable in which self cannot be defined by boundaries, in which choice and the desire for new experiences drives tourist consumption. Symbolic of the drive towards multiple identities is the fact that the consumer on average changes their hairstyle every 18 months (Future Foundation, 2007). From a tourist perspective, fluid identity is about collecting countries, trying new things and the desire for constant change. It means the tourist is both comfortable with a hedonistic short break in Las Vegas or a six-month ecotourism adventure crossing Africa. This fluid identity makes it difficult for destinations to segment tourists by behaviour or attitude. However, as wealth decreases identity becomes simpler *and* a new thriftiness and desire for simplicity emerges (Flatters & Wilmott, 2009). This desire for simplicity is driven by inflationary pressures and falling levels of disposable incomes, squeezing the middle-class consumer. As the economies of wealth slow down, whatever the reason, new patterns of tourism consumption emerge, whether it is the desire for domestic rather than international travel or what some call the *staycation*. A fluid identity means tourists can afford enriching new experiences and indulgence at premium five-star resorts. They can afford to pay extra for socially conscious consumption, whereas a simple identity means these trends have slowed, halted or reversed. As resources become scarcer, the mind set of a whole generation of tourists changes alongside their behaviour. Between now and 2050 the world will go through a cycle of economic prosperity and decline that is the nature of the economic order. When wealth is great, a fluid identity is the naked scenario, however, when a recession emerges, belts are tightened, and tourists, like other consumers search for a simple identity. This chapter examines the values, behaviours and thinking of the future tourist, whether it is a *Fluid* or *Simple Identity*.

Fluid Identity

This tourist is both interested in a two-week eco tourism vacation where they will undertake an authentic and sustainable experience, but at the same

Figure 4.1 The author's fluid identity and the desire for new experiences

time they will take a short break in Las Vegas, whether it is retail therapy, gambling or something more erotic (see Figure 4.1). Why? Tourists cannot be labelled according to their attitudes and beliefs – what they say and what they do, are two totally different things. They constantly evolve and seek something new just like David Beckham and his hairstyles (Yeoman, 2008). This is why segmenting tomorrow's tourist is becoming a lot more difficult. One version of the future is rising incomes and wealth accumulation distributed in ways that alter the balance of the power to even more centricity, along with the age of richness in new forms of connection and association, allowing a liberated pursuit of personal identity which is fluid; an identity which is less restricted by background or geography but more by achievement. In the fluid environment, communications channels and technologies are fast moving and instant, which produces a culture of choice enhancement.

Fluid identity produces consumer volatility of proliferated choice where a high entropy society exists (Future Foundation, 2007). Tourists have the means for endless choice and creative disorder. They have the power to express opinion and they do so, whether it is through www. tripadvisor.com or www.youtube.com. In fact, they form their opinion not on trusted sources from authority but from peer review, hence the importance of consumer-generated content and the advocacy of local authentic information as provided, for example, by the citizens of Philadelphia at www.uwishunu.com.

Consumers are excellent at using networking tools to get a better deal with, or complain about, poor service. A fluid identity allows tourists to be frivolous, promiscuous and just plain awkward. A fluid identity means tourists want to sample a range of new experiences, hence the rise of the long tail (Anderson, 2008) and emergence of bespoke tourism products, for example, specialist cruise markets at www.insightcruises.com.

A fluid identity emerges because society is less rigid, individuals have become less defined by class and human relationships are not restricted by accident of birth; the combination of breaking class distinction through education, income and the mind-expanding influence of modern travel and entertainment, broadens preordained identities and choices. The emerging tourists from Brazil, Russia, India and China are the new tourists who are now not restricted to one town, one church, one marriage and one football team, especially generations Y and Z. Fluid identity results in massively propelled ad hoc communities of new friends and connections some via social media and others through shared interest activity groups. Ethan Watters (2004) calls this *Urban Tribes*, groups of like-minded people and friends doing activities together whether it is a girlie weekend of pampering or a boyish rugby game. It is the idea that an infinite number of options are available, which propels the idea of fluid identity.

Globalisation shapes people's lives and the mixture of cultures produces exposure to new ideas and different identities. The tourist is the centre of the globalisation of experiences, where holidays in exotic locations that are deep inside countries are becoming the norm. No longer is an international holiday confined to a resort, but instead it is more authentic engaging with local cultures and living. Globalisation is brought nearer to us all through social media and personalised communications, in a society that is fast, instant and networked. No longer is the internet bound to a wire or a desk, but is mobile and wireless. Everyone seems to be online 24 hours a day, anywhere, as technology has become more accessible and costs of transactions are falling. The power of personal mobile technology means more features, interactivity and multi-functionality delivering a different way in which tourist providers have to engage with future tourists. One of the challenges for tourist destinations is how they protect their brand equity when it quickly can be destroyed or poked fun at on YouTube or Facebook. It means brands have to work harder to maintain trust because of disruptive discourse shaped by word of mouth or being followed on www.twitter.com.

Tourists' sense of timing and patience is changing; society is now just a click away from a screen and it is not one that likes the notion of delayed satisfaction. Patience is now measured in nano-seconds driving an immediacy culture. The tourist has become programmed, wanting more all the time in an instant. In Tokyo, 30% of hotel reservations are on the day of arrival as smart phone augmented technology allows tourists to look at a hotel through the smart phone camera and gauge availability, then book accommodation through a related website such as Expedia (Hatton, 2009) all driven by applications such as the Wikitude AR Travel Guide (www.wikitude.org).

Longevity is a key trend associated with fluid identity, as consumers live longer with wealth they expect richer experiences and more. They visit places and do things that their parents could not afford or would not have heard of. They will search for experiences that hold back the wrinkles of old age, whether it is a spa treatment in Hungary or a medical procedure in South Africa. Health and medical tourism become more important in this scenario along with any service that rejuvenates the soul or a tired body. Longevity also changes life courses, so change becomes the norm and unpredictable. Although tourists may have their favourite place, they like refreshment and renewal. This means they ask themselves who they are and a multiplicity answers suffice. Michael Willmott (Willmott & Nelson, 2005) calls this phenomenon complicated lives, in which the choice explosion of holidays and travel means tourists have brought upon themselves complexity and complications resulting in some anxiety. At one level, this means many tourists are opting out and taking career breaks and travelling the world; on another scale, authenticity becomes important as tourists look for simplicity. At another level, destination brands have to find a means to ensure they can help the tourist unclutter this world through brand search optimisation, high brand value and choice management. Although choice is regarded as a positive value within a consumption culture, choice making support is important, such as the www.amazon.com book recommendation service.

Tourism destinations need to understand their tourists, not engaging in a relationship which is about mass selling, but focusing on what tourists want at the right time and in the right place. To a certain extent, fluid identity is about wealth and a have-it-all society; these tourists can afford holidays several times a year and a multitude of short breaks. These tourists can afford to be concerned about the environment so they do not mind paying a little bit extra. In a have-it-all society, the desire is for sociality, economic gain, family involvement, leisure and self improvement, which are less lineated by stages of life or gender. All these desires are reflected in holiday activity, whether it is an extended family holiday at Walt Disney or a cultural short break in Paris. The expectation among the tourists with a fluid identity is they want a richer and more fulfilling life, but at the same time there are pressures of expectation, hence the previous mentioned link to a disruptive discourse in this identity.

Although rising wealth means more opportunity it also means a fear of loss, in which society is portrayed as in decline. Here the consumer turns to therapies and anti-depressants, is anxious about the future and thinks society has lost its way. Writers, such as Frank Furedi (2006) label this 'the culture of fear'. From a tourism and media perspective there seems to be a focus on a health scare or terrorism incident, which impacts upon destinations. The incident is portrayed as overtly bad news, which results in countries issuing travel advisories telling tourists not to travel to such and such a place.

A heightened sense of personal freedom has undoubtedly increased the growth of world tourism, where identity is built on liberal attitudes reinforced through education and knowledge. The exposure of tourists to a multi-cultured society allows greater expression of individuality, whether this is sexual behaviour or unconventional lifestyles; however the degree of liberalism differs around the world. Fundamentally, as economies grow they become more liberal in outlook and seek to push out the boundaries of their identity. As such, they will try new things and visit new places, destinations in the far away places that seemed inaccessible to previous generations.

The manifestations of a fluid identity are wide ranging, from overt and status-driven to the anonymous and elusive. Yet the common characteristic for the tourist is that they simply do not want to just consume, but also to experience consumption in several ways, reflecting increasing aspirations and higher-order expectations (Yeoman, 2008). One noticeable trend shaping a fluid identity is the movement from conspicuous consumption to inconspicuous consumption, by tourists from mature economies who are well versed in travel. It has become the norm not to parade wealth and success with deliberate ostentation, but to be more conservative, wiser and discreet. From a tourism perspective, inconspicuous consumption has developed as the experience economy has matured from theatre to the desire for authenticity, where tourists search for deeper and more meaningful experiences. This trend has changed the meaning of luxury in society away from materialism to one more about enrichment and personal development; for the tourist it is about self-actualisation in the Maslow hierarchy of needs (Maslow, 1998). Luxury has therefore become more accessible to the growing middle classes in a world in which they can hire a Ferrari for the weekend (www.gothamdreamcars.com/) or even hire the latest designer handbags (www.bagborroworsteal.com).

Related to the changing nature of luxury is the importance of cultural capital, as this is how tourists talk about destinations and experiences. The importance of cultural capital defines identity and status, it becomes the critical currency of conversation, that is, 'have you been to South Africa', 'I swam with the dolphins in New Zealand' or 'I built a bridge for a community in India.' It is the knowledge and experiences of the arts, culture and hobbies that help define who people are rather than their socio-economic grouping. Sociologists such a Rifkin (1984) and Bourdieu (Bourdieu & Nice, 1987) argue that consumers are moving from an era of industrial to cultural capitalism, where cultural production is increasingly becoming the dominant form of economic activity and securing access to the many cultural resources and experiences that nurtures human psychological existence becomes an important aspect in shaping identity. This means the definition of culture changes, the tourist is both happy with a high brow opera and low brow comedy, hence the rise of the creative class and no brow culture associated, for example, with the success of Edinburgh's festivals that embody the diversity of cultural capital and breadth of experiences.

The emergence of fluid identity means tourists are programmed to be suspicious and rather cynical of all marketing and advertising. It is as though the tourist is instinctively mobilised to mount resistance and rebuke. It also becomes increasingly difficult to label and segment tourists by demographics, attitudes and economic well-being as fluidity becomes the norm in this scenario. Fluid identity represents a challenge for tourism destinations because of constant change and resistance.

A fluid identity is represented in the following scenario:

Michael Hay is a 28-year-old business executive from London. Michael is a seasoned traveller, who likes to take two long haul holidays a year and several short breaks. This year Michael is visiting Tokyo and wants to climb Mt Fuji and see the snow monkeys near Nagano. He chose Japan because friends had previously visited the country; they often talked about the food, the people, how everyone was so helpful, how safe the country is and what a wonderful experience it was. Michael had considered China, but he had watched so many viral videos, that he was put off from visiting China at the present. Prior to visiting Japan he had read a couple of guide books which formed the basis of a vague itinerary. He looked at the destinations website for information and could vaguely recall Tourism Japan had sponsored some sort of sporting event.

His seven-day vacation to Japan begins in Tokyo, he hasn't booked accommodation and is relying on his Nikon 300UXP contact lenses,[1] such is the speed of the technology that at the flick of the eye, details of the JP five-star hotel is sought using the latest augmented reality technology and availability is confirmed and a reservation made. In addition, a five-day tour of central Japan is organised by his online travel agent based upon his requisites, attraction booking, hotel accommodation and transport connections. Japan is a place known for its organisational efficiency and excellent transport infrastructure making it easy to get around. Michael is even going to road test a classic 2020 Ferrari, something that requires manual control and skill not like today's automatic personal vehicles. Each day, Michael is trying something new, whether it is a Japanese spa treatment, staying in a traditional Ryokan or hiking up Mt Fuji. All in all, a wonderful action packed holiday, everything from adventure to tranquility.

This scenario is shaped by many of the trends associated with fluid identity including, wealth, a networked society, resistance to marketing, strong brand image, culture of fear, choice management, personal recommendation, variety of experiences and its cultural capital. The importance of the scenario highlights how individuals shape their life using technologies as short cuts and choice managers; however, the biggest influence of choice is personal recommendation and the ability to lead a fluid identity lifestyle depends on wealth.

Simple Identity

The Global Financial Crisis (GFC) plummeted the value of the High Net Worth population by US$32.8 trillion or 19.5% according to the World Wealth Report (2009) published by Capgemini and Merrill Lynch, so the rich are less rich. Flatters and Wilmott (2009) argue that in most developed economies pre-GFC, consumer behaviour was the product of 15 years of uninterrupted prosperity, driven by growth in real levels of disposable incomes, low inflation, stable employment and booming property prices. As such, new consumer appetites emerged in which the consumer could afford to be curious about gadgets and technology and tourists shelled out for enriching and fun experiences in exotic locations. Tourists could afford several holidays a year and rent premium experiences such as hiring a Ferrari for the weekend in exotic locations like Japan. The GFC changed that, propelling tourist trends into slow down, halting or even reversing the trajectory of growth in world tourism. So, is this a sample of the future, an era of the pension crisis, scarcity of oil, inflation and falling levels of disposable income in which tourism expenditure falls year on year? If so, what will the future tourist look like? Rather than having a fluid identity it will be more akin to simplicity.

During an economic slowdown, tourists tend to travel less, stay nearer home (increase in domestic tourism) and seek simplicity, such as www.exploreworldwide.com who offer value-based holidays that focus on basic facilities, meeting locals, lots of free time and budget in exotic locations throughout the world. This trend is accelerated in a scenario of falling incomes as a simple and functional product that will suffice. A simple identity means offering advice becomes extremely important, whether it is a website that advises travellers of the optimal time to purchase an airline ticket or price comparison technologies which are found on many online booking services (e.g. www.farecast.com).

Combined with simplicity is thrift, in which tourists trade down. For example, the Pod Hotel in Manhattan (www.thepodhotel.com), where accommodation usually costs US$300 a night, the Pod offers single beds from US$89 a night, including bunk beds. The use of technology and social media assists tourists in the search for bargains, whether it is the use of augmented technologies in smart phones or contact lenses that provide availability and prices as we view them in the street or recommendations from a network of friends on social media sites. Thrift and simplicity also combine to drive the trend of visiting friends and relatives (VFR); as incomes fall, getting back to basics and developing human relationships is very important and the most important aspects of tourists' lives are friends and relatives.

Research by the Trajectory Group (Flatters & Wilmott, 2009) highlights that affluent consumers have revealed mounting dissatisfaction with excessive consumption. Many desire a wholesome and less wasteful life. As such, there is a desire to get back to nature, to something that is tranquil, basic, rooted, human and simple (Yeoman, 2008). As a consequence, the desire for more authentic and simple luxury experiences accelerates. Tree house hotels are an example of simple luxury, since they offer a unique experience in a natural setting. This is a new experience which is not seen as conspicuous consumption, but overtly inconspicuous. The Costa Rica Jungle Hotel is based in a rain forest around Arenal Volcano, surrounded by wildlife and birds (treehouseshotelcostarica.com/). Other examples include haycations, where which holidaymakers pay to stay and work on farms. Holidaymakers are turning to haycations to experience a world far removed from their daily life. At Stoney Creek Farm (www.stonycreekfarm.org), tourists are charged up to US$300 a night to work on the farm. This is an experience where tourists pick their own food, then cook it that evening and in a location with no mobile phone reception. During times of recession tourists are searching for back to basics experiences that are simple, with a sense of community and authenticity. About 50% of the tourists to Stoney Creek Farm are locals from the same county. This is a typical example of inconspicuous consumption and a desire for a simple identity.

In a simple identity, ethical consumption declines as paying a premium for a Starbucks coffee falls by the wayside, even if they use organic coffee which supports children in a Third World country. From a tourism perspective, many of the ethical tourism projects in Third World countries such as Africa and India that depend on independent travellers will suffer.

Tourists also have become canny at searching for bargains; economists call this mercurial consumption, whether it is using price comparison software, or grabbing last minute offers from websites such as www.grabaseat. co.nz which offer last minute air travel deals to New Zealand consumers, or www.5pm.co.uk which offers diners the chance of discounted meals after 5 pm that evening. Technology and social media network-enabled purchasing strategies further accelerate this trend to mercurial consumption.

Attitudes to travel also change, as tourism has to compete with other forms of leisure expenditure, whether it is the latest technology gadgets or virtual holidays. There is a generation of Japanese youth who prefer their X-Box over climbing Mt Fuji. The desire for new experiences is more about insperience (Trend Hunter, 2008), where technology provides a better experience in which consumers desire to bring top-level experiences into their domestic domain.

There have been many predictions about the end of the high street travel agent in the last decade, but in fact during times of economic slowdown, when tourists are trying to unravel complexity and give up excess, they go back to travel agencies to reduce choice through an efficient filtering process and maximise time management. In addition, the desire for new experiences slows down as simple, repeat trips in usual places also increase (Buhalis, 2009).

In an economic slowdown, the role of authority changes as governments intervene to stabilise markets, bring assurance and confidence to markets, create jobs and increase public expenditure. As such, many countries have increased destination spending on marketing, particularly in domestic markets to entice tourists to stay at home, hence the term *staycation*, as international markets fall. The tourism industry in particular, will turn to government to offer support and strategic leadership when the private sector is failing. Therefore, trust in authority increases and destination brands that offer value, honesty and can deliver on brand promise become more important.

New Zealand is the adventure capital of the world, whether it is bungee jumping, jet boating, bugging or skydiving. During an economic slowdown extreme experience seeking stalls as they are seen as expensive, frivolous, risky and environmentally destructive. Extreme adventure is partially about how tourists differentiate between them. But conspicuous consumption is out of favour and the trend of simplicity and discretionary spending is in, so perhaps we have seen the last bungee jump in New Zealand as this trend is unlikely to bounce back (pardon the pun).

The GFC has focused the consumer mind on the boardroom, in particular the executive bonuses of companies such as AIG, Royal Bank of Scotland or General Motors. Excess has become a dirty word, and as such, travel and the meetings industry have taken a hit as too, as many think that this sector is about excessive and unnecessary expenditure.

A simple identity is all about simplicity seeking, thrift and an environment in which green yet mercurial tourists will hold tourism business and brands accountable. In a world of scarcity of resources this scenario becomes the norm.

A simple identity is represented in the following scenario:

Sheena Michaels is 68, lives in London and is a part-time social worker. She is well travelled, has just completed an Open University degree in Technology and is a volunteer with a number of local community projects. Circumstances force Sheena to work part time because of her pension shortfall and she thinks that this will continue until her health dictates otherwise. London is recognised as a cultural centre for tourism. Lack of money means Sheena has to watch what she spends. Websites such as www.culturalprice.com tell Sheena in advance when it is the right time to book a theatre ticket and Sheena's social media network of friends advise on special deals, etc. Sheena would like to travel but nowadays tends to stay in the local region taking day trips in the surrounding hinterland. When she does go on holiday, it is staying with friends and families. This year she managed to take a short break in Barcelona, staying with friends and capturing much of the city culture, especially the galleries. Today, Sheena is travelling to the Soho Theatre Quarter in central London as it is the opening day of the Quarter's festival and many of the acts are performing free street shows. She manages to take in several short acts including an eight-minute performance of all Will Shakespeare's plays by the Royal Company and a lunchtime comedy performance by Leo Blair on 'the exploits of a Prime Minister's Son'. Eventually, Sheena and friends find a café for a cup of tea and just watch the world go by.

This scenario is shaped by many of the trends associated with a simple identity including: a networked society, simplicity and thrift, pricing technologies, highly educated tourists, community, use of leisure time and personal recommendation. The scenario highlights the importance of how individuals trade down and are thrifty with spending.

Concluding Remarks

Tourism and leisure

Meeting the global consumer's leisure expectations in the future requires any business to speak to multiple demands and interests. Millions still want to have fun and price sensitivity is a key concern; but tourism is extremely important as consumers want to engage their creative side or feel a sense of self betterment. One challenge for tourism is the blurring between reality and virtual reality. Tourism is all about real experiences, expression of identity or visiting a fancy restaurant; but for most, in-home alternatives are becoming more feasible. We can now interact with the increasingly responsive and intuitive world of digital technology. Pre-programmed internet-enabled televisions loom on the mainstream retail horizon, potentially allowing millions of global consumers to engage much more directly with the programmes (and products) they watch. Soon, though, we may become accustomed to seeing screens which carry live feeds revealing what our friends are thinking or through which we receive recommendations about programmes we might prefer to watch instead. In this sense, leisure will become more intelligent and this is a challenge for tourism. For the tourism industry, the emphasis is on the experience, whether it is a bungee jump or a cultural moment. This emphasis is easier when identity is fluid because of wealth but very hard when it is simple and consumers lack money.

The importance in immersive technologies

In the near future, we will not just research the location of our holiday online but step inside and investigate the detail. Through maps of the local neighbourhood we will be able to explore the local nightlife in real-time, interact with the head chef to customise our menu and see whether a holiday destination is perhaps overpopulated with too many tourists. Real-time customer reviews will add an additional layer of information to our displays while better visualisations, sound and video streams will make the insight into our travel destination more vivid and compelling. These technologies will never replace real travel but will open a (limited but) valuable experience to those that might currently be excluded digitally. Experiences such as the natural beauty of the Galapagos Islands or a sunrise over Machu Picchu will become more realistic, complex and potentially interactive experiences on our screens. The technology will make the experience of space travel available to the mass market in the medium term.

The affluence interruption

Following the great global financial crisis, you could have expected a rebalancing of power as tourists demanded more. Indeed, there is a blur between a fluid and simple identity as the material and psychological shock of affluence interruption has paradoxically emboldened tourists further. It is a more considered – but no less demanding – approach to consumption that now characterises the behaviour of many as meticulous and waste-conscious, with deal-hunting, price comparison and a focus on value-for-money becoming the norm. Against such a backdrop, it is those tourism products delivering quality, affordability, relentless product/service innovation and allusions to premium-ness that will hold the momentum in a future world. In the 2010s, tourists and authorities alike grow ever more anxious about the implications of indulgence, even those forms which are, in a sense, culturally sanctioned. But those tourists with a fluid identity will continue to have a desire for treating themselves. The pleasure principle maybe more progressively redefined for a more health-conscious, consequence-aware era. But, that concern is particularly pronounced among relatively urbanised and wealthy individuals in emerging nations, where rising incomes have in recent years led to a dramatic increase in consumption possibilities.

So ...

Tourism is an unpredictable industry, shaped by events, the world economy and the socio-political environment. Tourists are fickle and when times are good will spend large amounts of disposable income on tourism. To a certain extent, tourists retrench and focus on lower-order basic needs when times are hard so tourism declines. Given the Global Financial Crisis and the forthcoming demographic and pensions time bomb, we could see year on year decline in tourism expenditure with 2050 being the flip point. When tourists do have money, they possess a fluid identity of constant change in a fast-moving world, in which they are easily bored, seek novelty, desire thrills, want something new, are aspirational and require enrichment. Tourism has always been about fun, relaxation, entertainment, enrichment and enjoyment, but whether it will be simple or fluid, only time will tell.

Note

(1)   A new generation of contact lenses built with very small circuits and LEDs promises bionic eyesight. The University of Washington, in Seattle, has engineered a lens akin to the ones portrayed in the Terminator movies. Arnold Schwarzenegger's character sees the world with data superimposed on his visual field, virtual captions that enhance the cyborg's scan of a scene. In stories by the science fiction author Vernor Vinge, characters rely on electronic contact lenses, rather than smartphones or brain implants, for seamless access to information that appears right before their eyes. These lenses do not give us the vision but have the potential to deliver the vision of an eagle and the benefit of running subtitles. See http://www.spectrum.ieee.org/biomedical/bionics/augmented-reality-in-a-contact-lens/0, accessed 10 October 2011.

Technology

5 Edinburgh 2050: Technological Revolution

Learning points

- In order to understand the future of technological advancement, reality can be viewed best through the paradigm of science fiction.
- This chapter explains the key drivers of technological change, the interface with tourists and tourism consumption.
- Real and personal information will still be the number one influence on holiday purchases in 2050 even in a technological world.

Introduction: The Role of Technology

Graham Whitehead, the renowned BT futurologist said, 'consumers will see more technology change in the next ten years than was witnessed in the previous hundred years' (Whitehead, 2005a, 2005b). Exponential change in technology has altered how consumers use information and how this impacts on tourism. The internet has changed distribution patterns and mobile technologies are about to change how tourists 'see and book'. As Google's Claire Hatton (2009: 638) said '30% of hotel bookings in the cities of Tokyo and Seoul are on the day of arrival through the mobile phone and this trend can only grow'. Today's typical tourist is pointing their mobile phone at a hotel, using augmented reality (AR) platforms to view information and then making reservations via websites such as Expedia. The provision of information on tourism products is available through a variety of channels and technological platforms, bringing with it a range of benefits such as convenience with user-friendly interfaces, up-to-date information and affordability to the end user. These developments increasingly drive the integration of technology within our everyday lives with mobile internet, navigation systems and smartphones, which attempt to constantly keep us connected to the digital world. This chapter explains how future tourists will interface with technology through a scenario of the life of Maria who is enjoying the Edinburgh Festival in 2050. The core of the chapter identifies 10 technological driving forces which will shape the future.

How Technology has Changed Everything

The internet is one of the main drivers of product design as many mobile devices are increasingly equipped with mobile internet capabilities. Connectivity to the internet allows faster and more immediate access to information. A survey conducted by TNS Global (2008) indicated that many see the internet as 'an encyclopaedia of information', where three out of the top five activities engaged by online users are related to information gathering. Survey results also indicate that 81% of respondents used a search engine to find information, 63% researched a product or service before, 61% visited a brand or product's website and 50% used a price comparison website. These figures suggest that consumers are increasingly turning towards the internet to obtain information on products, brands and pricing. Within the tourism industry, the internet is being targeted to become the most important channel for holiday sales, information and recommendation where two out of five reservations are completed online and 55% of all European travellers use the internet for information about their travel destination, travel providers and special offers (Isabel, 2009). Recognising this trend, in 2007 Tourism New Zealand shifted its marketing activities from predominantly print media, to embrace digital and screen technology. This includes advertising through televisions, cinemas, outdoor screens and billboards and more significantly, the internet and social media (Tourism New Zealand, 2010).

Technology has become part of our everyday lives, creating a digital society. While one of the main reasons for this is the exponential advancement in technology, another key driver is the presence of the digital generations (Generation Y onwards), and their demand for fast, innovative technology products. High-speed broadband with larger bandwidth have allowed greater capacity of network traffic and data sharing while new gadgets, increasingly equipped with mobile internet, reflect the level of demand and comfort societies have towards technologies. This trend is echoed in book sales with Amazon's sales of Kindle e-books outnumbering its sales of hard-covered books (Miller, 2010). Technology has also allowed the development of online user-generated content, altering the way information is provided, gathered and perceived. Information provision has evolved from the traditional single-directional push of information from suppliers to consumers to a multi-directional share of information between suppliers and consumers, and between consumers themselves. Deloitte predicts that in 2011, more than 50% of computing devices sold globally will not be PCs. Instead, sales of smartphones and tablet computers would come to 425 million, well above the sales of 390 million PCs (CNA, 2011a). This implies that user-generated content will increasingly penetrate the online world of information, reflecting two future scenarios of a 'Free Information Society' and of 'Real Information Society' as proposed by Yeoman and McMahon-Beattie (2006). A free information society highlights that information is freely available and consumers no longer need to purchase information, whereas a real information society reflects how technology supports personal information rather than replacing it.

In today's society, digitised information is the norm. Many guidebooks such as *Lonely Planet* have embraced mobile devices by providing digitised guidebooks through the format of mobile applications designed for smartphone operators like Nokia, Apple, Google and Android (Lonely Planet, 2011). However, the continuous development of technology is bringing societies to a flip point, where technologies become increasingly integrated in our daily routine. Driving this is ubiquitous computing. Ubiquitous computing refers to technologies which interact with humanity out in the open rather than users connecting with the computer; it is the interaction of one user with many interfaces through technology that is interwoven into the external environment. This concept puts forth many possibilities for interaction with information technologies without the use of devices, for example, the possibility of gathering information through a pair of contact lenses. As technology slowly recedes into the background and becomes an invisible interaction in our daily lives, the future of information provision may no longer require mobile devices.

So, Imagine This . . .

Maria, a 29 year old from Madrid loves culture, art and festivals and every other year visits the festivals of Edinburgh. She is thinking, what shall I do this year? Using her mobile phone, she watches the latest video on www.visitscotland.com, an interactive film which follows the exploits of Hamish, holidaying in Edinburgh, whether it is bungee jumping off the Forth Road Bridge, a performance of the Chicago Ballet at the international festival or the Russian veteran political satirist Vladimir Vladimirovich Putin. As Maria watches the film, she 'tags' the things she wants to do, places to stay and makes arrangements for flights, all of which is brought together as an individual itinerary. Maria then confirms everything speaking to Mary, VisitScotland's intelligent agent, a 3D hologram image on her phone.

On arrival at Edinburgh airport, Maria wants to check some local information; the cyborg information assistant is a wealth of knowledge advising Maria on local restaurants and pubs. Arriving in the city centre, Maria checks into her hotel using a biometric eye registration system.

Before leaving for a tour of the old town, she has purchased a 'witchery tour' app for her contact lens so that she can visualise what medieval Edinburgh would be like in 1650. This is all possible given the ubiquitous nature of the city's information network. That night, dinner is at the Rhubarb restaurant with friends before heading to the Festival Theatre to watch Mr Putin's 'vodka politiks' comedy routine. The evening finishes about 1.00 am with drinks at the Balmoral Champagne Bar, a seven star bar which features mind reading bar attendants who offer immaculate service.

Drivers of Technological Innovation

In *Physics of the Future* Michio Kaku (2011) demonstrates that in 2100 we will control computers via tiny brain sensors and, like magicians, move objects around with the power of our minds. Artificial intelligence (AI) will be dispersed throughout the environment, and internet-enabled contact lenses will allow us to access the world's information database or conjure up any image we desire in the blink of an eye. This chapter is not about 2100 but 2050 and considers the key drivers of technological innovation that will shape tourism. Ten drivers have been identified that shape Maria's scenario:

Driver 1: Ubiquitous computing and the urban environment
Driver 2: Gestural interfaces
Driver 3: Beyond Moore's law – Optical computing
Driver 4: Virtual reality and augmented reality
Driver 5: Biometrics
Driver 6: Interactive visitor centres
Driver 7: Technology and life
Driver 8: Artificial intelligence and singularity
Driver 9: Brain computer interfaces
Driver 10: Haptic technologies

Driver 1: Ubiquitous computing and the urban environment

Technologies in modern societies are highly interlinked with many of its urban elements, albeit in a rather haphazard way. Traffic cameras, for example, are connected to the internet allowing users to track live traffic conditions; transport systems timings are also linked to online systems providing information to users. Although technologies are highly assimilated in many of today's urban environments, it still requires some form of platform – such as a mobile device – in order to send and collect mobile data.

The concept of ubiquitous computing was first invented by a researcher, Mark Weiser, who developed the idea of 'invisible computing' – that is, computing without computers (Greenfield, 2006). This concept is character-ised as wireless, mobile and networked, where technologies are embedded into the external environment, allowing users to become more connected to their surroundings and other people. Ubiquitous computing allows integra-tion of devices and technology applications, in a world where everything is enabled and shared. For Maria, it is the seamless working of technology which enhance her 'witchery tour' experience. Ubiquitous computing is sometimes also referred to as the post-desktop model of human–computer interaction or the third wave of computing. Quite opposite to virtual reality (VR), users no longer require a technological device to interact with technol-ogy; rather, this interaction is spatial and external. The evolvement of ubiq-uitous computing will create an urban environment that will see the disappearance of devices into a situation where multiple users are potentially interacting with multiple interfaces at a given time and place.

Adam Greenfield (2006) introduced the concept of a networked city, where elements of the urban environment such as the objects and surfaces of everyday life will have the ability to sense, process, receive, store, display transmit and even take physical action upon information. Elements such as clothes, architectural space and public spaces have information gathering, processing, storage and transmission devices capability (Lift Asia, 2008). A networked urban environment will empower people to have more control of the type and amount of information presented to them. For example, a user at present will be able to obtain information on the type of cuisine a particular restaurant offers, but in a ubiquitous urban environment, the user can choose to obtain information on whether the restaurant is open at that moment, or whether there is a queue for tables. In a world of ubiquitous computing we may eventually see the demise of artefacts such as maps and guidebooks as information shifts from 'way-finding' to 'way-showing'. Users enabled by technology, will be able to navigate their way through urban environments without the use of maps or guidebooks – a trend that is already present in Tokyo. Apart from that, the use of mobile devices to pres-ent contextual information over an object through the AR is already present. As urban environments become ubiquitous and increasingly networked, more of such information which is locked as conditioned data, will be avail-able at the users' fingertips (Howells, 2009).

A networked urban environment empowers people in their process of information gathering. However, there are implications related to privacy, reliance on technology and social acceptance as society moves from a com-munity to a network. It may take decades to synthesise the ubiquitous com-puting society. Nonetheless, we do know that the future urban landscape will be an interactive space where people and information seamlessly inter-act. The ubiquitous computing environment will not only affect the way we interact with information but will also influence the behaviours and move-ments of people within the built environment.

Modern urban environments also present opportunities for different forms of information provision. Korea, for example, launched the 'Haru 2010 Campaign', which utilises Korean drama media and technology to allow people to create personalised guidebooks (just like Maria in the scenario above). Visitors to the website can watch the drama and TAGs appearing on screen to gather information about tourism in Korea and their related travel interests. By watching the entire episode, visitors can also find out about their own tour styles and download guidebooks which can be easily transferred to other social networking sites such as Twitter and Facebook (Haru, 2010). This campaign, clearly targeted at Generation Y and beyond, is an example of how destination marketing organisations are utilising technology to engage with visitors from various platforms such as television media, internet and social networks.

Driver 2: Gestural interfaces

Developments in ubiquitous computing have led to innovations in gestural interfaces. A gestural interface is a platform that bridges communication between humans and machines by inventing measures which allow computers to understand human body language. The screens of these interfaces are embedded with optical sensors that track the movement of the user's fingers such that they do not have to come into contact with the display (Salton, 2009). Science fiction movies such as *Minority Report* illustrate the possibility of future gestural interface, where things can be controlled without devices. At present, products such as Kinect by Xbox 360 (www.xbox.com/Kinect) have incorporated gestural interfaces with sound, voice and facial recognition in its gaming console. This 'natural user interface' allows the system to track and interpret movement, creating a control-free entertainment experience. Future gestural interfaces will enable humans to interact with machines without having to use any mechanical devices; it is the next big thing in computer interfaces.

Information in its traditional form is typically confined to print media, or digitally on screen. However, with a gestural interface, information can be interacted with externally through simple hand gestures. 'SixthSense' for example, is a wearable gestural interface that augments the physical world with digital information, and allows natural hand gestures to interact with that information. It bridges the gap between intangible digital information and the tangible world and frees information from its confined state of paper or a digital screen. The gadget is comprised of a pocket projector, a mirror and a camera in the form of a pendant like a mobile device. They are connected to the projector, which enables surfaces such as walls and other physical objects to become digital interfaces by projecting information onto it. Users then can interact freely with this information with hand gestures. 'SixthSense' incorporates applications that help users interact with particular information. For example, the map application allows a user to navigate a map displayed on a nearby surface using hand gestures; the drawing application tracks movements of the index finger, allowing the user to access their email account with the drawing of an '@' sign and a gestural camera allows photos to be taken when the 'framing' gesture is detected. The gadget is also able to augment physical objects to portray additional information (SixthSense, 2009) (Figures 5.1 and 5.2).

Certain gestural interfaces, like Microsoft's Kinect, use a peripheral embedded with a small camera to capture gestural information. However, this limits the sensitivity and performance of the interface at short distances. In order to overcome such limits, cameras need to be set far behind the screen, but this then makes the interface bulky and expensive (Salton, 2009). Developments are being made to alter gestural interfaces into a thin LCD device – such as a mobile device – and to enable interaction without gloves or devices. Although still in its development phase, gestural mobile devices are slowly being introduced into the market. These products are equipped with gesticulation-sensitive interfaces that enable the user to flip through a photo gallery, or zoom in and out using a fist (Shankland, 2011). The future of gestural interfaces may come in many forms; whether wearable or hand-held, these interfaces will enable quicker, digitised user interaction.

Figure 5.1 The SixthSense application with newspapers
(*Source:* Pranav Mistry and MIT Media Lab)

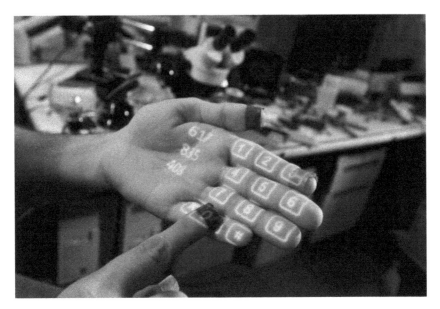

Figure 5.2 The SixthSense application with telephones
(*Source:* Pranav Mistry and MIT Media Lab)

Driver 3: Beyond Moore's Law: Optical computing

In order for innovations in technology to happen as described in the scenario above, a quantum leap is required in the terms of capacity processing power that goes beyond Moore's Law. The exponential advancement in technology is largely due to innovations and improvements made in computer science. Moore's Law is a trend that is typically used to describe the rate of long-term advancement in computing as a driving force behind technological changes. In 1975, a prediction was made by Intel co-founder Gordon E. Moore that the number of components in integrated circuits would double every year, increasing yields and driving costs per transistors down. This prediction, since dubbed 'Moore's Law', has been amazingly accurate (Intel, 2005). This law, premised on the quantity of transistors in an inexpensive integrated circuit, has defined a development path for chip makers. Today, the ability to squeeze more transistors into a chip is achieved by decreasing the size of transistors, reducing them to as small as 22 nanometres. However, physical miniaturisation cannot continue forever and new developments utilising new materials are evolving (Fildes, 2010).

Researchers are now looking at the use of optical transistors to improve the efficiency of electronic computing. An optical computer, or photonic computer, is a device which replaces the traditional use of electrons with photons of visible light. As light particles travel the fastest, the speed of processing powers in computers substantially increases without incurring additional heat or electricity as was the case with the traditional use of copper wire electrons in computer hardware. This means that future computers would be able to perform operations more effectively, making it faster than a conventional electronic computer. Photons are ideal for piping information over long distances through optical fibres (*The Economist*, 2010). Although the high cost of using optics have prevented a wide-scale development of optical computers, demand for devices and processing powers is increasing and as a result, a number of new optical alternatives are emerging.

Intel, for example, has embraced the use of silicon-based lasers to boost computer processing speeds. The system which is capable of shifting data at 50 Gb/s, is achieved by combining four silicon-based lasers each carrying a 12.5 Gb/s data stream along a single optical fibre, at the end of which the beam is split once again and set to four photodetectors for decoding for a total of 50 Gb/s along a single fibre (Halfacree, 2010). This system potentially lowers the cost and size of optical use inside a computer. IBM has also developed optical interconnects by mounting fibre-optic cables straight onto chips that direct traffic between multiple processes to speed up the flow of data and processing power of computers (*The Economist*, 2010). Apart from optical computing, new developments in transistors – which are fundamental components in modern electronic devices – are also driving data processing, capacity and computer powers. Hewlett-Packard has built the memristors which can be used to crunch data and build advanced chips. In a traditional device, data must be transferred and processed between two separate devices; but on a memristor, these two functions can be done on the same device. The memristor's ability to mimic synaptic activity in the brain means that it can be used to develop real brain-like computers in future (Fildes, 2010). These developments in optical computing may move beyond the Moore's Law predictions, creating computers with super processing speeds at low prices.

Driver 4: Virtual reality and augmented reality

One of the strands in the scenario is Maria using a 'witchery tour' app to experience and interpret medieval Edinburgh. Maria's experience is driven by developments in VR and AR, which have blurred the defining areas of the real world and the computer-generated world. VR is defined as 'the use of a computer-generated 3D environment – called a 'virtual environment (VE)' – that one can navigate and possibly interact with, resulting in real-time stimulation of one or more of the user's five senses' (Guttentag, 2009: 638). VR scenarios and real-world scenarios are situated at extreme ends of a spectrum; this means that when a user is fully immersed in a VE, they do not have any interaction with the real world. AR on the other hand, is situated between a VR and a real-world scenario where technologies enhance rather than replace reality. AR adds graphics, sounds, haptic feedback and smell to the natural world in which it exists, revolutionising the way information is presented to people (Bonsor, 2009). Provision of information through AR is not new, with many mobile devices such as the iPhone and Android capable of presenting information through mobile applications. For example, a mobile application, Layar, uses the mobile phone's camera and GPS capabilities to overlay information such as histories or photographs of nearby sites and restaurants on screen. Increasingly, many industries are embracing the use of AR for a variety of uses including information provision, medical surgeries and retail sales.

In the future, the use of AR in information provision may no longer require the use of hand-held devices such as mobile phones, but rather come in the form of wearable devices. Developments are underway to incorporate AR into contact lens – the project 'Twinkle in the Eye', undertaken by the University of Washington. The research on AR contact lenses will allow texts to be displayed, speeches to be translated into captions in real time, or offering visual cues from a navigation system. Hence, the story of Maria and the contact lenses. These contact lenses will be integrated with control circuits, communication circuits and miniature antennas using custom-built optoelectronic components, including hundreds of LEDs that are used to form images in front of the eye such as words, charts and photographs. The hardware will be semi-transparent, allowing the device to present information to the circuit and allowing users to navigate naturally in their surroundings at the same time. The potential of an AR contact lens will unlock a new platform of visual information, unfettered by the constraints of physical display (Parviz, 2009).

Besides contact lenses, AR has also been incorporated into other wearable products such as spectacles. In Japan, a pair of lightweight AR glasses – the AV Walker – has been created by Olympus and phone-maker NTT Docomo, and is able to overlay the world with digital content such as directions or a travel guide. Designed with a tiny retinal display at one arm of the spectacle frame, the display will be able to project text and images directly into the user's peripheral vision at the same time, allowing the user to be aware of their natural surroundings. Attached to the AR software, an acceleration and a direction sensor, the display will be able to project information on the object the user is looking at. This includes a virtual tour guide, directional information and even weather information and forecasts when the user lifts their head up to the sky. The AV Walker has an added benefit of accessing surrounding information without having to alter the user's natural behaviour (Fitzpatrick, 2010). Wearable products are increasingly being incorporated with electronic gadgets. The Lady Gaga Polaroid Digital Camera, for example, is a combination of digital camera and sunglasses. The camera sunglasses are embedded with two 1.5″ LCD displays which act as a wearable 12 megapixel camera with the ability to snap pictures, preload with pictures and videos and enable real-time photo sharing. The displays are situated below the wearer's line of sight, enabling the combinational use of a sunglass, camera and a mobile display screen. The use of AR in information is not new. However, with advancement of technologies, this platform will be further integrated with our daily lives, revolutionising the way we interact with information.

Driver 5: Biometrics

The use of retinal eye scanners and biometrics is present in today's technology, but with the increased use of technology in security it is a trend that will accelerate into the mainstream, as Maria demonstrates in the scenario given. The concept of biometrics was first introduced in the 19th century by Alphonse Bertillon, who practised the idea of using a number of body measurements to identify criminals. By the late 19th century, this concept had gained much popularity from major law enforcement departments. Today, biometrics is not only used by enforcement departments, but also in various civilian applications such as medical industries. One of the key reasons for this wide-scale application is rising cases of fraud and identity theft, which came alongside technological advancement. A biometric system, which is a 'recognition system that operates by acquiring biometric data from an individual, extracting a feature set from the acquired data, and comparing this feature set against the template set in the database' (Jain *et al.*, 2004: 2) can significantly decrease these numbers by increasing security measures. Today, biometric systems are used widely in commercial, government and forensic applications (Jain *et al.*, 2004).

Biometrics can be categorised into two forms – physiological and behavioural. Physiological biometrics identifies using physical traits of a person, such as fingerprints, hand geometry, the iris, voice and facial features. Fingerprints appear to be the most common identification method, accounting for 67% of all applications (TechCast, 2011a). The use of fingerprint identification is a common form of biometric authentication, with many countries such as the European Union, United States, New Zealand and others incorporating it as part of their biometric passport – a combination of paper and electronic passport – application. Popular biometric passport applications include fingerprint, facial and iris recognition for identity authentication. The convenience of biometric fingerprint scanners have encouraged its commercialisation, enabling additional security to mobile devices such as laptops and mobile phones where users can lock/unlock and protect stored data and access emails (TechCast, 2011a). Its application has also expanded with tourism operators such as Disney incorporating fingerprint scanning to fight illegally resold park passes and tickets (Utter, 2006).

Behavioural biometrics is based on the reflection of an individual's psychology, which includes aspects such as voice, typing rhythm and gait recognition. This type of biometric data is said to garner wider acceptability as it is less intrusive compared to physical biometrics (Gamboa & Fred, 2004). Expanding on the scope of behavioural recognition, further developments have been made within this area of biometrics, including an attempt to direct a mobile robot under real-world conditions into a target position by means of pointing poses only. The reason for incorporating pointing as an action is because of its natural and intuitive nature known to humans. Gestures also allow an intuitive way for humans to instruct robots without any use of input devices (Martin *et al.*, 2010).

ABI research findings indicate that people are feeling increasingly comfortable using biometric security, which could result in a $3 billion spending increase in biometrics over the next five years (Blanco, 2010). Biometric identification methods will continue to evolve, with research on tongue scanning identification currently being tested at Hong Kong Polytechnic University (Blanco, 2010). However, there are issues which need to be further dealt with in order for biometrics to be utilised at its full potential. This includes issues of privacy and security as experts indicate that biometric theft has implications more serious than just forging a signature.

Driver 6: Interactive visitor centres

TNS Global (2008) indicates that one in 10 respondents connect to the internet at least once a day via mobile handsets. Among them, over a quarter of its Japanese and Chinese respondents access the internet over mobile at least once a day. In an Australian survey, 56% of respondents used their mobile phones to obtain information while 21% visit a website at least once per day (AIMIA, 2009). These figures reflect the rising rates of mobile usage and increased mobile penetration, coupled with developments of technology that has prompted the shift of traditional information to digital information; from passive to interactive. As younger generations of consumers embrace the use of mobile media to seek information, make bookings and navigate themselves in an external environment, destinations are incorporating technology with information provision to enhance the visitors' experience.

The collaboration between Google and New York City saw the launch of an interactive visitor information centre and a digital platform where visitors can retrieve information about the city, on the go. The website, NYCGO. com, is a Google-fuelled local search and reference site, which provides information on attractions and activities in New York City. The website contains useful visitor information such as maps powered by Google, travel deals from Travelocity and local content from *Time Out New York*, nightlife culture magazine *Paper*, the *New York Observer* and eco-living guide *Greenopia* (McCarthy, 2009). A unique characteristic of this website is that it allows visitors to download information on hotels, restaurants and access discount packages directly from their mobile smartphones such as iPhone and Blackberry. Users are also able to send details of attractions and locations of activities to their mobile phones via text messages. These locations are powered by Google Maps, which then allows users to navigate the city on the go by quickly accessing walking, driving or subway directions to their destinations. This digital platform is supported by an interactive visitor centre which features interactive map tables that are powered by Google Maps API, allowing visitors to navigate venues and attractions, as well as create personalised itineraries which can be printed, emailed or sent to the users mobile device. The centre also features a gigantic video wall where users can view their personalised itineraries in virtual 3D – powered by Google Earth. This collaboration between Google and New York City shows that destinations are starting to embrace the use of technologies to explore and support the visitors' experience.

However, not only are destination visitor centres embracing technologies for service. The Ciudad Grupo Santander bank in Madrid has created a futuristic visitor centre encompassing robotic butlers, an AR model and interactive walls. As visitors walk into the bank's main lobby, knee-high autonomous robots, known as Santander Interactive Guest Assistants, will be available. The interactive system allows visitors to choose a language they are familiar with, and the robots then greet and guide them to their intended location, even within a crowded space. Within the building, walls are created with a motion, touch-screen-based interaction design that has the ability to sense and react to what is around it, communicating financial information in interactive ways. Besides that, a model of Santander's financial centre was made and built with an AR set-up using state-of-the-art lasers and a large database of photographs. With a digital information layout and mobile transparent-like screens, users can manoeuvre them and explore information, facilities and architectural tales of the centre, acting as a guide on its own (Ashby, 2010; YDreams, 2010). As public spaces become increasingly incorporated with digital features, as reflected in the New York City's visitor centre and Ciudad Grupo Santander, the future of visitor centres may see human staff eventually replaced by robotic staff for 24/7 service, along with digitalised platforms to present information in an interactive manner, as occurs in the scenario with Maria.

Driver 7: Technology and life

It is recognised that different generation cohorts reflect different attitudes and beliefs that are shaped by external factors. Generation Y, born between 1977 and 1997 have been heavily recognised as a generation wholly different from earlier generations with the key influencing factor being technology, to the point that life is lived through a screen (as Maria demonstrates in the scenario). Tapscott (2009) coined the term 'Net Generation' in relation to the Generation Y, because they have grown up in an era where technology advanced at an exponential rate. Unlike the baby boomer generation, the Net Generation did not have to accommodate to new forms of technology; rather, they assimilated easily and without much difficulty to new and advanced technologies. In fact, the Net Generation has a range of unique characteristics, which up till today, are driving the innovation and developments of technologies and revolutionising the meaning and use of the internet. These characteristics, which include their love for customisation, desire for freedom of choice and speech and innovative ideas have transformed the internet from an information-provision platform, to an information-sharing platform; from passive media into interactive media. The Net Generation's high assimilation to technology is reflected from their ability to multi-task, such as talking to friends, listening to music and surfing multiple websites all at the same time (Tapscott, 2009).

Tapscott (2009) had also identified that this generation do not observe, but rather participate in online activities. Unlike previous generations of passive internet users, the Net Generation uses the internet to 'inquire, discuss, argue, play, shop, critique, investigate, ridicule, fantasize, seek and inform' (Tapscott, 2009: 40), which is what drives information on social media sites. Research conducted by Beresford (2006) on the usage of social media networks in the United States indicates that younger users aged 18–24 (Generation Y) consult social networks before making decisions and that no online activity (other than email) ranked higher in importance than online social networking. This indicates that social networking sites are increasingly being integrated into Generation Y's lives so much so that they become a trusted resource for their decision making.

The Net Generation is a generation which likes to share information and stay connected with friends and families, and they use technology ranging from mobile phones to social networks to do so (Tapscott, 2009). The advancement in mobile technologies, such as mobile internet, means that mobile phones are no longer perceived as just communication devices, but rather a vital connection to their social networks, enabling them to stay connected online wherever they go. Smartphones such as iPhone and Blackberry are mobile phones that have access to general internet and support user applications. According to the Australian Interactive Media Industry Association, 77% of respondents use their mobile phones for a purpose other than voice or SMS, 56% use it to search for information and 21% use it to visit a website at least once a day (AIMIA, 2009), reflecting the evolving role of the mobile device. Increasingly, users are also integrating smartphones into their daily lives, utilising it as an alarm clock, replacing computers and using it to access emails and surf the internet, using it as a GPS guide during trips, loading their favourite music on the go rather than listening to radios, as well as obtaining up-to-date, personalised news feeds through their mobile devices instead of reading the newspapers (Tapscott, 2009). It is forecasted that there will be more people accessing the mobile web more than the desktop web by 2015 (Lock, 2010). The Net Generation contribution is what drives the increasing amount of consumer-generated content online as more people – at a decreasing age – contribute to innovations of mobile applications with the youngest iPhone application writer being nine years old (iPhoneTechZone, 2009).

As future consumers of tourism, Generation Y (or the Net Generation) has a distinct set of characteristics, attitudes and behaviours significantly different from previous generations. Technology and mobile devices are an assimilated part of their growing up years and have been highly integrated into their daily lives. They are absolutely comfortable in creating, interacting and utilising multiple platforms of media at the same time, relying on it as a significant platform for keeping in contact with friends and families. They are the main drivers behind the vast amount of consumer-generated information online, revolutionising the way information is presented to consumers.

Driver 8: Artificial intelligence and singularity

AI has been recognised as an attractive direction to the development of future technology. Alan Turing, who conceptualised the 'Turing Test' in 1950, described the defining moment in AI as when computer behaviour becomes indistinguishable from human behaviour (TechCast, 2011b); this is when *singularity* has arrived. In the scenario, humans are being replaced by Cyborgs in the Visitor Information Centre at Edinburgh Airport. The use of AI is increasingly being used in a variety of sectors such as medical and manufacturing, as well as software and technologies designed with part-AI systems. Google, for example, has used AI in their search engines and translation software, which allow the translation of words and phrases between different languages (Gomes, 2010; Saenz, 2010). The vast amount of information online from various origins in different languages means that Google Translator will be able to translate information within seconds, allowing users who are not proficient in a language to understand this information. Besides that, full AI systems such as the Smart Call Agents are powered by artificial general intelligence (AGI) engine or 'brain', which unlike automatic conversation solutions, reasons and learns from experiences and are able to generate personalised speech for each caller in a more natural conversation. This system had the ability to undertake and handle phone calls typically required by human operators, as it is equipped with speech recognition technology, integrated with an intelligence engine and able to recognise phone-quality speech input (SmartAction, 2011).

AI technologies are set to develop further in the future as more futuristic systems are being experimented with. For example, the research on telepresence systems is currently being undertaken. This research encompasses four different prototypes of telepresence systems, one of which allows people to communicate using interactive real-time 3D communication. It involves, for instance, the development of a virtual human that can be sent in the form of an 'autonomous avatar' when the actual person is unable to attend a meeting. This virtual human will be able to recognise the real participants in the meeting, register what is being said and report to the absentee after the meeting. Other prototypes include the development of an 'avatar' – a mobile robotic mannequin that takes on the appearance of its far-away human host – that can be remotely controlled and navigated from a distant environment (CNA, 2011b).

It is possible that the continual development of AI may eventually result in technological singularity, which is a situation of intelligence explosions where humans will no longer be able to predict their future as intelligence entities surpass human biological intelligence. This possibility drives the rapid advancement of technologies encompassing the possibility of creating systems more intelligent than humanity. Although AI systems have significant contributions in terms of convenience and service to humanity, a technological singularity will have major social implications on society including issues such as population job loss, economic impacts and others. It is vital then that society ensures and manages the balance of negative and positive implications artificial agents bring.

Driver 9: Brain computer interfaces

Brain computer interface (BCI) is a 'communication system in which messages or commands that an individual sends to the external world would not pass through the brain's normal output pathways of peripheral nerves and muscles' (Wolpaw et al., 2002: 769). Instead, these thoughts are sent through an external device which translates them into actions. BCI has been widely recognised within the medical arena for its capabilities to allow movements in people who may be paralysed or 'locked-in', or have severe neuromuscular disorders such as spinal cord injuries by replacing movements made from their nerves and muscles through producing electrophysiological signals which then converts them into physical actions (Wolpaw et al., 2002).

The crux of BCI technologies is the development of a direct communication channel between the human brain and machines that does not require any motor activity (Leeb et al., 2007). Two different BCI interfaces – invasive and non-invasive – exist. Invasive BCI typically requires an electrode implant into the user's brain, although this increases signal to the external device it potentially presents health risks as well. However, a more common approach is undertaken through non-invasive BCI that requires users to wear headgear covered in electrodes which has better signal (The Wheelchair Guide, 2008). Non-invasive BCI, or electroencephalography (EEG) is the most studied aspect of non-invasive interface due to its fine temporal resolution, ease of use and low set-up cost. It allows users to choose the brain signals they found easiest to operate the BCI. Research conducted by the University of

Rochester found that users are able to control elements to the external virtual world through EEG readings, including switching the lights on/off and bringing a mock car to a stop. A common application example is for wheelchair users, who, after being equipped with a BCI, are able to control their wheelchair through thought.

BCI has also been used to aid patients who are partially disabled, such as incorporating the use of a robotic arm. This form of invasive BCI, as mentioned earlier, requires an implant of electrodes into the user's brain in order to produce signals high enough to stimulate movement. Research conducted indicated the ability of a tetraplegic human to control an artificial hand using invasive BCI. The user was able to open simulated email, draw a circular figure on a paint programme, adjust a simple hardware interface such as volume and others with control of his robotic hand by thinking about these movements together with the computer cursor, lights and television (Hochberg et al., 2006).

The ability for technologies to connect to brain waves has resulted in an emerging field of synthetic telepathy. This is demonstrated in the scenario at the Balmoral Champagne bar, where the bar staff have mind-reading abilities. Synthetic telepathy involves the development of a 'telepathy chip', which is a neural implant that allows users to project their thoughts and feelings, and receive the same thing from others without the use of verbal words or actions (Goertzel, 2009). The initial development of synthetic telepathy revolved around military use, when the US Army Research Office awarded the University of California, Irvine a US$4 million grant for research to work on the project 'Silent Talk'. The objective of the project is to allow soldiers to engage in 'user-to-user communication on the battlefield without the use of vocalised speech through the analysis of neural signals' (June, 2009; UCI, 2008). The research seeks to develop technology that would detect the signals of 'pre-speech', analyse and transmit the statement to an intended interlocutor, which then using non-invasive brain imaging technology such as EEG decodes these thoughts, translates them into brainwaves and eventually transmits them to the intended target (Drummond, 2009).

Although BCI technologies, to a large extent, have created possibilities to do things that were previously deemed impossible, it also entails a range of psychological, social and ethical implications. Hence, it is necessary for organisations to properly manage the effects of negative implications so that they can be effectively minimised.

Driver 10: Haptic technologies

Improvements in technology have revolutionised the way devices are designed, evolving from buttons to touchscreen interfaces. This evolution is greatly attributed to developments in haptic technology, which is defined as 'the systems required – both hardware and software – to render the touch and feel of virtual objects' (Harris, 2011). Haptic is derived from the Greek word 'Haptesthai', meaning touch. The concept of haptic technology builds on users' sense of touch, allowing them to touch and feel objects within the virtual world. For example, applications of haptic technology in video games have allowed players to feel and manipulate gaming tools where they are able to feel, for example, the resistance of a longbow's string as they release a virtual arrow in the game.

Haptic technologies form the foundation of the design of touchscreen mobile devices, allowing users to interact with the mobile interface with their sense of touch. Nokia, for example, created a touchscreen platform that creates the feeling of movement in and out when the user pushes a 'button' on the interface, creating an audible click at the same time. Apart from that, this form of technology is also widely used in teleoperation, or telerobotics, where the human operator controls the movements of the robot, or when they have a sense a presence located in the robot's environment (Harris, 2011). It allows the operator to control the movement of the robot even at a distance. Other sectors which utilise this form of technology include the medical industry for surgeries and the aviation sector for aircraft maintenance (Hillsley, 2004).

The field of haptic technologies is set to grow and potentially contribute increasing reality in virtual worlds. Haptic technologies have multiple advantages. Haptic interfaces integrate a much more satisfying user experience as our sense of touch conveys rich and detailed information about an object. When combined with the other senses, particularly sight, it dramatically increases the amount of information which is sent to the brain for processing. This increase in information eventually reduces user error, time taken to complete tasks, energy consumption and magnitudes of contact forces used (Harris, 2011). The possibilities of incorporating haptic technology and VR mean that future computer platforms will allow users to touch, grip and even manipulate 'impossible objects', significantly changing the way users interact with computer platforms. Users will be able to 'feel as well as see virtual objects on a computer, and so can give an illusion of touching surfaces, shaping virtual clay or moving objects around' (Hillsley, 2004). For example, researchers at the University of Tokyo have developed 3D holograms that can be touched with bare hands. Acoustic radiation pressure, for example, can be used to create a touch sensation, refuting the notion of holograms being made only of light. The technology adds tactile feedback to holograms which allows physical interaction with virtual images (as seen in the scenario with Maria's holographic mobile phone). In particular, it does not require a special glove or special control; users can just 'walk up and use', depicting how information provision may change in time to come (Physorg, 2009). Without doubt, haptic technology will continue to be largely infused into our daily lives, such as it being incorporated into clothing textiles so that individuals can feel the texture of clothing when purchasing through the internet (Ruvinsky, 2003).

The importance of real and personal information in tourism

What if the technology does not work or would you not just want to speak to a real person instead? Yeoman and McMahon-Beattie (2006) in the paper *'Tomorrow's tourist and the information society'*, had drawn two different scenarios on the future of information provision in tourism. The 'Free Information Society' is one which highlights that information is freely available and future consumers no longer need to purchase information. On the other hand, the 'Real Information Society' uses technology to support personal information, rather than replace it entirely. The development of information technology with changing consumer attitudes and behaviours towards information search is revolutionising the way information is presented and collected within the tourism experience.

Without doubt, the advances of technologies as earlier discussed will shape the way information is provided and gathered in a manner that is quite different from how it is done today. Interactive media platforms incorporated with designs such as mobility and VR/AR will create a different experiential platform for tourists at a destination. In fact, potential developments such as telepresence may reduce the need for people to travel, since they are able to appear robotically as 'avatars' at another location. It can be argued however, that although having gone through significant advances of technology, real and personal information in tourism still plays a crucial role in the tourist's experience.

Tourism is an industry where people and culture are essential components of the tourism product, particularly in the provision of information in tourism. Unlike other commodities, tourists need to travel to the destination in order for consumption of various tourism products; it is intangible and cannot be seen or felt prior to purchase. This means the type of information collected prior to purchase is particularly influential. Although increasingly, more people are turning towards online user-generated content for information as it is perceived as being the neutral opinions about experiences, this does not increase the information's reliability. On the contrary, locals who are knowledgeable about their own destinations will be able to provide personalised information more accurately to visitors. This is also one key reasons why word-of-mouth is a particularly effective distribution channel in the tourism industry, where information provided by locals and people who have experienced the product are highly regarded. Technology in this case should enhance the visitor's search for information, allowing it to become easily accessible and convenient, rather than replacing it as a whole.

Many tourists seeking authentic experiences regard interaction with local people as a way of experiencing the local culture of a destination. Technology then becomes a large obstacle between tourists and authenticity. If in the free information scenario tourists are able to gather information entirely from various media platforms, the possibility of them engaging the use of a local visitor centre is minimal, thereby reducing the authentic aspect of the experience. However, personal recommendations from locals at the destination has been deemed as 'very important', and classified as 'tacit, episodic, difficult to code and to make explicit' (Yeoman & McMahon-Beattie, 2006), illustrating that personal information in the tourist experience plays a significant role in influencing the tourist's experience.

Consumer demographics are evolving, significantly reshaping attitudes and behaviours in their information search. The use of technologies for information searching will continue to rise as consumers become more comfortable with interacting with different media platforms. However, this will not be cause the demise of the use of local knowledge at visitor centres, as word-of-mouth recommendations and personal information continue to remain the most influential form of information for tourism destinations.

Concluding Remarks

From the internet to ...

Some would think that the world of the future has arrived today: the internet changed society. The mobile phone changed it again. In the future, the internet is everywhere; in wall screens, furniture, billboards and even in contact lenses. If you blink you will be online. Scientists at the University of Washington (Parviz, 2009) have perfected the virtual retinal display (VRD) in which red, green and blue laser light can be shone directly onto the retina. Contact lenses will have facial recognition capability so you will be able to recognise your friends via Facebook. In fact, you will have a world of information in the blink of eye. According to Kaku (2011) these pattern recognition systems have a 90% success rate. At a business meeting or social function, you will never be embarrassed because you forgot someone's name.

The goal of ubiquitous computing is to bring the computer into your domain by putting chips everywhere. The purpose of VR is to put us into the computer. Today, we can live in a virtual world, for example, www.secondlife.com. You can control your world and be part of someone else's world as an avatar. VR is already the staple of video games. In the future as computer power expands, tourists will visit unreal worlds that seem real. Does this mean the end of the holiday as we know it as real experiences are no longer necessary? VR is already changing the shopping experience, for example, Westfield shopping centre in West London unveiled a 'tweet' mirror which allowed customers to see images of themselves and post the content straight to their chosen social networking site. Those who used the service were thus able to see how they looked in particular garments and then seek real-time advice from their online friends and family members. More, if a customer decided not to purchase an item, the image was nevertheless sent to their email address, together with a link to the website of the clothing brand in question, should they later change their mind. This is yet another example of increased interconnectivity in today's world, a retailer allowing consumers to connect with their social networks while in-store, as well as create digital images to make the process of shopping more fun and engaging.

Haptic technologies allow us to feel the presence of objects that are computer generated. The technology, first developed by scientists to handle highly radioactive materials with remote-controlled robotic arms, has moved on. By simulating the sensation of pressure you can feel shape and texture, that is, as you move your finger across a surface, haptic technologies will simulate the feeling of a wooden table. Haptic technologies combined with objects that are seen in VR goggles, complete the illusion of an alternative reality.

AR is already changing provision of information, as Hatton (2009) points out, '30% of hotel bookings in the cities of Tokyo and Seoul are on the day of arrival via the mobile phone'. Combining this trend with AR on mobile phones, tourists can find out anything about a hotel by simply pointing the phone at the building then making a decision about whether to book or not, and so forth. In the future, tourists will walk into museums and go to an exhibit and their contact lens will give a description of each object. A virtual guide will give you a cybertour as you pass. AR will allow you to see reconstructions of historical sites which are no longer there – along with an interactive recantation of battles of events from history. Hikers will never get lost in the future as they will know their exact position in a foreign land along with the names of all the plants. Tourists will be able to speak the local language via software translator. Imagine an American tourist ordering Peking Duck in a restaurant in Kunming using the right Mandarin dialect. Researchers at Carnegie Mellon University in Pittsburgh have pioneered computer-assisted translation (CAT) which attaches electrodes to the neck and face of the speaker, these pick up the contraction of the muscles and decipher the words being spoken. This approach does not require audio equipment, since the words can be mounted silently. Then a computer translates these words and a voice synthesiser speaks them out loud. In the future, language barriers will no longer be a barrier (Kaku, 2011). Finally, like the Greek gods, we think certain commands and our wishes will be obeyed. Today, the brain can control a computer; in the far future tourists will be able to dream about a destination and then play that creation on their computer, and create an itinerary and test experiences. Scientists at the Advanced Telecommunications Research Computational Neuroscience Laboratory (http://www.cns.atr.jp/en/) in Kyoto use fMRI scans to record where the brain stores images and reproduce those images as jpeg files. The tourism industry will be radically changed by future technologies. We can only imagine exactly what these changes might be.

What does all this mean?

Rapid technological advancement means machines and humans will be indistinguishable by 2050, as the point of singularity arrives. What does this mean? Some might say that in 2050 the robots will be going on holiday and the humans will be captive in the zoo. This may be the case, but the importance of soft singularity, or the component parts of it, is that rapid change is occurring driven by gains in artificial technology. Technology is one of the key drivers of the future, where flying cars, internet capable contact lenses, resurrection of extinct life, the end of death, space tourism and everything else Star Trekky is possible. This is where AI will be dispersed across a world in which information sources will be connected, where tourists tracked by GPS could not get lost.

National Tourism Organization's (NTO) have fundamentally switched marketing expenditures from print to digital and more recently towards mobile applications. As Tapscott (2009: 40) points out, generations of consumers live life through the screen in which they 'inquire, discuss, argue, play, shop, critique, investigate, ridicule, fantasize, seek and inform ... a noticeable movement from passive to interaction'. The South Korea tourism organisation marketing campaign (www.haru2010.com), is an example of this interaction towards new marketing applications in which change drives individualisation and personalised experience for tourists. Information, once linear and based on words, now has multiple dimensions, whether video or audio. In the not-too-distant future, haptic technologies will provide real 3D holographic feel as if you were talking to a real person. This rapid pace of change is happening now, ubiquitous computing is allowing technologies to join together, shape information and provide a seamless environment. Today, as Hatton (2009) points out, AR applications through mobile phones allow new dimensions in the distribution channel, where information and bookings are immediate and transparent. The MIT Media Lab project 'SixthSense' brings to life information with pictures in which a newspaper can have video and audio or a tourist could take photographs without a camera. Technology companies are talking about movement from the personal computer to the mobile phone, but the likely future is even more fantastic with connectivity achieved via smart contact lenses or even mind-reading telepathy.

This chapter recognises that technology has already changed how tourists engage with tourism and it will continue to do so. In the future we, like Maria, may use an artificially intelligent agent to seek authentic information, as if the robot was a real person; it is also likely that we will see increased use of biometric keys expediting and ensuring the safety of our trips.

6 Singapore 2050: Medicine, Science and the Meetings Industry

Learning points

- As the pace of discovery in science and medicine rapidly increases, new paradigms of complexity form. As a result, medical practitioners need to update their skills and knowledge more often at smaller and more frequent educational meetings.
- Science, medicine and technology represent 46% of all worldwide meetings.
- Singapore's science and research strategy is in sync with countries meetings, incentives and events industry.
- This chapter explains structural change in the meetings industry including the emergence of new meetings technologies and the importance of knowledge clusters.

Introduction

In most cultures God possesses the ultimate power; the power of life over death, the ability to heal the sick and prolong life. Is the future of medicine without death? Maybe! Use of the term 'complexity' has grown exponentially in the scientific literature. As society develops and grows, it finds new solutions; discovery is the heart of medicine, technological revolution seems endless and therefore humankind seems to be facing a world in which the pace of discovery is infinite. As a result, complexity and the pace of discovery are changing the world of science, technology and medicine, to the extent that simple human mortals cannot keep pace with this change. The meetings industry is benefiting from the increased complexity and rate of change. For example, medical doctors, instead of meeting every five years to keep abreast of change, now have to meet every two years (HCEA, 2009). Improvements in cancer treatments are a good example of how and why change is occurring.

Table 6.1 Five-year relative survival (%) during three time periods by cancer type

Type	1975–1977	1984–1986	1996–2002
All	50	53	66
Breast (female)	51	59	65
Colon	51	59	65
Leukaemia	35	42	49
Lung and bronchus	13	13	16
Melanoma	82	86	92
Non-Hodgkin lymphoma	48	53	63
Ovary	37	40	45
Pancreas	2	3	5
Prostate	69	76	100
Rectum	49	57	66
Urinary bladder	73	78	82

Source: European Federation of Pharmaceutical Industries and Associations

Table 6.1 shows that medical treatments for cancer have radically improved survival rates. The frequency of survival after five years has increased from 50% in 1975 to 66% in 2002. In other fields of medicine, new and better treatments are emerging. Over the last decade we have seen life expectancy massively increase for patients diagnosed with HIV due to new treatments and drug therapy combinations. One in five people in advanced economies by 2030 will probably celebrate their 100th birthday (Shoemaker & Shoemaker, 2009). A typical 50-year-old woman living in the United States in 1990 could look forward to an average of 31 additional years of life, bringing life expectancy to 81 (Shoemaker & Shoemaker, 2009). If we assume a cure for cancer, her average life expectancy increases to 84 years; adding a cure for heart disease she can look forward to 89 years of life. After we conquer strokes and diabetes, the increment rises to 47, yielding a full life expectancy of 97 years of age. No one knows for sure how far the boundary of death can be pushed, but optimistic scientists consider 130 years to be feasible by 2050.

It would seem logical that the complexity of change occurring in the field of science and technology can only be of benefit to the future of the meetings industry. However, the way the world changes is never simple. With reference to Singapore's public policy drive to champion scientific innovation this chapter explores how the future of the meetings industry will be shaped by science, medicine and discovery (Figure 6.1).

The Meetings Industry

Medical science has been the largest sector of the meetings industry for the last decade according to statistics from the International Congress

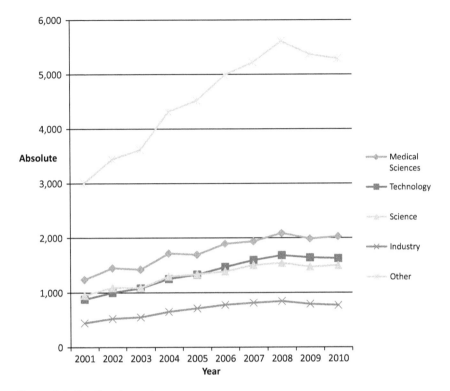

Figure 6.1 Meetings by sector
(*Source:* ICCA)

and Convention Association (ICCA, 2011). In 2010, medical science represented 18.1% of all meetings; combined with technology and science these sectors accounted for 46% of all meetings. According to the ICCA the following statistics provide a glimpse of the meetings industry worldwide:

- Over the last 10 years the number of meetings has risen from 5262 in 2001 to 9120 in 2010.
- The number of international association meetings that rotate the world has been decreasing over the last 15 years.
- Europe is still the most popular destination with the majority (54%) of the meetings hosted there in 2010. However, Europe's market share has been decreasing over the past 10 years and so has the relative popularity of North America, due to an increase in the attractiveness of Asia/Middle East mostly and Latin America.
- The United States and Germany are the number one and number two countries in terms of meetings per country, while Singapore is ranked 24th.

- Vienna has been the most popular city to host meetings for the last six years to 2010. European cities dominate the top 10 with Barcelona, Paris, Berlin, Madrid, Istanbul, Lisbon and Amsterdam constant performers for the last 10 years. The only non-European cities to make the top 10 are Singapore (5th) and Sydney (10th). However, Taipei (11th), Beijing (12th), Buenos Aires (12th), Seoul (16th) and Hong Kong (20th) are pushing hard.
- The average number of participants per meeting reached its lowest point in 2010 with 571 participants per international meeting compared to 696 in 2001.
- Over the last 10 years there has been a big expansion of the market share of the smallest meetings (50–149 and 150–249 participants) at the cost of all meetings attracting over 500 participants.

Healthcare

In the United States, according to the Healthcare Convention and Exhibitors Association (HCEA, 2011) the average total attendance for the top 50 healthcare meetings was 19,512 (Table 6.2). Notably, six of the top 15 healthcare meetings are dental, with the Greater New York Dental Meeting retaining its top position for the second year in a row. Attendance changes can vary greatly from year to year for most healthcare associations, depending on the economy, education draw, event location and the number

Table 6.2 Top 10 Associations Meetings in the United States

Rank	Association name	Total attendance	Professional attendance
1	Greater New York Dental Meeting	58,135	34,637
2	Radiological Society of North America	58,044	27,190
3	FIME	47,125	36,626
4	American Society of Clinical Oncology – Annual Meeting	32,700	26,600
5	Society for Neuroscience	31,975	26,393
6	Chicago Dental Society	31,373	22,054
7	American Academy of Orthopaedic Surgeons	29,164	14,716
8	Healthcare Information & Management Systems Society	27,855	13,846
9	Massachusetts Dental Society – Yankee Dental Congress	26,792	22,674
10	California Dental Association – Anaheim	26,166	18,737

Source: HCEA (2011)

of attendees who participate from outside the United States. The top 20 healthcare meeting destinations in the United States hosted 43% of all reported healthcare meetings in 2010. While location selection may be a result of cyclical decisions or the required resources that a limited number of cities may offer due to the needs of large events, these locations provide a benchmark for where medical meetings were held in 2010 according to the HCEA (2011). The top five cities in 2010 were Orlando, Washington DC, San Diego, Las Vegas and Chicago.

How the Meetings Industry is Changing

A report by futurist Rohit Talwar (2010a) highlights how the meetings industry is changing. The study identified six critical global drivers shaping the world in which the meetings industry operates. The drivers are: political power shifts, environmental drivers, economic drivers, commercial drivers, social drivers and science and technology. The drivers are summarised below as:

(1) *Political power shifts*: The uneven distribution of hope for a more prosperous future means that business optimism is higher in developing nations where commerce has been less hard hit by the global economic downturn. Developing nations such as China and India are exerting increasing influence on global organisations. The opportunity to better understand and partner with such nations exists. In terms of country risk and international security, political unrest, terrorism and cyber crime emerge as three key issues in the report.

(2) In terms of *environmental drivers*, the main question for the meetings industry is, is there a commercial advantage to be gained from understanding and taking a leadership role in driving sustainable business practice? We can anticipate sustainability issues over basic items such as fresh water and food. Severe water issues are likely in some geographical locations. As climate change becomes an increasing focus of attention, greater emphasis will need to be placed on assessing the climate risk of a location. By 2020, the peak oil period is likely to be over and on the basis of current consumption patterns it is unlikely that well thought out alternatives will be available.

(3) *Commercial drivers*: In the current economic climate we see strategic development driven by research and development utilising innovative and collaborative practices. New models of interaction are emerging with a movement towards marketing strategies targeted at the individual consumer. There is a trend towards free or fantastic and 'freemium' products, including free products with premium purchases and paid for upgrades to a free service.

(4) Power shifts, uncertainty, and infrastructure investment are the main *economic drivers* of future change. The global prominence of emergent markets in developing countries means that established destinations and venues need strategies to compete with the 'thrill of the new'. On a 'purchasing power parity' basis Asia will contribute a larger share of the global economy by 2014 than Europe and America collectively, providing 50% of sales for some Western multi-nationals, compared to 25% in 2010. Demographics are also a factor. By 2050, one-third of the world's population will be over 60 with an estimated pension bill 10 times larger than the cost of the recent financial crisis. Economic uncertainty is a key driver in a world where many markets are fragile due to the scale of the recent bailouts. The prospect of prolonged economic downturn is another factor shaping future scenarios for the meetings industry. With high public deficits in developed countries and lack of funds in developing countries the global infrastructure investment landscape is uncertain. Infrastructure investment decisions over the next few years will affect the meetings industry in both developed and developing countries.

(5) A number of *social drivers* will impact on the future of the meetings industry. In 2050, event formats will need to cater for up to five different generations in one room. Cities will be the primary drivers of economic growth over the next decade and the primary focus of convention activity.

> For the next three decades, the world will be demographically split: in the global north, old cities full of old people; in the global south, new cities full of young people. (Brand, 2010: 58)

According to Stewart Brand (2010), by 2020 more that 50% of the global middle class could be from Asia. With increasing GDP and the rise of the Asian middle class by 2025, 24 of the top cities will be Asian and the remaining six from Africa; these are the up-and-coming global city magnets.

Learning is integral to the meetings industry. New understandings of how we learn and the opportunities afforded by technological advancement are likely to have a huge impact on the way events are run. We are living longer and staying healthier as we become more accustomed to manipulating our health. As new technologies such as pharmacogenomics and nanotechnology progress, cognition enhancing food and drugs may become an aspect of event management.

(6) Science and technology, specifically global technology, the mobile economy and the growth in data traffic will be mega drivers of change in the meetings industry. 'The internet of things' (Kirkpatrick, 2010) or the 'internet of objects' is a term used to describe the networked

interconnection of everyday objects, a growing set of technologies from which things that we would not recognise as computers, like cars and clothes, have computational power. This is an aspect of ubiquitous computing, one person, many computer interfaces. Videos will account for 91% percent of global traffic by 2013. This opens up a range of possibilities to track, capture and use information about the delegate experience, as well as offering new opportunities for generating revenue. Scientific innovation, the deliberate merging of disciplines and championing of hubs of scientific activity by national governments, such as in Singapore, may change the way technological innovation is undertaken and accelerate the pace of change in the decade ahead. Scientific output in Asia last year surpassed North America.

We are in a period of accelerating change, with revolutionary advances taking place in previously separate fields of science, technology and social science. As these come together, new understandings are reached. Normalisation of the interface between humanity and technology has occurred in most sectors of the Global North. We are in the ubiquitous computing era, the era of the cyborg, part human part machine. As technology continues to advance at an ever-increasing rate and the 'internet of things' develops we will see boundaries between the physical world and the virtual world begin to erode. This poses opportunities and threats for the meetings industry. Nonetheless, regardless of technological advance, there remains a need for non-interfaced, flesh-to-flesh communication. Basically, complexity becomes more complex. Medical science is changing as a consequence of new boundaries of science and technology emerging. So, what does this all mean for the meeting industry?

The Medical Meetings Industry in Singapore

The Singapore Meetings, Incentives, Conventions and Events (MICE) industry has grown tremendously over the past decade. In 2008, the Singapore MICE industry accounted for a quarter of all business events held in Asia and generated around S$6 billion in revenue. Following the economic recession, business/MICE travellers and receipts dipped to 2.7 million and S$4.2 billion in revenue, respectively, in 2009 (Statistics Singapore, 2012). The sector's importance to Singapore's tourism industry is reflected in *Singapore Tourism Board's (STB) 2015* plan, which aims to strengthen Singapore's position as a leading convention and exhibition city in Asia with a strong dynamic business environment, projected to contribute 35% of tourism receipts by then (Statistics Singapore, 2012; STB, 2010). STB also hopes to increase its MICE sector market share in the Asia-Pacific region to 13% in 2015 from 8% in 2007 (Statistics Singapore, 2012).

The biomedical sector in Singapore is one key area focused on by the Singapore government. It aims to develop the country into a Biomedical Hub; a push to make Singapore a globally competitive and trusted centre for scientific and related commercial activities. This move attracted big players such as Japanese drug maker Takeda and GlaxoSmithKline from the industry to set up their regional headquarters and offices in Singapore (Singapore, Business Times, 2009). Aligned with the government's move to develop the nation into a Biomedical Hub, Singapore Tourism Board (STB) is also targeting these big players in the medical trade to bring conferences into the country. With regional offices based in Singapore, these companies will be more inclined to organise MICE activities locally. By targeting non-MICE professionals (such as the medical sector), STB launched a 'Corporate Outreach Programme' in late 2006 to draw in the international corporate community in Singapore. This approach hopes to attract, anchor and grow events that add value to Singapore's key economic clusters – such as biomedical sciences – a move aligned with the government's long-term plan. This strategy is brought through STB working closely with private sector partners and related government agencies to create and develop several flagship events.

STB and Singapore Exhibition and Convention Bureau (SECB) put forth bids and secured a number of major events within the biomedical sciences and medical cluster from 2010 to 2015, including:

- The 3rd World Congress of the International Academy of Oral Oncology (IAOO) (2011).
- The 15th World Conference on Tobacco or Health (WCTOH) (2012).
- The World Congress on Cardiac Pacing and Electrophysiology (2015). (*Source:* Singapore Tourist Board, 2009)

Scenario: Conveying Complexity

Professor Michael Daniels is the world's leading authority in multiple sclerosis, having completed a PhD on using nanotechnology machines to repair the myelin sheath at Harvard University's Singapore campus in 2030. The world's biannual neurology conference is being held at Singapore's new state-of-the-art convention centre which can hold up to 5000 delegates, but with video conferencing it is expected that 35,000 doctors worldwide will listen to Professor Daniels' keynote address, as some delegates from Western countries are not allowed to attend medical conferences due to the perception of the authorities that meetings are an indulgence and are 'seen as a freebie'. However, the conference has been sold out 12 months in advance, as delegates are keen to update their skills and knowledge since medical science has developed so fast in the last decade. Medicine taught in medical schools seems like the 'dark ages' to many practising doctors today. For those that cannot attend the meeting or missed the video conference, the organisers have created an avatar presentation in a 3D hologram that can be emailed to any location in the world.

Key Issues

The key issues highlighted in the scenario about Professor Daniels are discussed in the next section of this chapter. The key issues are:

- The convergence of science and technologies.
- The cost of discovery and less discovery.
- Moving East.
- Science parks, elite universities and knowledge clusters.
- Assault on pleasure.
- The knowledge economy, complexity and pace of change.
- Virtual reality and meetings technologies.
- We will still want to talk to each other – face-to-face communications.

The convergence of science and technologies

The phrase 'convergent technologies' refers to the synergistic combination of four major 'NBIC' (nano-bio-info-cogno) provinces of science and technology, each of which are progressing at a rapid rate: (1) nanoscience and nanotechnology; (2) biotechnology and biomedicine, including genetic engineering; (3) information technology, including advanced computing and communication; and (4) cognitive science, including cognitive neuroscience. This is the foundation of Professor Daniels PhD in the scenario *Conveying Complexity.*

Convergence of diverse technologies is based on *material unity at the nanoscale and on technology integration from that scale.* The building blocks of matter that are fundamental to all sciences originate at the nanoscale. The same principles will allow us to understand and, when desirable, to control the behaviour both of complex microsystems, such as neurons and computer components, and of macrosystems, such as human metabolism and transportation systems. Revolutionary advances at the interfaces between previously separate fields of science and technology are ready to create key NBIC, including scientific instruments, analytical methodologies and radically new materials systems.

Roco and Bainbridge (2001) suggest numerous examples of what the convergence of science and technology outside of traditional disciplinary boundaries will entail. Fast broadband interfaces directly between the human brain and machines. Comfortable, wearable sensors and computers will enhance every person's awareness of their own bodies and the world around them. Humanity will be more durable, healthier, more energetic, easier to repair and more resistant to many kinds of stress, biological threats and ageing processes. Machines and in fact structures of all kinds, from homes to aircraft, will be constructed of adaptable, efficient and environment-friendly materials. A combination of technologies and treatments will compensate for many physical and mental disabilities and will eradicate altogether some impairment that has plagued the lives of millions of disabled people. Instantaneous access to information. The ability to ethically control genetics. New organisational structures and management principles enabling enhanced effectiveness in business, education and government. Factories that are 'intelligent environments' organised around converging technologies and increased human–machine capabilities. Agriculture and the food industry with greatly increased yields and reduced spoilage. Bacterium-sized medical nano robots that according to Robert Freitas (2010) writing in the *Futurist*, would act like an artificial mechanical white cell seeking out and digesting unwanted pathogens like bacteria in the bloodstream.

The cost of discovery and less discovery

According to PricewaterhouseCoopers' (2007) study into the future of the pharmaceuticals industry, it has a core problem of innovation that is going to cripple product development in the future, and especially in meeting the medical needs of the elderly population. Even allowing for inflation, the industry is investing twice as much in research and development as it was in 1997 to produce two-fifths, 40% of the new medicines it then produced.

Specialist medicines hold huge clinical and commercial promise but they are used to treat conditions that affect only 3% of the general population (Consumer International, 2007). Prevention, on the other hand, is a much more stable market. As global populations grow and age, and demand for better healthcare management increases, the emphasis on treatment rather than prevention will become increasingly unsustainable. For example, in the US Merck's breakthrough vaccine for cervical cancer sells for US$360 compared to around US$20,000 for a course of interferon used in the treatment of multiple sclerosis. Older people consume more healthcare than young people everywhere. PricewaterhouseCoopers (2007) estimates that by 2020, the OECD countries will be spending 16% of their GDP on healthcare, while the United States will spend a huge 21%.

This innovation deficit in the pharmaceuticals industry has enormous implications for the meetings industry. It will either mean companies will reduce the need for research, therefore resulting in less meetings, or it will drive further innovation in order to build a new model, which means more meetings.

Moving East

Asia is coming to the fore as a hub of NBIC innovation. The number of PhDs awarded in the natural sciences and engineering has levelled off or declined in the United States, United Kingdom and Germany since the late 1990s. Conversely, it has been rising steadily in Asia and in addition Asian students continue to travel overseas for their doctoral studies. Many of these foreign students returned to their countries of origin, once they graduated. The scientific literature published outside the established scientific centres of the United States, EU and Japan is likewise growing rapidly. China's output rose by a huge 530% and that of the Asia-8 (South Korea, India, Indonesia, Malaysia, the Philippines, Singapore, Taiwan and Thailand) by 235%, boosting their combined share of the world total from less than 4% in 1988 to 10% in 2003 (PricewaterhouseCoopers, 2007). Additionally, much of the scientific research performed in the West is becoming prohibitively expensive. Many of the leading pharmaceutical companies are establishing partnerships in Asia; for example, Wyeth has opened an early development centre with Peking Union Medical College Hospital in Beijing and Roche has set up a research base at Zhangjiang Hi-Tech Park in Shanghai. Although the research base for many of these pharmaceutical companies is still going to be in Europe and the United States, a long-term shift in knowledge will flow eastwards along with medical meetings by 2050.

Science parks, elite universities and knowledge clusters

In the scenario *Conveying Complexity,* Professor Daniels studied at Harvard University's Singapore campus. The government of Singapore is helping the pharmaceutical and biotech industry through the Biomedical Sciences Initiate, started in 2000, which brings universities, manufacturing and industry together in a knowledge cluster. The economic value of the cluster increased manufacturing output in Singapore in the biomedical sciences from US$5 billion to US$20 billion in 2008, a fourfold increase (Shoemaker & Shoemaker, 2009). Singapore's ability to quickly put together various resources and infrastructure needed to attract foreign investors and grow; the industry has proved to be the key. The crown of this achievement is Biopolis, a still evolving and growing research and development complex that houses the country's leading major public biomedical research institutes and private laboratories. This knowledge cluster enables the entities to share research facilities equipment and amenities, which helps to overcome a major challenge that both start-ups and established companies face: the need to manage research and development costs and shorten time-to-market. At Biopolis, tenants can take advantage of its 'plug-and-play' infrastructure and access shared facilities and state-of-the-art equipment. One of the successes of the cluster has been the ability to attract an impressive number of top scientists from the United States and the rest of Asia, and it is becoming a hub for the biosciences meetings industry. Singapore has adopted a 'Queen Bee' approach to building its research base by enticing key international players and it assumes that others will follow.

The Singapore government has set out to make the country the hub of science in Asia, as a consequence The Singapore Tourist Board has developed a meeting industry strategy working with universities to attract medical and science conferences. For example, an aspect of the strategy is a meeting ambassador programme used to leverage leading medical experts such as Professor Neal Copeland who heads the Singapore Institute of Molecular and Cell Biology or Professor Edward Lui of the Genome Institute of Singapore to act as ambassadors for the tourism industry thus connecting science with tourism through the meeting industry (Talwar, 2009).

Assault on pleasure

There is hardly any aspect of the modern world that does not attract some form of moral or political debate; today the meetings industry is at the forefront of that debate. In the scenario, some delegates could not attend the congress because there were restrictions on hospitality spending and the perception of meetings by political leaders. In a free society where the individual should have choices, the range of options is declining. Authorities are increasingly intervening to restrict options and to prohibit activities, including smoking, gambling and anything perceived to be connected with indulgence and fun. From a consumer's perspective political correctness has reached the point at which they have to worry about what they do and how they behave. Since the fall of the Berlin Wall and subsequent demise of communism, capitalism has existed in a vacuum; there is nothing to counterbalance its excessive side. Therefore, politicians have focused on individual issues and the individual's lifestyle rather than the wider world. Telling someone how to live their life has become the order of the day (Yeoman, 2008) in which a new puritan order is born. From a tourism perspective, it is about taking the fun out of society as it is perceived as excessiveness. Yeoman (2008) coins this trend as an *Assault on Pleasure*, the ultimate outcome of which is a global environment in which tourism is banned.

An article in the *US Today* highlights the *Assault on Pleasure* trend:

What do Reno, Orlando and Las Vegas have in common? To some pockets of the federal government, they just seem like too much fun. Instead, employees at some big agencies, like the U.S. Department of Agriculture, are being encouraged to host meetings in more buttoned-down places such as St. Louis, Milwaukee or Denver. When a conference planner for MGM Mirage's New York-New York Hotel & Casino in Las Vegas tried to book a conference with the Federal Bureau of Investigation, she received a polite refusal. The Department of Justice 'decided conference[s] are not to be held in cities that are vacation destinations/spa/resort/gambling,' according to a May email from an FBI employee obtained by the U.S. Travel Association and viewed by The Wall Street Journal. 'Las Vegas and Orlando are the first 2 on the chopping block.' According to an Agriculture Department employee familiar with the guidelines, the agency issued internal travel guidelines in the spring that encourage employees to hold meetings in cities that display three key attributes: a travel hub; low in cost; and 'a non-resort location.' ... Resort locations aren't banned, 'but you have to provide robust justification' to supervisors for approval to hold an event there, the employee said. (Audi, 2009)

Furthermore, many countries and professional medical organisations have responded to this driver by creating regulations to curb perceived excessivenesses. In March 2009 (Hosansky, 2009), the state of Massachusetts finalised its Pharmaceutical and Medical Device Manufacturer Code of Conduct, which regulates interactions between drug and device companies and healthcare practitioners, placing restrictions on meeting venues, gifts, meals and entertainment. It also requires companies to disclose any gifts or payments to healthcare practitioners worth $50 or more. This practice is replicated across the world whether it is European Federations of Pharmaceutical Industries and Associations (EFPIA) code of practice or similar codes in Australia, New Zealand, Japan or Canada. The meetings industry is certainly influenced by the *Assault on Pleasure* driver.

The knowledge economy, complexity and pace of change

The foundation and creation of the knowledge economy lies with Moore's Law. Moore's Law describes a long-term trend in the history of computing hardware, in which the number of transistors that can be placed inexpensively on an integrated circuit has doubled approximately every two years (Brock, 2006). From a medical science perspective, Moore's Law can be applied to the fields of cardiovascular science and cardiovascular medicine, both of which are advancing at a similar breakneck pace. New drugs and therapies appear, only to be superseded or refined within a matter of a year or two. These advances have had a wide-ranging impact on the practice of both anaesthesia and critical care medicine (Howell *et al.*, 2004). As a consequence, over the last decade there has been a rapid expansion of continuous professional development for medical doctors as horizons of medical science and technology expand as doctors try and keep skills and knowledge at the forefront (Bapat, 2009).

Virtual reality and meetings technologies

Virtual reality, one of the promises of the information revolution, is a term that applies to computer-simulated environments that can simulate places in the real world, as well as in imaginary worlds, the ability to immerse oneself in an artificial environment that simulates the sensory experiences. Virtual reality rooms have been around since the early 1990s, often as simple desktop systems. Today, organisations from governments to the military, and the commercial sector are investing in virtual application making. Second Life, Google Earth and a host of other 3D virtual worlds are creating an even more ubiquitous virtual environment called the 'metaverse'. According to Techcast (2010) the virtual reality market is valued at US$30 billion. 3D movies are becoming the first choice of many theatre goers, with the 3D version of *Avatar* grossing US$77 million in its opening weekend in 2009. As more cinemas install 3D technologies, revenues from 3D movies as a proportion of total sales range between 25% and 37%.

Human beings are fascinated with the virtual world. The success of 3D movies such as *Avatar*, holographic images like Marina Macaus's fire eating mermaid and the advent of pop star Hatsune Miku, the world's first virtual diva, are testament to this. While the virtual world may pose a threat to the meetings industry as increasingly attractive virtual reality options surface, it also offers opportunities. The creations of the metaverse, a virtual space made up of virtual worlds, augmented reality and the internet, are becoming increasingly seductive. In a technologically advanced postmodern world we are at home with the hyper real as our consciousness becomes increasingly comfortable with the melding of reality and fantasy. Virtual avatars can be manipulated to elicit particular responses, for example, red to increase competition, white to increase harmonious interactions (Merola & Peña, 2010). On the one hand Hatsune Miku is merely anime, on the other, a pop star with a host of fans who will travel to see her perform live and respond to her in the same way they would to a flesh and blood star. A virtual reality world takes us beyond our physical senses to the world of feeling.

One of the common applications of virtual application technology in the meetings industry is telepresence. Telepresence refers to a higher-level set of video-telephony technologies which allow a person to feel as if they are present, to give the appearance that they are present, or to have an effect, via telerobotics, at a place other than their true location. Telepresence requires that the user's senses be provided with such stimuli as to give the feeling of being in that other location. Additionally, users may be given the ability to affect the remote location. In this case, the user's position, movements, actions, voice, and so forth may be sensed, transmitted and duplicated in the remote location to bring about this effect. Therefore, information may be travelling in both directions between the user and the remote location.

Kersey described some benefits of telepresence:

> There were four drivers for our decision to do more business over video and telepresence. We wanted to reduce our travel spend, reduce our carbon footprint and environmental impact, improve our employees' work/life balance, and improve employee productivity. (Kersey, 2008)

Rather than travelling for face-to-face meetings, it is now commonplace instead to use a telepresence system, which uses a multiple codec video system (which is what the word 'telepresence' most currently represents). Each member/party of the meeting uses a telepresence room to 'dial in' and can see/talk to every other member on a screen/screens as if they were in the same room. This brings enormous time and cost benefits. It is also superior to phone conferencing (except in cost), as the visual aspect greatly enhances communications, allowing for perceptions of facial expressions and other body language. These cues include life-size participants, fluid motion, accurate flesh tones and the appearance of true eye contact (Human Productivity Lab, 2010). This is already a well-established technology, used by many businesses today. The chief executive officer of Cisco Systems, John Chambers (Saunders, 2009) at the Networkers Conference compared telepresence to teleporting from Star Trek, and said that he saw the technology as a potential billion dollar market for Cisco.

Looking further into the future, virtual reality will move from a 2D telepresence to 3D imagery. For example, research by the Institute for Creative Technologies (ICT) at the University of Southern California have already developed a 3D teleconferencing telepresence device at the Army Science Conference in Florida. Dubbed 'Live 3D Teleconferencing' (http://gl.ict.usc.edu/Research/3DTeleconferencing), ICT's set-up captures a single participant in 3D and then transmits that image to a viewer. All of this is happening within microseconds. The video card and processor are rendering so quickly that they are creating 72 different facial views per second, enough different images so that each pass of the mirror shows one of the viewer's eyes in a slightly different image. It is this optical illusion that creates the 3D effect you see in the video. What does all this mean for the meetings industry? The projection of speakers to conferences in a 3D image or even the creation of celebrity conference avatars like Hatsune Miku as the ultimate virtual reality experience.

We will still want to talk to each other: Face-to-face communications

As Larsen *et al.* (2006) point out, the last decade has seen a striking increase in the use of technology and social media as a means of communications.

Even in this era of technologies the social context of personal relationships is still an important driver for the meetings industry. Sociological research on personal networks pays increasing attention to people's meeting opportunities (Mollenhorst et al., 2008) and in particular, to the importance of social networks and informality in order to build trustful relationships. Bjorkman and Kock (1995) emphasise the importance of social bonds in buyer–seller relationships in China, focusing on personal relationships and recommendations as the most important influencers in purchasing decisions. This importance is underpinned by Anderson and Kumars' (2006) study of buyer–seller relationships in business executive's found relationships. They found that such relationships are formed through physical presence in which competence and trust are seen as the key variables. Mair and Thompson's (2009) review of the UK association conference attendance decision-making process highly emphasises networking and the quality of the speakers at events. In particular, asking the question what is 'the likelihood of attending the conference again in the future' is highly correlated to networking as a motivating factor. Mair and Thompson's (2009) review of reasons for conference attendance suggests personal interaction, with other like-minded people, keeping up with changes in their field and learning new skills are all part of networking.

Concluding Remarks

To sum up, the future of death ...

God may hold the ultimate power; the power of life over death, the ability to heal the sick and prolong life. But, for the mere mortal, life is full of disease and illness. Will death be a thing of the past by the year 2050? Change is happening within the fields of medicine. One of the major drivers of change is quantum theory and the computer revolution (Kaku, 2011). Quantum theory has given us amazingly detailed models of how atoms are arranged in each protein and DNA molecule. Atom for atom, we now know how to build the molecules of life structures. Gene sequencing, once a long, tedious and expensive process, is now fully automated and robotic. In the past it cost millions to sequence all the genes in the human body; now it costs a fraction of the price. The future is genomic medicine and personal treatments. We will know in advance what diseases to expect and life expectancy. Tissue engineering is another hot topic in medicine, making possible the human body spare parts shop in which scientists could grow skin, blood, heart values, bone and ears in the lab from your own cells. So far, the medical field has grown a couple of types of tissues and a few simple structures, but by 2050, livers, pancreas and hearts will be the norm. Another field of rapid change is stem cell technology, where cells have the ability to change into any type of cell in the body. According to Kaku (2011) although a skin cell may have the genes to turn into blood, these genes are turned off when an embryonic cell becomes an adult skin cell. Each cell in our body has the complete genetic code necessary to create our entire body. As our cells mature they specialise and specific genes are inactivated. However, embryonic stem cells retain the ability to regrow any type of cell throughout their life. Stem cells have the potential to cure a host of diseases such as diabetes, Alzheimer's or the common cold, making mere mortals lives disease free. If we could grow various organs of the human body, then we could regrow a human being, creating an exact copy or a clone, a future without death.

What does this all mean?

As this chapter and the scenario *Conveying Complexity* highlights, spurred by the conscious convergence of previously separate technological and scientific disciplines the pace of change is increasing rapidly. The tourism industry is responding to changes in tourist needs through tailored services. In the meetings industry new global destinations and a raft of new players are shifting the competitive dimensions. Boundaries will shift with venues increasingly competing with professional conference organisers to offer event management and new alliances. As demonstrated in this chapter, the range of choice and range of meeting technologies are expanding rapidly with hybrid events of physical and virtual sessions, exhibits and other experiences becoming commonplace. This hybrid event means a new experience for the delegate. However, cost will be a significant factor in the future.

Change is particularly evident in the medical sciences where, for example, preventative medicines are vaccinating us against previously incurable diseases such as cancer. The pace and complexity of change in the medical arena, the largest sector of the meetings industry for the last decade, means that meetings are occurring more frequently in an effort to try to keep abreast with the complexity of change.

Increasingly, innovation is shifting eastwards as government and industry investment in the NBIC provinces of science and technology increases in these countries. For example, Singapore's creation of a knowledge cluster in the pharmaceutical and biotech industry increased manufacturing output in Singapore in the biomedical sciences fourfold. Capitalising on this investment the Singapore Tourist Board has created a meetings strategy to attract medical and science conferencing. While innovations in connective technology, the assault on pleasure in the modern world, increasing costs and a concern for the environment may adversely affect the meetings industry, it is likely that increasing technological complexities will necessitate the continuance of face-to-face meetings.

The end of the meetings industry ...

What if the world ran out of oil and at the same time technological advancement changed the future of humanity? A number of changes would have to occur. One of these is haptic technologies. Haptic technologies provide the illusion of real objects through tactile feedback that takes advantage of the user's sense of touch by applying force, vibration or motion. This mechanical stimulation makes virtual objects become real. In the medical industry, doctors are already using haptic to undertake remote surgery using teleoperators. A particular advantage of this type of work is that the surgeon can perform many operations of a similar type, and with less fatigue. In the future, keynote speakers may be holographic projections and delegates may be avatars interacting remotely in real time with one another.

7 Amsterdam 2050: Sex, Robots and the End of Human Trafficking

Learning points

- This chapter identifies the key drivers of change that will shape the future of sex tourism in Amsterdam, whether it is the desire for beautiful women or emotional connection to robots.
- Robot sex in 2050 means the end of human trafficking, a radical reduction in sexually transmitted infections (STIs) and that organised crime no longer has a place in the sex industry.
- Society recognises that humans have an emotional connection with robotic pets, toys and dolls.

Introduction

Would you pay to have sex with a robot? Even if it was akin to something from *Stepford Wives?* Is this the future of sex tourism in a futurist world? A revolution of humanoid social robots (or androids) is quietly taking place in our society, autonomous, interactive and human-like entities of various sizes and shapes are leaving research laboratories in large numbers, making their way into the world of our everyday lives. Automated teller machines (ATMs), vending machines and automated telephone response systems are standing in for human attendants to serve real people; online search agents, game bots and chat programs are working for and playing with human users; and robotic dolls and pets are cuddling up with children and talking to the elderly. The rise of a synthetic social world, where human individuals and humanoid social robots co-mingle, calls for a new conceptualisation of society. The traditional view of society as consisting of only human individuals needs to be revised. For one thing, the boundary between humans and human artefacts is no longer inviolable due to the increasing technological prostheticisation of human bodies. Technologies are becoming an integral part of the human condition. Furthermore, robotic replacement of human individuals in the processes of social interaction and communication creates a human–machine nexus that is indispensable to the operation of everyday life. Society comprises not only human individuals as delimited by their biological bodies, but also technological extensions of individuals, including their robotic surrogates. In the film *Terminator 3*, the android terminator manifests itself simultaneously as young naked flesh but also as a declining and ageing self-depreciating actor, being chased by the next level up android, which happens to be young, blond and a female killing machine. Her ability to totally reconfigure her body, at a moment's notice, imbues her with an unusual allure (Barber, 2004). By the same token, considering the female 'Borg' character 'Seven of Nine' from the Star Trek: Voyager series; 'falling in love' with a machine appears to be inevitable, her pert attributes are continuously subjected to nano-probes and aesthetically placed biotechnical devices. The film, *Veronica 2030* is about a female android called 'Julia', created to provide sexual pleasure for humans. When she accidentally gets transported back in time from the year 2030 to 1998, she becomes a lingerie model and engages in various erotic adventures. These fictional characters are constructed to be physically pleasing with a high degree of sexual arousal, especially for male audiences all in the search for fantasy and perfect sex (Barber, 2004).

David Levy (2007) suggests in his book *Love+Sex with Robots* that by 2050 technological advancement will allow humans to have sex with androids, something akin to the *Stepford Wife* concept of a woman with a perfect body and who can perform great sex with a man. In 2006 (Levy, 2007), Henrik Christensen, chairman of EURON, the European Robotics Research Network predicts that people will be having sex with robots in five years and in 2010 the world's first sex doll was showcased at the AVN Adult Entertainment Expo in Las Vegas. Priced between $7000 and US$9000 Roxxxy is a truly interactive sex doll offering a range of replicated personalities from Frigid Farah to Wild Wendy.

Robot sex offers a solution to a host of problems associated with the sex trade. Given the rise of incurable STIs, including emergent strains of gonorrhea and HIV/AIDS throughout the world and the problems associated with human trafficking and sex tourism, it is likely that we will see an increase in demand for alternative forms of sexual expression. In 2050, Amsterdam's red light district will all be about android prostitutes who are clean of STIs, not smuggled in from Eastern Europe and forced into slavery, the city council will have direct control over android sex workers controlling prices, hours of operations and sexual services. Android prostitutes will be both aesthetically pleasing and able to provide guaranteed performance and stimulation for both men and women. This chapter discusses how such a scenario could come about based upon a futurist perspective of sex tourism in Amsterdam.

Sex Tourism

Tourism and sex have always gone together for various reasons (Yeoman, 2008). It is theorised that Columbus brought syphilis from America to Spain in 1492 (Clift & Carter, 2000). Soon after, epidemics of syphilis spread across Europe, mainly associated with the movement of men. In 1494, the 50,000 troops dispatched to the Alps by Charles VIII were handicapped by syphilis and consequently withdrawn to France. Between 1495 and 1496, cases of syphilis were reported in several countries, from England to Hungary, and throughout Germany and Russia.

Tourism, romance, love and sexual relations have always been linked and will continue to be so in 2050 and beyond. For as long as people have travelled, they have engaged in romantic and sexual encounters of various kinds. Sometimes sex or the prospect of sexual encounters in the destination or along the way plays a central role in the decision to travel and the choice of destination. At other times, sex represents an incidental aspect of a trip or plays no role whatsoever in the decision-making. Sometimes sexual activity is regarded as being a socially acceptable and mutually beneficial reason to travel, as in the case of honeymoons or romantic getaways. Sex tourism is one of the most emotive and sensational issues in tourism. It is an extremely problematic area to define. Opperman (1999) defines sex tourism within the context of purpose of travel, length of time, relationships, sexual encounters and travel. Destinations such as Las Vegas, Thailand and Amsterdam are sex tourism destinations whether by intention or not.

Amsterdam's Sex Industry

During the Middle Ages, prostitution in the Netherlands was not prohibited. The attitude of worldly and religious authorities towards prostitution was pragmatic. Many cities tolerated prostitution to protect chaste female citizens from rape and defilement. There were, however, a number of conditions imposed on prostitutes and their clients. Prostitutes were not allowed to be married. Married men and Jewish men were prohibited from hiring prostitutes. Prostitution in Amsterdam has always been tolerated as this posting proclamation for the city council in 1413 states:

> Because whores are necessary in big cities and especially in cities of commerce such as ours – indeed it is far better to have these women than not to have them – and also because the holy church tolerates whores on good grounds, for these reasons the court and sheriff of Amsterdam shall not entirely forbid the keeping of brothels. (Brants, 1998: 622)

The tolerance of, and liberal attitude to, prostitution in the Netherlands has its origins in the principle of *gedoogbeleid* (policy of tolerance) and a belief that the enforcement of the anti-prostitution laws would be counterproductive to the goal of protecting the city's women. This principle is realised in policies that emphasise harm reduction. This genuine Dutch policy of tolerating formerly illegal activities for harm reduction purposes has been and still is also applied towards illegal drugs in the Netherlands.

The red light district is the image most people have of the legal prostitution system in the Netherlands; however, in reality, these areas represent a mere fraction of the commercial sex markets as larger illegal sex markets have developed in the shadows of this legalised structure. The perception of the commercial sex markets as safe, legal and regulated in the Netherlands has created an expectation by the buyers that purchasing sex is merely part of the tour. This creates heightened demand and thereby a need for a constant supply of women and children to be the human product in this market. Thus, the secondary market of commercial sexual services using trafficked women and children thrives in the background of the legalised system (Shared Hope International, 2007).

The layout of the red light district in Amsterdam capitalises on the concept of the commercial sex market as a 'shopping mall' where the buyer can pick and choose the woman who will provide the sexual services. This market has as its centrepiece, the well-known windows displaying a variety of women brought to Amsterdam from all over the world to be exploited in a legal environment. The General Ban on Brothels (*Bordeelverbod*) law was lifted on 1st October 2000, making prostitution and pimping legal occupations in the Netherlands with removal of each from the penal code. Since then, Amsterdam's red light district (in Dutch, *de Wallen*) has become a multi-million dollar business, with a yearly turnover of €83 million. Though the infamous red light district was in operation for centuries, concerns were mounting that it had become infested with drug and human trafficking crimes. Policymakers believed that legalisation would force brothels to clean up their acts, scale back and even eliminate the employment of illegal migrants. Legalised brothels would also mean an increase in revenue for the government, as the regulated brothels would pay taxes. Instead of curbing and deterring sex crimes, the legislation had the opposite effect, resulting in the expansion of commercial sex markets into a larger, concealed market in the hands of Albanian and Turkish organised crime groups, Moroccan pimps and many other criminal entrepreneurs. As a consequence, Amsterdam City Council and the authorities have taken action to tackle the human trafficking problem and reduce the size of the red light district in the city by 50%.

Amsterdam's Red Light District

In 2004, about 8000 prostitutes worked in Amsterdam. Based upon these estimates, 25% of them worked in the windows, 25% in brothels, 1% as streetwalkers and the remaining 49% in closed or private situations such as escort services, bars, private houses or at home. More than two-thirds of the women are of foreign origin. Amsterdam's red light district is a major tourist destination for buyers seeking commercial sexual services. Though it has existed for several centuries and has been a boost to the economy by attracting tourists and collecting taxes from brothels, today the district is losing its lustre. The Amsterdam City Council ordered 100 of the 350 windows to close by the end of 2006. The City Council continues to examine the status of other commercial sex venues as it confronts human trafficking (Shared Hope International, 2007).

The red light district is located in the heart of the oldest part of Amsterdam, covering several blocks south of the church *Oude Kerk* and crossed by several canals. The name *de Wallen* refers to the names of the two canals in the area, the *Oudezijds Achterburgwal* and the *Oudezijds Voorburgwal*. The district has existed since the 14th century and formerly housed many distilleries, mainly catering to sailors. In response to proposals by the head of Amsterdam's largest political party to discourage women from marketing themselves in windows, several commercial sex venues in Amsterdam's red light district held an open house on 18th February 2006, and again on 31st March 2007, with the intent to 'de-stigmatise' and promote the red light district locally (Shared Hope International, 2007).

In the *Singel* area of the red light district, windows are contained within a thriving commercial district surrounded by high-end homes. The windows are controlled by an organised group of young, teenaged-looking Turks and Moroccans who perform a revolving check of the windows and an older group of 20-year-old men of Indonesian origin who run a pattern that takes them over the Singel canal and back down *Oude Nieuwstraat*. The women in this area are mostly Latin or South American (from Colombia, Cuba, Brazil or Venezuela). *Middelpunt* is the Window Administrative Office in the Singel Area where girls retrieve and return keys for rented windows. East European, African and Turkish pimps are easily recognised as they loiter singly and in groups while keeping a protective eye on their charges in the windows. Approximately 30 windows are located in Singel's *'de Pijp*,' an area to the south of the main red light district on *Ruysdaelkade* behind the *Rijksmuseum* disturbingly – and some question whether deliberately – accessible to the many tourists travelling to the *Rijksmuseum* and the Van Gogh Museum:

> 'Loverboys' and pimps go about their business – trafficking in women – without being bothered in the red light district of Amsterdam, while the police look on, said two policemen of the bureau Beursstraat, one of whom has been replaced elsewhere within the police at his own request. 'We are in the midst of modern slavery,' says Ron, who until recently has been a vice officer in the red light district. Police are doing far too little to end forced prostitution with all its excesses, say the policemen.

The policemen do not want their names in the paper, because they have been threatened by criminals several times. Two groups of pimps are active in Amsterdam's red light district: the 'loverboys' and a group known as the 'Turks'. They carry on a lucrative business in trafficking women from the Eastern bloc. According to policeman Ron, criminal reports by women 'are gathering dust everywhere in the Netherlands'. In 2003, four detectives were put on the group of Turks. 'The investigation turned into a fantastic disaster,' says Ron. Investigations are not allowed to take any longer than three months. The four detectives were notified by their superiors in June that they had to close the case. Some arrests followed, but the public prosecutor found the evidence inconclusive. (NRC Handelsbad, 2009)

In the last few years the city government of Amsterdam, under mayor Job Cohen, has started cracking down on prostitution in the capital, resulting in the closure of famous sex clubs such as the Yab-Yum, Casa Rosso and the Banana Bar, as well as buying one-third of all prostitution windows at the De Wallen and turning them into studios for artists and fashion designers. Concerned about money laundering and human trafficking, Amsterdam officials under mayor Job Cohen denied the license renewals of about 30 brothels in the Amsterdam red light district De Wallen in 2006 (UNDOC, 2009).

Mayor Job Cohen (Asthana, 2007) announced plans to close half of the city's 400 prostitution windows because of suspected criminal gang activity. The mayor is also closing some of the city's 70 marijuana cafes and sex clubs. This comes at the same time as the government's decision to ban the sale of magic mushrooms and the closure of all coffee shops situated near schools:

> It is not that we want to get rid of our red-light district. We want to reduce it. Things have become unbalanced and if we do not act we will never regain control. – Mayor Job Cohen (Asthana, 2007)

Scenario: Perfect Sex

So, in 2050 will sex tourism in Amsterdam look like this?

The Yab-Yum is Amsterdam's top sex club for business travellers (both men and women) located beside a 17th-century canal house on the Singel. It is modern and gleaming with about 100 scantily clad blondes and brunettes parading around in exotic G-strings and lingerie. Entry costs €10,000 for an all-inclusive service. The club offers a full range of sexual services from massages, lap dancing and intercourse in plush surroundings. The Yab-Yum is a unique bordello licensed by the city council that is staffed not by humans but by androids. This situation came about due to an increase in human trafficking in the sex industry in the 2040s which was becoming unsustainable, combined with an increase in incurable STIs in the city, especially HIV, which over the last decade has mutated and is resistant to many vaccines and preventive medicines. Amsterdam's tourist industry is built on an image of sex and drugs. The council was worried that if the red light district were to close, it would have a detrimental effect on the city's brand and tourism industry, as it seemed unimaginable for the city not to have a sex industry. Sex tourism is a key driver for stag parties and the convention industry. The Yab-Yum offers a range of sexual gods and goddesses of different ethnicities, body shapes, ages, languages and sexual features. The club is often rated highly by punters on www.punternet.com and for the fifth year in a row in 2049 was voted the world's best massage parlour by the UN World Tourism Organisation. The club has won numerous technology and innovation awards including the prestigious ISO iRobotSEX award. The most popular model is Irina, a tall, blonde, Russian exotic species who is popular with Middle Eastern businessmen. The tourists who use the services of Yab-Yum are guaranteed a wonderful and thrilling experience, as all the androids are programmed to perform every service and satisfy every desire. All androids are made of bacteria-resistant fibre and are flushed for human fluids, therefore guaranteeing no STIs are transferred between consumers. The impact of Yab-Yum club and similar establishments in Amsterdam has transformed the sex industry alleviating all health and human trafficking problems. The only social issues surrounding the club is the resistance from human sex workers who say they cannot compete on price and quality, therefore forcing many of them to close their shop windows. All in all, the regeneration of Amsterdam's sex industry has been about the success of the new breed of sex workers. Even clients feel guilt free as they actually have not had sex with a real person and therefore do not have to lie to their partner.

The drivers that are shaping this scenario are:

Driver 1: The growth of the sex industry
Driver 2: Why do men pay for sex?
Driver 3: Beautiful women
Driver 4: Human trafficking
Driver 5: Incurable STIs and HIV/AIDS
Driver 6: Sex toys enhance sexual pleasure so we will have sex with a robot
Driver 7: Our emotional connection to robots
Driver 8: Destination brand and the importance of sex tourism in Amsterdam

Driver 1: The growth of the sex industry

Davies in the *American Sociological Review* poses the conundrum of prostitution: 'Why is it that a practice so thoroughly disapproved, so widely outlawed in western civilisation, can yet flourish so universally?' (Davies, 1937: 744). The sex industry is growing, with the average consumer from an OCED country spending US$20 per year on visits to massage parlours and escort services (Harcourt & Donovan, 2005; Yeoman, 2008). One reason for this continued growth is that sex is a mainstream entertainment product. Sex is packaged as excitement, from the sparkling neon lights of visible erotic landscapes, to lap dancing encounters to adult channels on satellite television. The desire for sex is ever present, and while there is an element of pleasure in the danger of erotic adventure for most it is of no more moral consequence than the desire for food. Like food, this product is prepared, and presented in an ever-expanding variety. Sex is everywhere, present in everything from a Pot Noodle advertisement to the more overt and deliberately erotic. As Yeoman (2008) points out, Las Vegas is the most successful tourist destination in the world and it is built upon pure sex and adult fun.

The sex industry goes beyond heterosex in the dead bug position, oral sex and hand jobs; it includes, domination, fetishism, role play, romance, touching, bondage, stripping, tantric and virtual sex. The list of desires and matching services is endless, creative and inventive. It is an industry that will never go away; however, there are clear tensions, particularly around health, morality, human rights and privacy that will change the presentation of the industry and degree to which it is accepted. Men, and to a lesser degree women who buy sexual services are somewhat outside the respectability of the modern citizen. It is not something that is acceptable to do or talk about in the majority of communities, even though we live a more liberal society (Yeoman, 2008). The pleasures associated with commercial sex are contested in the moral debate, pragmatic policing and the law. There is a political desire to prevent certain types of prostitution that are framed as harmful (Saunders, 2008), namely street prostitution and at the same time, there is less political will to interfere in the private sex lives of individuals, while some forms of sexual activities, such as lap dancing have seen unprecedented explosions in many cities across the world in the last decade.

Driver 2: Why do men pay for sex?

Half a century after Freud's 1938 proclamation that pleasure is the goal of sex (Hoffman, 2005), psychologists started to study reasons for making love. John DeLamater (1989) asked the question 'What would be your motives for having sexual intercourse?' Women typically gave reasons relating to love, while men focused on the physical pleasure. When the question was more focused, inquiring the subject's most recent sexual activity 51%

of women and 24% of men gave reasons connected to love and emotion and while 9% of women and 51% of men gave reasons connected to lust and physical pleasure. A study of 1000 women by psychologists Cindy Meston and David Buss (2007) revealed that 84% women have sex to ensure a 'quiet life' or as a bargaining tool for household chores. Stating the obvious, men want and like sex as a desire, fantasy and a physical encounter and therefore, would be more likely to pay for it.

The ideas of satisfactory sex being available whenever it is desired is extremely appealing to enormous numbers of men, but for a variety of reasons many people do not enjoy a satisfactory sex life, whether they are in or not in a relationship. Whatever the reason, this void in life has a simple remedy that for thousands of years men have adopted, which is paying for sex, hence the creation of the world's oldest profession, prostitution.

Obtaining accurate estimates of the percentage of the population that visits prostitutes is fraught with difficulties, largely due to the stigmatising view of prostitution. In 1948, Alfred Kinsey (1998/1948) estimated that 69% of the white male population of the United States had been with a prostitute. If this is considered high, it should be considered along with another historic study by Timothy Gilfoyle (1994), who estimated that between 10% and 25% of all young women in New York City were prostitutes in the 19th century.

The prevalence of men who buy sex has been studied by sexologists and epidemiologists and is well documented (Saunders, 2008). The likelihood that someone will purchase sex is a factor of demographics, lifestyles and other motivations but can be divided into 'push' factors – elements of men's lives that are lacking and 'pull' factors' – aspects of the sex industry that are attractive and are promoted as 'entertainment'.

Men's ability to buy sex is related to disposable income and economic position, but this does not necessarily translate into the desire to exercise power or domination over individual women. Stein (1974) notes that buying sex and intimacy represented time out from performance pressures, one of the reasons why passive sexual roles are often sought by consumers of sexual services. Buying time with sex workers translated into something to show for their hard slog at the office, something tangible, transporting them into a warm, secure place where they are the focus of lavish attention for their body, mind and soul (Saunders, 2008).

Men, who integrate the sex industry into their moral economy and their everyday lives, often over a considerable number of years, are married and usually have little intention of ending this long-term commitment. Stein (1974) argued that the New York City call girl market existed for the middle classes who were committed to marriage but not sexually or emotionally fulfilled by the relationship. Meston and Buss (2007) suggest in their research, today and in the future, marriage, for some clients, is not really the institution of romantic love, fidelity and pure commitment, but bears more resemblance to the economic foundation of marriage in feudal times where women swapped sexual services for an easy existence, security and sustenance.

Campbell (1998: 164) suggests that loneliness and the inability to form a sexual relationship are important factors in men's decisions to visit sex workers. Bryant (1982) stated reasons for seeking commercial sex often go beyond sexual gratification:

> It's more for intimacy ... I am a hermit if you like, I am lonely guy. I don't have many real friends or I don't see that often. There you are for five years, most of the time sleeping in your own bed .... it's nice to have a cuddle (Steve, 47, divorced, IT)

> I think it's probably more about being single and the traits of my personality. I mean I'm naturally shy, was as a child. I continued into my teenage years and I guess I have the typical things like poor self image, that sort of thing (Ron, 51, divorced, teacher)

Reasons for visiting sex workers can change over a lifetime. There appears to be no fixed pattern according to Saunders (2008); instead involvement fluctuated as men's lives changed and personal relationships took on new forms. Where older men made decisions about how to improve their quality of life, 'push' factors (age, lack of relationships, sex or intimacy) worked together with the 'pull' factors of the sex industry (the fact that temporary sexual relationships with beautiful women can be purchased in safe environments that are sympathetic to the needs of older men). Commercial sexual relationships for many men are based around social relationships (desirable commodities such as companionship, socialising, common interests, rituals of courtship, romance, pseudo-conventionality and the purchase of intimacy) which act as 'pull' factors for experimenting with new sexual lifestyles and relationship formations.

To understand why men buy sex we need to look beyond the psychological and psychiatric perspectives that tend to individualise the desire to buy sex, to sociological understandings that include the 'push' and 'pull' factors that fuel the sex industry.

Men are attracted to the nature of sex industry and what it offers, the glitzy or gritty images and promises that emanate from adverts, websites, stereotypes, pictures and the allurement of fantasies created specifically for those who want to trade cash for pleasure. Brents and Hausbeck's (2007) case study of the legalised brothel industry in Nevada illustrates how the sex industry is beginning to use the marketing strategies, business forms and wider economic structures of late capitalism to sell an 'individualized, interactive touristic experience'. Strategies that aim to mainstream the sex industry, such as up scaling, market specialisation and expanding markets and services are evident in designer brothels and gentlemen's clubs in the Western world.

The sex industry is predicated on meeting the desired fantasy of the paying client. Sex workers (especially exotic dancers) work hard to exploit their femininity, sexuality, bodily capital and emotional labour to provide the customer with this ultimate fantasy. The very presence of the opportunity to buy something that is unobtainable in their real life is perhaps the greatest seduction for many. As Saunders points out:

> 'You have the opportunity to have sex with someone who looks on the web site an attractive girl .... You know, almost a girl of your fantasy really'. (Tony, married, pilot). (Saunders, 2008: 46)

The desire to suspend reality, experience something outside their mundane routine and take some 'time out' are strong pull factors that sex entrepreneurs exploit.

Driver 3: Beautiful Women

Men want beautiful women and women want to be beautiful. It is as basic as that (Morris, 2004; Yeoman, 2008). Sociologists tell us that humans, as animals, are programmed to appreciate a youthful, healthy appearance because this signals fitness for reproduction. But consumers are vain and cultural definitions of beauty also encapsulate a youthful appearance. It is no surprise, therefore, that health concerns encompass physical appearance (Morris, 1994). It goes without saying that, since time immemorial, women's appearance has been influenced by the ideal of feminine beauty prevalent at the time – from the voluptuous curvaceousness of the early Greeks to the waif-like frailty of the 1990s supermodels, which has led to the contemporary emphasis on looking thin. Generally speaking, women's attitudes towards their looks have been conditioned by the prevailing stereotypes, which are reinforced by the media and by society as a whole.

Women's fascination with beauty and appearance is a universal development that seems to have intensified in the last few decades (Yeoman, 2008). The rise of the metrosexual phenomena and the fact that rhinoplasty and Botox are currently the most popular cosmetic surgery procedure for men are testimony to the fact that men have not escaped the push towards physical perfection. All in all, the pressure to look good has intensified for both sexes over the years, leading to an age of the image where visual appearance is prized above all else. However, for women it is a fact that beauty fascinates and there is a strong desire for the body beautiful in contemporary society. This is partly fuelled by consumers' aspiration to look like the supermodels, actors and action heroes they see in the media. These portrayals of the 'ideal' body have a profound impact on self-perception, self-esteem and how they rate their own attractiveness. Many people feel intense additional pressure to look good because modern culture increasingly equates internal and external characteristics, that is, slim=success and self-discipline, obese=laziness and a lack of will power. Visual appearance is prized above all else (Yeoman, 2008).

Anthony Elliott (2008) explains in his book, *Making the Cut: How Cosmetic Surgical Culture is Transforming Our Lives*, that the increasing demand for cosmetic and plastic surgery is shaping the social and cultural values that drive our consumer culture. Elliott argues;

> at an international level, bodies today are pumped, pummeled, plucked, suctioned, stitched, shrunk and surgically augmented at an astonishing rate. At the core of this, he says, is a new economy that judges people less on their achievements, less of their records of success, and more and more on the willingness to adapt, to change, to transform themselves. Plastic surgery provides the most seductive answer to the new socioeconomic dilemmas. (Elliott, 2008: 15)

Further, Elliot explains the media and fashion industry's portrayal of the 'ideal'. Reality TV shows including *Dr. 90210, Extreme Makeover* and *Nip Tuck* capture a fair share of attention from those who want to believe that the ultimate transformation can and does happen. Even with the downturn in the economy, people continue to flock to the most affordable treatment possible on their quest for perfection. Medical spas and 'affordable' treatment such as Botox injections and microdermabrasion offer more people a chance to join the self-reinvention revolution. Despite a slowing economy and tighter consumer budgets, the future looks bright for the cosmetic and plastic surgery industry (Yeoman, 2008). The American Society of Plastic Surgeons (ASPS) recently published their predictions for 2015, and estimated that over 55 million procedures – one for every five Americans – will be performed. Analysts claim that more people will be taking advantage of better technology and more competitive prices (Cosmetic Surgery Review, 2008).

As a consequence, within the field of plastic surgery, one of the most popular procedures for women is breast enhancement, with more and more women wanting larger breasts, all for the sake of physical beauty and men (Yeoman, 2008). Larger breasts can be attractive to men in Western societies because women with higher breast to under-breast ratios typically have higher levels of the sex hormone, estradiol, which promotes fertility (BBC, 2004). Maybe men live in a 'have-it-all society', as sex is a physical driver rather than an emotive experience; men just want perfection in which they search for bodily perfection and younger looking women. It is men who have a desire for blonde Russian brides who haunt websites such as www.hotrussianbrides.com or www.club10.com. As such, the film *Stepford Wives* is a symbol of that demanding, have-it-all society for the body beautiful. Without doubt, the robot Stepford wives are perfect examples of physically beautiful, passive, fetishised objects of the male gaze (Helford, 2006).

Driver 4: Human trafficking

Human trafficking is the acquisition of people by improper means such as force, fraud or deception, with the aim of exploiting them. The Netherlands is listed by the UNODC (2009) as a top destination for victims of human trafficking. Countries that are major sources of trafficked persons include Thailand, China, Nigeria, Albania, Bulgaria, Belarus, Moldova and Ukraine. Currently, human trafficking in the Netherlands is on the rise according to a study published by the UNODC (2009). The report shows a substantial increase in the number of victims from Hungary and China. There were 809 registered victims of human trafficking in 2008, 763 were women and at least 60% of them were forced to work in the sex industry. All victims from Hungary were female and were forced into prostitution (UNODC, 2009).

Within the Netherlands, victims are often trafficked by the so-called 'lover boys' – men who seduce young women and girls and coerce them into prostitution. Women and girls are trafficked to the Netherlands from Nigeria, Bulgaria, China, Sierra Leone and Romania, as well as other countries in Eastern Europe (UNODC, 2009).

Many victims of human trafficking are led to believe, by organised criminals, that they are being offered work in hotels or restaurants or in child care and are later forced into prostitution with the threat or actual use of violence. Estimates of the number of victims vary from 1000 to 7000 on a yearly basis. Most police investigations on human trafficking concern legal sex businesses. All sectors of prostitution are evident in these investigations, but particularly the window brothels are overrepresented (UNODC, 2009).

At the end of 2008, six people were convicted in what prosecutors said was the worst case of human trafficking ever brought to trial in the Netherlands. The ill treatment of women in the case meant that victims were compelled to have breast enlargement surgery (*USA Today*, 2008).

Experts said the case could have an impact on the Dutch prostitution policy. Jan van Dijk, an organised crime and victimology expert at the University of Tilburg, said:

> The honeymoon of the new prostitution legislation is over; we are really reconsidering whether we're on the right track. (*USA Today*, 2008)

Driver 5: Incurable STIs and HIV/AIDS

By the very nature of prostitution there is a connection to incidents of STIs (Clift & Carter, 2000), 9% of STI tests in the Netherlands are for sex workers (Koedijk *et al.*, 2009). The number one STI in the Netherlands is chlamydia representing 44% of incidences at registered clinics, whereas HIV infection represented 1.8% of all incidences (Koedijk *et al.*, 2009). A report by the Laar *et al.* (2005) for the Netherlands Ministry of Health found 3.1% of female prostitutes working in Amsterdam to be infected with HIV (the figure jumped to 17.1% for transgender sex workers). Of main concern is the number of imported foreign prostitutes from Eastern Europe working in the red light district, hence one of the reasons why Amsterdam City Council is reducing the size of the red light district. Figure 7.1 highlights that the majority of registered HIV infections in the Netherlands relate to non-Dutch citizens, and this is rising given the country's liberal attitudes and rising migrant population. In all, 42% of registered HIV patients were born outside the Netherlands and 52% infected abroad, with many cases originating from

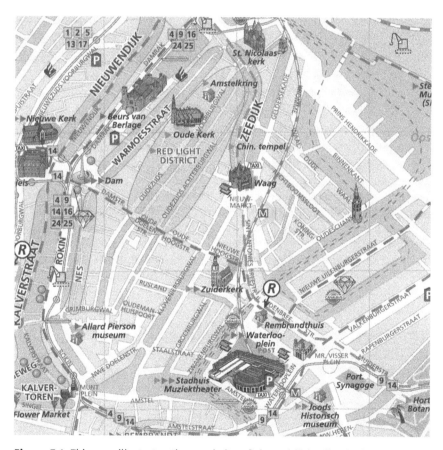

Figure 7.1 This map illustrates the proximity of the red light district in 2007 to key tourism sites, including the Rembrandt Museum, Music Theater, Train Station and several historic churches (Shared Hope International, 2007)

Africa, Surinam, Netherlands Antilles or Turkey. The total percentage of HIV cases from these ethnic groups is 2%, 10 times greater than the national average (Koedijk *et al.*, 2009).

The fall of the Berlin Wall and communism in Eastern Europe has immigrated labour towards Western European countries such as the United Kingdom, Netherlands and France. As a consequence, many poorer migrants have brought diseases with them, including STIs. According to the UN Global Aids Epidemic Report (2008), 90% of HIV cases in Eastern Europe and Central Asia are in the Ukraine and Russia with the rate of infection steadily rising in these countries. The overlap of sex work and intravenous drug use features prominently in the region's epidemics. For example, 39% of female sex workers in the Samara Oblast, part of the Russian Federation, and 37% in St Petersburg study are intravenous drug users (Benotsch *et al.*, 2004). A hypothesis could be constructed among sex workers and clients about the fear of infection from the disease (Furedi, 1997) based upon a culture of fear, as HIV has a social stigma attached to it; however, since the 1980s the presence of HIV/AIDs in the world has not stopped sexual activity.

The Sexually Desiring Women's Ability to Pay for Sex

The 'have-it-all nature' of late capitalism drives women's as well as men's consumption patterns. Historically, men's ability to buy sex is related to disposable income and socio-economic position; increasingly, however, women are in a position to be able to procure sexual services themselves. The rise of the Cougar phenomenon, the well-dressed and financially secure woman out on the prowl for a younger man, and the increasing popularity of Host Clubs in Japan offering mainly non-penetrative sex to their patrons are testimony to women's desires. The world's first women's brothel conceptualised along the lines of the designer brothels and gentlemen's clubs of the Western world is set to open in Auckland in 2012 (Tan, 2010). Building on women's propensity to shop as a leisure activity the brothel will provide consumers various options in terms of physical aesthetic, sexual style and ambient surroundings to weigh up and consider. Emphasising safety and certainty for its patrons, the brothel provides women with a range of options and choices of sensual and sexual experiences. Women are accustomed to buying intimacy in the form of body work and beauty services. Moving towards more sexualised forms of pleasure and intimacy as they become available would seem inevitable.

While beauty and physical perfection are strong drivers of women's desire, emotional intelligence and sexual knowledge and skills are also required. Male sex workers will need to possess a complex range of skills, a range that interactive technology, even more than the average flesh and blood human male, has the potential to provide. In addition, women are more accustomed than men to having technologically enhanced orgasms; vibrators have been readily available since the turn of the 19th century. The leap from blow up doll to robot sex may be uncomfortable for men while the efficiency, effectiveness, reliability and social acceptability of existing technology requires less of a stretch of the feminine imagination.

Driver 6: Sex toys enhance sexual pleasure so we will have sex with a robot

The world's most advanced country associated with technological advance is Japan; it is also the country that leads the way in high-end sex dolls. Connell (2004) writes in the *Mainichi Daily News* with the headline *Rent-a-Doll Blows Hooker Market Wide Open* explains how one leading purveyor started a 24/7 doll escort service in southern Tokyo.

'Originally, we were going to run a regular call girl service, but one day while we were surfing the Net we found this business offering love doll deliveries. We decided the labour costs would be cheaper and changed our line of business. Outlays are low, with the doll's initial cost the major investment and wages never a problem for employers. We've got four dolls working for us at the moment. We get at least one job a day, even on weekdays, so we made back our initial investment in the first month. Unlike employing people, everything we make becomes a profit and we never have to worry about the girls not turning up for work'. Doll no Mori charges start at 13,000 yen (around US$110) for a 70-min session with the dolls, which is about the same price as a regular call girl service. The company boasts of many repeat customers. 'Nearly all our customers choose our two hour option'. Within little more than a year of the doll-for-hire idea taking root in Japan, sex entrepreneurs in South Korea also started to cash in. Up market sex dolls were introduced to the Korean public at the Sexpo exhibition in Seoul in August 2005, and were immediately seen as a possible antidote to Korea's Special Law on Prostitution that had been placed on the statute books the previous year. Before long, hotels in Korea were hiring out 'doll experience rooms' for around 25,000 Won per hour (US$25), a fee that included a bed, a computer to enable the customer to visit pornographic web sites, and the use of a doll. This initiative quickly became so successful at plugging the gap created by the anti-prostitution law that, before long, establishments were opening up that were dedicated solely to the use of sex dolls, including at least four in the city of Suwon. These hotels assumed, quite reasonably, that there was no question of them running foul of the law, since their dolls were not human.

Levy (2009) reports that if consumers from the most advanced technology economies in the world will have sex with dolls, then it is envisaged that humans will jump species to have sex with robots. The early successes of the sex doll businesses are a clear indicator of things to come. If static sex dolls can be hired out successfully, then android prostitutes become a feasible proposition.

Driver 7: Our emotional connection to robots

Some readers may be familiar with Robbie the Robot from the film *Forbidden Planet* who served his master with human-like qualities, or Sonny the robot in a more recent film *I-Robot*. Today, robots are far from human-like in what they can do. Many robots are used for drudgery-related tasks, such as cleaning, manufacturing, mail carts and bomb disposal. There is a series of robots that are used in the home for mowing the lawn, vacuuming and security. This creeping army of technological gain is invading the realm of human social life, sharing the living environment with people, communicating emotionally with humans and learning 'right' and 'wrong'. Some of these sociable robots are even capable of interacting with humans with facial expressions, gaze directions and voices, mimicking the affective dynamics of human relationships. This emerging movement of social roboticisation is causing a fundamental change in the meaning of social interaction and the nature of human communication in society (Zhao, 2009).

Cog and Kismet (Turkle, 2005) became the first two research prototypes for such humanoid robots. In addition, in the 1990s a barrage of humanoid robotic pets, toys and dolls, such as Tiger's Furby (www.furby.com), Sony's Aibo (www.us.aibo.com) and Hasbro's My Real Baby (see www.irobot.com/toys/default.asp) hit the consumer market, all designed to trigger human emotions with believable social interaction. Human beings are increasingly becoming cyborg creatures, intimately attached to our various forms of technology. With the launch of the Xbox Kinect, PlayStation Move, Wii Remote and the invention of Motion Plus sensors a new generation of more sophisticated gaming and entertainment technology is currently hitting the market. Controllerless technology and more sophisticated sensors are taking us to a level of interactive sophistication previously only imagined in science fiction.

Parallel to the development of various mechanical social robots was the emergence of socially intelligent software agents that communicate with human users in natural human language. The first well-known chatter bot (Levy, 2007) was 'Eliza', a computer program capable of conversing with people in text by playing the role of a psychiatrist. The spread of the internet in the 1990s contributed to the rise of numerous online conversational agents, such as 'Julia' (www.lazytd.com/lti) and 'Alice' (www.alicebot.org), which chat with people round the clock on topics ranging from politics to sex. We are now living in a world that is being cohabited by an ever-increasing number of humanoid social robots.

The current state of the art of android robotics, whose appearance is designed to resemble humans, includes such as Honda's ASIMO, Waseda University WABOT and Toyota's trumpet-playing robot. These robots are functional and without human emotions. A proposition in David Levy's book, *Love+Sex with Robots* (2007) is that if Sonny, the android robot from *I Robot* has come about it must be recognised that future robots are likely to have similar potential to interact. The mere concept of an artificial partner, husband, wife, friend or lover is one that for most people at the start of the 21st century challenges the notion of relationships. Previously, the relationship between robot and human had always been considered in the terms of master to slave, of human to machine. But with the addition of artificial intelligence to the machine-slaves conceived in the 20th century, something more is possible. By endowing robots with capability of communicating with humans and making them human like, android robots moves us to an era when robots will interact with us not only in a functional sense but also in a personal and pleasurable sense.

Sherry Turkle, writing in her book *Second Self* (2005) eloquently makes the point that it is not about what the computer will be like in the future. But what will we be like? What kind of people are we becoming? How will humanity need to change in order to think of android robots as lovers? It is the capacity to fall in love with a robot and the natural process of having sex with them, not thinking it is unethical or demeaning. We can love animals, we do love machines, so a logical next step is the proposition of having sex with one or even marrying one.

Driver 8: Destination brand and the importance of sex tourism in Amsterdam

What would Amsterdam be without the red light district? According to the destination's website:

> The majority of people have heard about Amsterdam's Red Light District well before their visit. Leaving nothing to the imagination, most stereotypes about this area are true: there are plenty of sex shops, peep shows, brothels, an elaborate condom shop, a sex museum and of course prostitutes in red-lit windows. In addition to the fact that there is much more to the city than this district, there are a few more truths to be known about this (in) famous part of Amsterdam.

> Prostitution has enjoyed a long tradition of tolerance in Amsterdam and, as with soft drugs, the Netherlands' approach is to legalise the trade and impose regulations. Basically, they know people are going to do it

anyway, so they may as well keep it safe for those involved. In addition to preventing forced prostitution, this open and honest approach means sex-workers here have their own union, plenty of police protection, an information centre (for visitors as well), frequent monitoring and testing and professional standards. (http://www.iamsterdam.com/en/visiting/spotlight/redlightdistricts, accessed 20 September 2011)

The red light district is part of Amsterdam's brand equity and values according to research for the Amsterdam City Council and Tourist Board (Gehrels *et al.*, 2004). Research identifies the city's sex and drugs culture as a strength which has a teasing appeal. More liberal attitudes allow expression and freedom, at the same time the red light district is seen as a potential weakness based upon the words 'dirty', 'disorderly', 'not appealing to families' or 'saturated drugs image'. Kavaratzis and Ashworth (2006) argue that one of the main elements of the city's international image is associated with the liberal attitude towards soft drugs and prostitution.

The image problems of Amsterdam can be traced back 40 years and are to some extent a consequence of earlier highly successful branding long before the term itself was in use. The image formed in the 1960s was composed of two dominant elements. First, there was the urban tourism image of Vermeer townscapes and tightly packed canal side buildings, which has become so established as to lock the city into a single historic period and single morphological product. Second, together with London and Copenhagen, Amsterdam acquired an international status as 'swinging' youth centre based upon sexual liberation and narcotic indulgence. The intrinsic problems of these images stem in part from their very strength. The established image made product diversification difficult and the tourism image of the capital was sharply discordant with the official nationally projected 'Holland waterland' image (Gehrels *et al.*, 2004) and the popular 'clogs, windmills and tulips' foreign image of the Netherlands. In part, however, it can be attributed to fashion changing faster than brand image.

In addition,

an easygoing tolerance slipped effortlessly into personal insecurity and public disorder. Acceptance of soft drugs and of sexual variations became a serious hard drugs problem and a sordid commercial sex district on the 'Wallen' and the city's continuing polycentric vitality as a focus for homosexual tourism is equivocal for its general tourism promotion. (Ashworth & Tunbridge, 2000: 221)

The current easyJet promotion of its Amsterdam flights aims quite explicitly at a youth party market (especially 'stag and hen' parties) stressing the advantages of cheap alcohol, possible sexual encounters and indulgent policing. This is the dilemma; the success of Amsterdam is about short breaks driven by cheap flights. Both the studies by Genhrels *et al.* (2004) and Kavaratzis and Ashworth (2006) highlight change is necessary but as the city cannot afford to lose its drugs and sex image, it is a process of balance.

Is Making Love to a Robot a Feasible Future?

Sexually transmitted diseases, human trafficking, men's desire for the body beautiful, women's increasing propensity to buy sexualised intimacy and the importance of the sex industry to Amsterdam's tourism leads to the suggestion of androids as sex workers. Even the real sex workers of Amsterdam may not be able to compete with such technologies. Levy quotes a reference from the UK *Guardian*:

> In 1983, the Guardian newspaper reports that New York prostitutes share some of the future of other workers – those technology developments may put them out of business. All the peepshows now sell substitutes – dolls to have sex with, vibrators, plastic vaginas and penises – and as one groused in New York, 'it won't be long before customers can buy a robot from a drug store so they won't need us'. (Levy, 2007: 215)

So, is such a suggestion feasible? For starters, virtual sex or cyber sex is one of the successful stories of the internet, the top selling searches and purchases on the internet are sex and tourism (Yeoman, 2008). Haptic technology refers to technology that interfaces to the user via the sense of touch by applying forces, vibrations and/or motions to the user. This mechanical stimulation may be used to assist in the creation of virtual objects (objects existing only in a computer simulation), for control of such virtual objects, and to enhance the remote control of machines and devices. Regina Lynn (2004) on technology sex blog describes the haptic technology application *sinulator*:

> The UPS guy delivered my sinulator the morning of the day I was giving a party. I signed, sent him on his way and returned to my preparations. It wasn't until hours later, draped around the room with about 20 friends, that I remembered my new toy.

> The Sinulator is a device that lets you connect a sex toy to your computer so that other people can control it for you over the internet. After announcing to the room that I had one of these, I really had no choice but to open the box and pass the thing around.

> Here's how it works. Your Sinulator package includes the transmitter, a vibrator and a receiver. You download the client application from Sinulator. com. During installation, you connect the transmitter to a USB port.

When you're all installed and have the client running, you attach your toy to the wireless receiver and switch it on. Finally, you go to Sinulator. com and choose a name for your toy. After that, anyone who knows your toy's name can set your toy a-buzzin' using the Sinulator control panel. Neither of you have to register or divulge any personal information – not even an e-mail address.

The control panel looks like a grown-up version of a driving toy for baby, with buttons and levers and sliders that you manipulate with your mouse. I laughed when I first saw it – now you can have sex and drive a race car at the same time! If that's not a popular male fantasy, I don't know what is.

But it gets even better. You probably want to stick to the dashboard if you're at the office, but for home use, the Interactive Fleshlight is where it's at. The Fleshlight is a standard, sleeve-style vibrator for men, with a twist: It's also a transmitter. It measures the speed and force of each thrust and communicates those metrics to the software, which translates them into vibration and pulse on the other end.

... In other words, a man can be thrusting in Cleveland while a woman is penetrated in Seattle, and the cybersex experience gets one step closer to the holodeck.

The rise of a synthetic social world where human individuals and androids robots co-mingle, calls for a new conceptualisation of society. The traditional view of society as consisting of only human individuals needs to be revised. For one thing, the boundary between humans and human artefacts is no longer inviolable due to the increasing technological prostheticisation of human bodies (Stelarc, 2000).

Moving into androids that can express emotions and subtly read the body language of a lover has foundations in the RoCo project at MIT (http:// robotic.media.mit.edu) in which a novel robotic computer is being designed with the ability to move in subtly expressive ways that respond to and encourage its user's own postural movement. The design of RoCo is inspired by a series of Human Robot Interaction studies that showed that people frequently mirror the posture of a socially expressive robot when engaged in a social interaction. Future developments include how the benefits of RoCo's movement might apply to establishing a kind of social rapport with people, the process of satisfaction is achieved based upon learning companion technology. When the technology is applied to androids, movements can be programmed based upon non-verbal cues and developing signals for intimacy (Breazal, 2004).

The act of having sexual intercourse with an android sounds physically challenging, along with the challenge of emotional connectivity. However,

emerging technologies and personal robots are combining functional ergo-
nomics and emotional reaction. The personal robotics group (http://
robotic.media.mit.edu) at MIT is using an uBot5 mobile manipulator developed by the Laboratory for Perceptual Robotics UMASS Amherst. The
mobile base is a dynamically balancing platform. It is capable of traversing
indoor environments at human walking speed. The two 4-degrees of freedom arms are based on a series elastic DOMO/WAM style arm design with
force sensing to support position and/or force control. These arms are
designed to be able to pick up a 10 pound object fully extended when used
together. The arm length permits a large bimanual workspace on the
ground plane. The arms are used in mobile dexterity research including
group manipulation tasks such as having several MDS robots carry a large
object together. The robot head is capable of expression such as nodding,
shaking and orienting, therefore having the capacity to substantially mimic
the human body.

Sex is all about sensitivity and the Huggable project at MIT will allow
robots to respond to touch such as force, pressure, pain including those
designed to elicit different types of responses such as 'teasing pleasant',
'teasing painful' and 'touch pleasant' (Stiehl & Breazeal, 2005). Combined
with research being undertaken Professor Heike Mertsching at Fraunhofer-
Gesellschaft Institute (2009) is to produce artificial skin for the next generation of soft-skinned androids. Alternatively, a new generation of
artificial skin for robots is being developed by scientists at Tuff's University
using silicon which offers a higher probability of success in the near term
(Keller, 2009).

Standard humanoid robots mimic the human form, but the mechanisms
used in these robots are very different from those in humans, and the characteristics of the robots reflect this. This places severe limitations on the
kinds of interactions such robots can engage in, the knowledge they can
acquire of their environment, and therefore on the nature of their cognitive
engagement with the environment. However, a new kind of robot is being
developed called an anthropomimetic robot (http://eccerobot.org/). Instead
of just copying the outward form of a human, it copies the inner structures
and mechanisms – bones, joints, muscles and tendons – and thus has the
potential for human-like action and interaction in the world. The skeleton of
the robot is based upon thermoplastic polymorph which is distinctly bone-
like in appearance and density. The anthropomimetic robot is equipped with
two 'eyes' represented by two high-speed, high-definition cameras and
highly efficient image preprocessing and recognition memory system, while
the audio system mimics the acoustic and directional characteristics of the
human ears.

Honda's ASIMO not only looks humanoid it is now capable of recognising people, using facial recognition software and with the use of augmented
reality technologies. This means that robots not only recognise someone but

are able to access memory systems of their potential lovers likes and dislikes (Honda, 2009).

Concluding Remarks

The worst kind of tourism

Sex trafficking simultaneously exploits both the best and the worst aspects of globalisation. The champions of globalisation tout the growing ease of conducting business across national borders. Sophisticated communication tools and relaxed banking laws make it possible to exchange assets internationally with ease. Virtual enterprises can operate everywhere and nowhere, making themselves known only when and where they choose. Organised crime syndicates take advantage of these tools to create more efficient overseas networks. Although most trafficking originates with local operators, they deftly connect to an international sex industry looking to fill slots in brothels, massage parlours, strip joints and lap dance bars.

A club owner in Amsterdam can pick up the phone and 'mail-order' three beautiful young girls from Eastern Europe. Twenty-four hours later, a fresh shipment of three Russian girls will be touting for sex. Technology has become the single greatest facilitator of the commercial sex trade. In Japan, buyers are connected with prostituted women and children through a complex system of telephone booths and call centres (Yeoman, 2008). In both the Netherlands and the United States, commercial sex services and the victims providing those services are advertised extensively over the internet, with a simple search of English language websites advertising escort services yielding millions of results on Google. In fact, sex is one of the success stories for the internet. Cellular telephone technology is connecting buyers with victims and increasingly distancing the trafficker from the action of enslaving as he directs the transaction over the telephone. Technologies have also contributed greatly to the proliferation of pornography. The viewing of adult pornography by situational or opportunistic buyers is a primary gateway to the purchase of humans for commercial sex.

Sex tourism and sex trafficking appear to be pandemic throughout the world. The demand for commercial sexual services is driving markets and generating profits for the criminal traffickers. The average person trafficked into the sex industry earns approximately $67,000 per year in revenue for her/his trafficker (Shared Hope, 2007). The exact number of sex trafficking victims worldwide is unknown, with estimates ranching from 600,000 to 800,000. Isn't it about time this was stopped? Could robots be the answer?

It's possible

Could our patterns of consumption in late capitalism expand to include cyborg sex in an Amsterdam brothel? It is certainly hard to imagine David Levy's prediction that by 2050 sex and love with robots will be a human possibility. But then again, 25 years ago when Donna Haraway (1991/1985) imagined a cyborg future where technological extensions of the human self are an everyday reality, we could not possibly have imagined our own present day relationship with connective technology.

The future of sex tourism in Amsterdam needs an innovative solution and the use of androids as sex workers is that futuristic solution. The present situation of human trafficking, sexually transmitted infections, pressure from the local community and the threat to the destination brand means change is inevitable. However, the use of androids as sex workers has implications for society. For example, would humans actually do it? In advanced technology societies such as Japan and Korea, humans are already having sex with sex dolls and we already live in a society where technology has emotional appeal. Levy (2007) proposes that such a change will happen by 2050. For example, would such a proposition be legal? Most of us in a free-thinking society are unlikely to feel that the use of androids by adults in private is a practice that should be prevented by legislation, yet in Alabama, Texas, and some other jurisdictions in the United States, the sale of vibrators has been deemed illegal (Levy, 2009). Would your partner consider sex with an android as infidelity or is it just another form of masturbation? Would the use of androids out perform humans in sex as they could offer variety, in the terms of appearance, size, endurance, voice, conversation and performance of sexual acts that to some would be unimaginable? Will female consumers of sexual services prefer android sex? And finally, when do robots become humans and overtake humans, just like Sonny in *I Robot*? This chapter is not about these issues, but the future of sex tourism in Amsterdam using androids as sex workers. If such a proposition came true, Amsterdam would probably be the safest and best sex tourism destination in world and all the social problems associated with sex tourism would disappear overnight.

Robot sex is safer sex, free from the constraints, precautions and uncertainties of the real deal, but regardless of how good the sex is, will it ever take the place of human interaction?

8 New Zealand 2050: The Future of Professional Rugby and Sporting Events

Learning points

- This chapter identifies the key drivers of change that will shape the future of professional rugby and the sports fan experience, including demography, science and cultural capital.
- The economic power of sport redefines values and ethics, and genetic modification is de rigueur for athletes.
- By 2050, singularity would be achieved, and the functionality of the human brain would be quantifiable and matched by technology. Robots will be the new referees.

Introduction

Rugby Union is the No. 1 sport in New Zealand and the All Blacks are the country's leading brand (Coleman, 2009). However, by 2050, this could all be different as demographic change will result in an ageing population and a smaller cohort of young men entering the sport. Along with the paradox of choice scenario (Schwartz, 2004; Yeoman, 2008) in which populations participate in a diversity of sports rather than concentrating on one sport, rugby in New Zealand faces a critical situation moving into the future. How does future New Zealand Rugby maintain its position as the sport of choice for participation, spectators and broadcast audiences? How do the All Blacks maintain their enviable historical winning records? Maybe, technology and science will revolutionise and enhance the game. This chapter provides a futuristic presentation of what rugby in New Zealand will look like in 2050 focusing on the professional game: sport science, interactive technologies, stadium and home experiences.

New Zealand and Rugby Union

In New Zealand's short history, New Zealanders have thought of themselves as belonging to a great sporting nation. This image has been and is an important component of New Zealand's national identity. While the game of rugby was the country's premier national sport by the 1890s, it was the success of the New Zealand team on the 1905 tour of Great Britain that transformed an imported game into a national ethos. In short, rugby expressed the core values of New Zealand society. Rugby was one thing that New Zealanders believed they could do better than any other group of people in the world. By proclaiming rugby, an upper-class English game, as the colony's national game, New Zealanders were proclaiming both their loyalty to Britain and their independence from Australia, where cricket had become the major vehicle of nationalism (Crawford, 1998). Play Up and Play the Game was one of a number of British aphorisms of the 19th century that illustrated how sport became an expression of a national and religious ethos. The athletic emphasis, however competitive the game, was to play well, not necessarily to win. The difference for colonial New Zealand was that the dominant social activity was not cricket, a uniquely English synthesis of sport and morality, but rugby is more than a game.

Rugby Union is an extremely physical, contact sport played between two teams each consisting of 15 players (with substitutions allowed), using an oval-shaped ball. Matches are made up of two halves of 40 min each and take place on a rectangular field, with maximum dimensions of 100 m × 70 m plus up to 22 m in each 'in-goal' area. The aim of the game is to accumulate more points than the opposing team by scoring tries (currently worth five points) and by kicking conversions (two points), penalties (three points) and drop goals (three points). A try is scored if a player crosses the opposing team's line and grounds the ball in the in-goal area. Players attack the opposing team's line by running with the ball in hand, kicking the ball, and passing the ball (but not forwards) to another player in the team (Owen & Weatherston, 2002).

In 2011, the All Blacks were the world champions having beaten France 8-7 at the Eden Park final. The All Blacks are the most recognisable, and probably the most feared team in the world. Rugby in New Zealand is the exemplar of social and spiritual life, a game that demands skill and courage. Also, in New Zealand, rugby is the symbol of national identity and is the cornerstone of conversations, stories, life and culture; some would say there is not anything else (Jackson & Hokowhiti, 2002).

How will New Zealand Dominate the World of Rugby in 2050?

The story continues

The highlight of Roger's visit to New Zealand is to watch the Rugby World Cup between the All Blacks and Australian Wallabies at the Originals Stadium. Roger was staying at the stadium hotel where his bedroom overlooked the rugby pitch just like an executive box. The stadium seating featured the latest innovations in technologies and comfort, including built-in video screens at every seat for ordering food and drink; and vibration services designed to get the crowd on its feet. Roger has invited some friends to watch the match with him, along with a number of Stepford mistresses to keep them company. If Roger missed a bit of the game, he simply rewound the play and selected different camera angles. Roger could even send video clips of the game to friends instantly. The national coaches can ask the crowd which substitutes to use and fans can offer the manager advice on tactics using the interactive voting system. Players have built-in radio frequency identification chips (RDIF) chips that help the coach make predictions about player's positions, endurance and tactics. In 2050, rugby players are elite athletes whose performance is controlled by nutrition, science and genetic engineering. The development of youth players starts with designer babies at www.surrogacy-rugby-mothers.com.

All referees are now expert robots who never make a wrong decision. They are supported by an array of embedded technologies around the pitch from radio frequency chips which know when the football is outside play and global positioning systems which identify when a footballer is offside. Nanotechnology medicines are incorporated into players' shirts to allow for the healing of minor scrapes. Anyway, the All Blacks win 50-4, another milestone for the greatest rugby nation on Earth! Roger and friends celebrate the victory with a night of sin courtesy of the hotel's Stepford mistresses.

Will this future be based upon . . .

- A youth system based upon designer babies?
- Coaches who measure players' performance using artificial intelligence (AI) aids?
- The use of nanotechnology with self-healing properties for players' injuries?
- Prototyping technology similar to the TV programme, the Six Million Dollar Man?

- The use of stem cell therapy for speeding up the recovery period of players?
- A technical experience rather than a physical game?
- An interactive stadium for the supporter or will it be empty stadiums given the importance of HD technologies?
- Using technology to bring about perfect weather and avoiding storms?

... who knows!

Drivers of Change

The key drivers that shape this scenario include:

Driver 1: Demography

According to Statistics New Zealand (2009), the country's population is projected to grow from 3.88 million in 2001 to approximately 4.9 million in 2050 or by 25%. After 2050, the population is projected to decline as deaths outnumber the combined effects of births and net migration changes. In common with other developed countries, New Zealand's population is ageing. The process is expected to hasten after 2011, when large post-Second World War baby boom cohorts start to enter the so-called 'retirement ages'. Half of all New Zealanders are projected to be over the age of 45 years by 2050, compared with a median age of 35 years in 2001, a rise of 10 years. The proportion of children (under 15 years) is projected to drop significantly, from 23% of the New Zealand population in 2001 to 16% in 2051. The proportion of New Zealanders aged 65 years and over is projected to reach 25% of the nation's population by 2051, up from 12% in 2001. New Zealand's labour force is expected to grow from 1.88 million people in 1996 to 2.24 million by 2021, an increase of 360,000, or 19%. It is then expected to drop slowly to 2.11 million by 2051, as the large group of cohorts born between the mid-1950s and mid-1970s retire from the labour force.

The age structure of the labour force is projected to undergo significant change, resulting in fewer younger workers than in the past. By 2050, the youth segment of the labour force (18–24 years) is projected to make up a smaller share of the total labour force than in 1996: 12% versus 16%. In contrast, the older labour force (45–64 years) is projected to increase its share greatly, from 28% in 1996 to 40% in 2050, when they are projected to slightly outnumber those in the 25–44 years age group.

These diverse trends mean that the labour force is projected to take on an older profile in the future. Half of the labour force is projected to be older than 42 years by 2041, compared with a median age of 37 years in 1996, a rise of five years. Most of the increase is projected to take place over the next 10 years as the baby boomers enter older working age groups. Hence in the future, the professional sport of rugby will have a smaller pool of young people coming through the ranks of the game.

Driver 2: Singularity: The evolution to robots, science and man

Such is the pace of discovery and progress in technology, that according to futurist Graham Whitehead (2005b), the world will see more technological innovation in the next 10 years compared to the last 150 years. The advent of human-level AI, a machine capable of the richness of expression and nuance of thought, is on the horizon (Tucker, 2008). However, the development of cyborg-style professional athletes is the field of futurist Ray Kurzweil (2005), who proposes that the exponential improvement described by Moore's Law will ultimately lead to a technological singularity: a period where progress in technology occurs almost instantly based upon the assumption that new types of technologies will emerge such as optical or quantum computers. Kurzweil's proposition about singularity projects a point where the functionality of the human brain is quantifiable and matched by technology. Singularity means being on verge of robots as humans or at the intersection of technology and the human brain and could lead to the eradication of such diseases as Alzheimer's. This is the point in 2050 where the singularity cyborg emerges as a professional athlete, a half human/half robot. The arrival of singularity is explained through a series of predictions as seen in Table 8.1.

Driver 3: Desire for new experiences, the long tail and individualism

Edward Griffiths, Sports Minister in the UK government of 1970–1974 believed there had been a shift from collective to individual sports because society had become wealthy, and the desire for new experiences meant sport can be tailored to the individual (Yeoman, 2008). Individual sports are often perceived as less time consuming than team sports because many such activities are easy to take part in and require little initial skill. In addition, consumers' leisure portfolios have grown greatly over the last 25 years according to research by the Future Foundation (Yeoman, 2008), although leisure time has increased by only 20 minutes per day in the same period. Clearly, people are trying out many activities, making it difficult to gain expertise in specific sports. At the same time the rise of individualism has created an interest in a variety of sports, no longer is the choice just football, rugby, netball and athletics, but basketball, kayaking, whitewater rafting, bugging, zorbing, running and a variety of extreme sports. Consumers are participating in individual and a variety of sports, rather than traditional team sports. This shift from traditional, mass-based team sports creates the surge for niche or one of a kind experiences which Chris Anderson (2007) in his book calls the Long Tail or

Table 8.1 The journey to singularity

Timeline	The road to singularity
2010s	• Computers will disappear as distinct physical objects, meaning many will have nontraditional shapes and/or will be embedded in clothing and everyday objects. • Full-immersion audio-visual virtual reality will exist. • Computers become smaller and increasingly integrated into everyday life. More and more computer devices will be used as miniature web servers, and more will have their resources pooled for computation. • Eyeglasses that beam images onto the users' retinas to produce virtual reality will be developed. They will also come with speakers or headphone attachments that will complete the experience with sounds. These eyeglasses will become a new medium for advertising as advertising will be wirelessly transmitted to them as one walks by various business establishments. • Advertisements will utilise a new technology whereby two ultrasonic beams can be targeted to intersect at a specific point, delivering a localised sound message that only a single person can hear. This was demonstrated in the films *Minority Report* and *Back to the Future 2*.
2020s	• Personal computers will have the same processing power as human brains. • As one of their first practical applications, nanomachines will be used for medical purposes. • Accurate computer simulations of the entire human brain will exist due to these hyperaccurate brainscans, and the workings of the brain will be understood. • Nanobots capable of entering the bloodstream to 'feed' cells and extract waste will exist (though not necessarily be in wide use) by the end of this decade. They will make the normal mode of human food consumption obsolete. Thus, humans who have injected these nanobots into their bloodstream will evolve from having a normal human metabolism and become humanoid cyborgs. Eventually, according to Kurzweil (2005), a large percentage of humans will evolve by this process into cyborgs. • The threat posed by genetically engineered pathogens permanently dissipates by the end of this decade as medical nanobots – infinitely more durable, intelligent and capable than any microorganism – become sufficiently advanced.

(continued)

Table 8.1 (Continued)

Timeline	The road to singularity
	• A computer will pass the Turing test by the last year of the decade (2029), meaning that it is a Strong AI and can think like a human (though the first AI is likely to be the equivalent of a kindergardner). This first AI is built around a computer simulation of a human brain, which was made possible by previous, nanotech-guided brainscanning.
2030s	• Mind uploading becomes possible.
	• Nanomachines could be directly inserted into the brain and could interact with brain cells to totally control incoming and outgoing signals. As a result, truly full-immersion virtual reality could be generated without the need for any external equipment. Afferent nerve pathways could be blocked, totally cancelling out the 'real' world and leaving the user with only the desired virtual experience.
	• Using brain nanobots, recorded or real-time brain transmissions of a person's daily life known as 'experience beamers' will be available for other people to remotely experience.
	• Recreational uses aside, nanomachines in peoples' brains will allow them to greatly expand their cognitive, memory and sensory capabilities, to directly interface with computers, and to 'telepathically' communicate with other, similarly augmented humans via wireless networks.
	• The same nanotechnology should also allow people to alter the neural connections within their brains, changing the underlying basis for the person's intelligence, memories and personality.
	• Cyborgs surpass the performance of professional athletes.
2040s	• Human body 3.0 comes into existence. It lacks a fixed, corporeal form and can alter its shape and external appearance at will via foglet-like nanotechnology. Organs are also replaced by superior cybernetic implants.
	• There will be social splitting into different levels of use of reality argumentation, from those who want to live in a life of imagined harems, or those who dedicate their thoughts to philosophical extension. Human society will drift apart in its focus, but with ever-increasing capabilities to make imagined things occur.
2050s and beyond	• $1000 buys a computer a billion times more intelligent than every human combined. This means that average and even low-end computers are hugely smarter than even highly intelligent, unenhanced humans.

Table 8.1 (Continued)

Timeline	The road to singularity

- Singularity occurs as AIs surpass human beings as the smartest and most capable life forms on the Earth. Technological development is taken over by the machines, who can think, act and communicate so quickly that normal humans cannot even comprehend what is going on; thus the machines, acting in concert with those humans who have evolved into humanoid androids, achieve effective world domination. The machines enter into a 'runaway reaction' of self-improvement cycles, with each new generation of AIs appearing faster and faster. From this point onwards, technological advancement is explosive, under the control of the machines, and thus cannot be accurately predicted.
- Singularity means the arrival of the half human and half human professional sportsperson.
- Singularity is an extremely disruptive, world-altering event that forever changes the course of human history. The extermination of humanity by violent machines is unlikely (though not impossible) because sharp distinctions between man and machine will no longer exist thanks to the existence of cybernetically enhanced humans and uploaded humans. The physical bottom limit to how small computer transistors can be shrunk is reached. From this moment onwards, computers can only be made more powerful if they are made larger in size.
- Because of this, AIs convert more and more of the Earth's matter into engineered, computational substrate capable of supporting more AIs until the whole Earth is one, gigantic computer. At this point, the only possible way to increase the intelligence of the machines any further is to begin converting all of the matter in the universe into similar massive computers. AIs radiate out into space in all directions from the Earth, breaking down whole planets, moons and meteoroids and reassembling them into giant computers. This, in effect, 'wakes up' the universe as all the inanimate 'dumb' matter (rocks, dust, gases, etc.) is converted into structured matter capable of supporting life (albeit synthetic life).

Source: Adapted from Wikipedia (2011), Kurzweil (2005).

seen another way, a *Paradox of Choice* (Schwartz, 2004) of endless possibilities. According to the Recreation and Physical Activity Participation Amongst New Zealand Adults Survey (SPARC, 2009) rugby is not identified as a top 10 sport or leisure activity by participation. The top participation sports and activities are individual-based activities such as swimming, walking, gardening, fishing, equipment-based exercise, golf and jogging. Even team-based activities such as football and cricket have higher participation rates than rugby.

Driver 4: Economic power of sport and rugby

Today, sport is a key part of global business, which includes sports magazines, sports channels, sports medicine, professional football or people going to the gym just to exercise. According to the World Economic Forum (Elliott, 2009) sport represents between 2% and 3.7% of world GDP, therefore placing an economic value on sport of between US$1.36 Tr and US$2.5 Tr, making sport one of the most important industries in the world.

According to a study by Deloitte Sports Business Group (Hall, 2009) the direct economic impact of New Zealand hosting the 2011 Rugby World Cup is NZ$1.25 billion, with 70,000 extra tourists expected to come to New Zealand as a result. In addition, the total economic stimulus of hosting the tournament rises to NZ$5.6 billion taking into account a multiplier effect on New Zealand's economy. The economic importance of rugby is noted in television viewing figures, with Rugby World Cup being the world's third most watched sport on television after the Olympic Games and the FIFA World Cup. Viewing figures for the tournament have grown significantly since the inaugural World Cup in 1987, from 230 million to 4.2 billion in 2007, whereas attendance at the event has simultaneously grown from 600,000 to 2,240,000, respectively (IRB, 2009; Yeoman, 2008).

Driver 5: Cultural capital

Rugby has always been part of the soul of New Zealand life, as Michael King notes in the *Penguin History of New Zealand*:

> For New Zealand men as a whole, Maori and Pakeha, playing and following rugby was the great common denominator they could share as players and supporters and as a sure-fire topic for socially bonding conversation. In most New Zealand schools before the war it was the only male winter sport available, and in many of them participation was compulsory. And, as Jock Phillips has noted, rugby was, along with drinking in public bars, one of the twin pillars of New Zealand male culture. Interests in the game embraced people from every class and occupation, and from both town and country – 'urban professionals right through to farmers and working class ... it became a universal experience for nearly all New Zealand men'. (King, 2003: 388)

From a more modern perspective, Fraser Holland, Sponsor and Marketing Manager with New Zealand Rugby Union said:

> Rugby in New Zealand is the sport and the pastime of choice for approximately three quarters of the country, male or female, so that's an incredibly

wide demographic. Rugby has been a component of the New Zealand psyche and a component of New Zealand history and heritage for over a hundred years. For those who aren't New Zealanders, rugby was the international gateway for New Zealand, and as I said, more than seventy-five per cent of New Zealanders claim to be avid fans. Just to give you a little bit more of an insight, within that demographic roughly about eighty per cent of those people would rather watch an All Blacks test match when it is played than do anything else. So it's quite special. (Scherer, 2006: 98)

There probably is no place in New Zealand where rugby is not the centre of conversation. Jackson and Hokowhiti (2002) note that rugby has strong cultural identification both in New Zealand and abroad, to the extent as a consequence of globalisation of society that rugby and in particular the All Blacks Haka have become 'the' symbol of New Zealand. It is what people call a nation's cultural capital, which is embodied in peoples' long-lasting disposition of the mind and body of what New Zealand is (Jenkins, 2002).

Driver 6: Insperience economy and urban tribes

According to Trendwatching (2008), futurists have always being talking about homes of the future, whether it is butlers such as Robbie the Robot or talking fridges. So this is not a new trend. However, the insperience economy is a representation of a consumer society which is dominated by experiences and consumers' desire to bring top-level experiences into their domestic domain. The key aspects of this driver include the consumer's desire to turn their homes into a highly connected, comfortable place fully equipped to entertain others, as represented by Ethan Watters (2003) in his book *Urban Tribes*, where friends are the new families. The aspect is extremely important for rugby, which is predominately a male spectator sport in which men gather like tribes for the sporting occasions. In addition, in a society where time is of the essence, having an insperience means consumers do not have to venture out. This is especially vital for generation Y for whom that technology is paramount, and the bigger the better (Yeoman, 2008).

How Will These Drivers Change the Sporting Landscape?

The fan experience

Will all the stadiums be empty because the experience is better in your living room, driven by the insperience economy and demographic trends? According to Professor Roy Jones of Loughborough University reporting in the Orange Report into the future of football; 'His daughter couldn't understand why she couldn't rewind the action as she was used to watching football on Sky+ when attending a live football match' (Orange Report, 2008: 5). High-definition television (or HDTV) and its digital format is turning watching TV into a high-quality real experience, surpassing the stadium event itself. Fundamentally, HDTV yields a better-quality image than standard television, because it has a greater number of lines of resolution. The visual information is some 2–5 times sharper because the gaps between the scan lines are narrower or invisible to the naked eye. The larger the size of the television the HD picture is viewed on, the greater the improvement in picture quality. On smaller televisions there may be no noticeable improvement in picture quality. With the development of digiboxes (e.g. SkyPLUS and so on) where the viewer can rewind, replay, focus on specific angles, skip adverts, watch multiple channels simultaneously and when watching events such as rugby decide which camera to view; it is no wonder the comments of Professor Roy Jones have the ring of truth.

What about holographic viewing, in which fans can watch live rugby without the need for coloured glasses? Advances in 3-D displays and life-size interaction are not that far away according to Ting-Chung Poon (2006), to the extent that quantum ghost imaging would allow images to be created. Ghost imaging uses photons that do not bounce off objects, but instead bounce off other photons, which have themselves bounced off objects. The effect is a 'ghost' image of the object reflecting the second set of photons. This would allow real 3D images beyond the normal flat screen TV making watching a game of rugby a surreal experience and revolutionising the home entertainment experience (Figure 8.1).

JVC, a technology manufacturer, already produces a 3D projector intended for home theatres that requires no special glasses or screens to view its effects. The DLA-RS2 uses something called D-ILA projection, which is akin to LCD projection, to produce stereoscopic video in 1080p high definition. However, for the sports fan that wants a real experience outdoors, try the Cal Spas' Ultimate Outdoor Theatre (http://www.calspas.com), a complete home theatre system with an anti-fog, anti-glare 400 cm LCD HDTV touting surround sound, DVD/CD player, iPod Docking Station, Sirius Satellite radio receiver and game console inputs. It also comes equipped with a five-burner BBQ grill, a wet bar, weatherproof recliners with cup holders and two fire pits. The whole system has been designed for protection from the external elements, priced around US$30,000.

For the truly dedicated fan, the ultimate experience will be the hotel as part of the stadium complex. The Marriott Hotel at England's Twickenham rugby ground includes six suites overlooking the pitch. As Zin (1998) points out, the correlation between themed hotels and sports is reinforced by authenticity and the experience of the sporting event. Therefore, living, participating and feeling the rugby experience are important dimensions of this scenario.

Figure 8.1 Cal Spa's ultimate outdoor theatre
(*Source:* Calspa)

Beating the Weather

For stadiums looking to beat the weather, there is cloud seeding which induces rainfall by launching substances such as silver iodide or dry ice into the clouds to encourage condensation, thus creating a micro-climate in a specific geographical location (Bluhm & Siegmann, 2009). China used such a concept for the opening ceremony of the 2008 Beijing Olympic Games in order to avoid a big downpour. China has been using cloud seeding technologies since 1958 as part of their weather modification programme which launches thousands of specially designed rockets and artillery shells into the sky every year in an attempt to manipulate weather conditions. Run by the Weather Modification Department, a

division of the Chinese Academy of Meteorological Sciences, the programme employs and trains 32,000 to 35,000 people across China, some
of them farmers, who are paid to handle anti-aircraft guns and rocket
launchers (Orange, 2008).

Figure 8.2 Retractable roof: Houston's Reliant Stadium
(*Source:* Rainer Ebert)

It rains a lot in New Zealand and this disrupts play or causes the cancellation of rugby matches. So in the future, a high retractable roof will be deployed at venues. A retractable roof is a kinetic architectural element, in which a roof made of a suitable material is mechanically deployed from some 'retracted' or 'open' position into a 'closed' or 'extended' position that completely covers the field of play and spectator areas. They are generally used in locations where inclement weather, extreme heat or extreme cold are prevalent during the respective sports seasons, in order to allow for playing of traditionally outdoor sports in more favorable conditions, as well as the comfort of spectators watching games played in such weather. Retractable roofs allow for the playing of the outdoor sports in outdoor conditions in indoor venues

Figure 8.2 shows the retractable roof at Houston's Reliant Stadium. Reliant's 291 × 117 m roof divides into two panels that open in the middle of the stadium over the 50-yard line. The panels are made out of a translucent Teflon-coated fibreglass. Five trichord trusses support each panel and span between super trusses. The panels will slide over rails built on top of the super trusses at a rate of about 10.7 m/min.

As an alternative to grass and the desire to beat the weather, artificial turf is deployed in many stadiums. One of the most advanced artificial turfs is FieldTurf, a brand of artificial turf playing surfaces produced by Tarkett Inc., USA (Figure 8.3). In the late 1990s, the artificial surface changed the industry with a design intended to replicate real grass. The new system quickly began taking market share from Astroturf and is now the leader in the industry.

The surface is composed of monofilament polyethylene blend fibre stuffed into a polypropylene backing top layer and a bottom layer which includes a mixture of silica sand and cryogenic rubber infill. The fibres replicate blades of grass while the infill acts as a cushion. This cushion

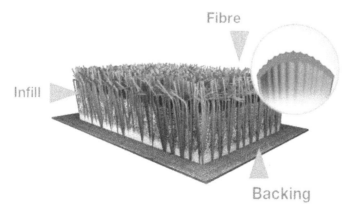

Figure 8.3 Field turf
(*Source:* Field Turf Inc)

improves safety when compared with earlier artificial surfaces and allows players to plant and pivot as if they were playing on a grass field. Proponents of the surface also cite its low-cost maintenance and durability. However, the emergence of the surface in association football stadiums has been controversial. Players and coaches have been critical of the toll it takes on a footballer's body and have expressed concerns that it does not play enough like actual grass. The surface has also been criticised for the infill not staying in place and the potential health risks related to the chemical properties of the surface.

The Future of Professional Sport

The intelligent manager

Coaches of the future would not simply trust their instincts, but will rely on technology and AI to make decisions. Systems such as ProZone (http://www.prozonesports.com) intelligent cameras will make decisions on tracking players' movements and effort (Orange, 2008). The camera can also be used for gait analysis to understand which players are getting angry or frustrated, which can lead to penalties, foul play or being sent off. This analysis could be used by the coach regarding substitutions. Supporting these intelligent cameras would be software systems such as www.datatrax.tv, which allow accurate 'realtime' tracking for all the players, officials and the ball for competitive matches and training sessions. Basically, the use of RDIF chips in players enables coaches to gather fitness information on every player on the pitch. Coaches can see who is tiring, who may need to be substituted and create a game plan shaped by this information. In addition, players would be wired up for coaches to monitor heart rate, endurance and fitness levels. All these statistical data would be used by computer expert systems to select teams and make tactical decisions. These systems are used by the South African Rugby Union as the basis for player's contracts, a truly performance-based valuation system (Orange, 2008). In addition, limited data would also be made available to spectators who could advise the coach on substitutions.

Perfection: No more blaming the referee

The economic and business value of world sport and rugby means that in the future referees cannot make mistakes, as the stakes are too high. In the 2007 World Cup, video refereeing was the norm, by 2050 science will provide perfect decisions. Technologies would be used to ensure the right decisions and spectators would be informed. Robot linesman will be used to spot a forward pass and a light-emitting system would identify where the foul occurred (Orange, 2008). The exact spot for lineouts will be worked out by RDIF in the balls, when a ball crosses a line. The RDIF chips would be used to inform the referee and a signal would be sent to the referee's watch or personal communications console. Chips embedded in rugby kits could be used to measure the strength of a pull on a shirt and so on. By 2050 players would not be able to fake injuries as expert system computers will be able to read faces and tell the referee if the player is lying. At the University of Witwaterstrand in South Africa, scientists have developed AIDEN, a computer card-playing robot that has taught itself to bluff and read other players faces to see if they are bluffing, hence referees would be able to spot those who is faking injury in the future (Mareli, 2007).

Sports medicine and science

Nanotechnology will be incorporated into football apparel to help heal minor scrapes and to improve shirt visibility. Agion antimicrobial technology is already used in shoes to keep them clean and help prevent athlete's foot. Nanotechnology could allow shirts to be made of fabric that can destroy airborne germs and pollutants. Such fabrics have already been created by Professor Juan Hinestroza of Cornell University:

Several leading players are already using nutrient-releasing patches during play which replace the minerals lost by the body during sweating … it is technically possible, through the use of nanotechnology, that such minerals could be incorporated into the fabric of a kit and absorbed in the same way. However, this would only work if the kit was in continuous contact with skin so it would have to be tight-fitting. It would also be difficult to monitor the quantities of minerals being absorbed and there could be issues with allergies, so it would probably mean each player would need their own bespoke kit. (Avila & Hinestroza, 2008 as quoted in Orange, 2008: 11)

Combined cryotherapy and magnetic therapy chambers will cut recovery times by as much as 300% facilitating much faster recovery between games and giving the ability to train more often. The advances in genetic and metabolic typing will also give rise to completely individualised pre-match drinks and non-invasive 'electrosonephoresis injections' which will optimise energy levels. Timed release nutrients will ensure energy is optimised throughout a game and the concept of fatigue resulting from depleted glycogen stores will become history. Sports consultant David Reddin notes that:

players will be genetic super-athletes covering up to 50% more distance than today's players – up to 20 km per game, speed of movement will increase by 10–15% owing to advances in power training, over-speed training and nervous system nutrition .... Injuries will be almost non-existent due to advances in gene therapy and the ability to predict an injury before it occurs. Even during a game sensor technology built into a player's kit will measure forces and tolerances and allow managers to proactively manage their team. (Orange, 2008: 11)

Philip Newton, Director of Lilleshall Sports Injury Clinic, says:

we could see gene therapy being used to treat injuries in the future, speeding up recovery times. Players will keep their children's umbilical cords for more than just souvenir purposes and child prodigies will be having biopsies to safeguard against the future, creating a surge in stem cell banking facilities for elite athletes. (Orange, 2008: 11)

Cyborgs: The new generation of athletes

A cyborg is a cybernetic organism (i.e. an organism that has both artificial and natural systems). The term was coined by Manfred Clynes and Nathan Kline (1960) who used it in an article about the advantages of self-regulating human–machine systems in outer space. The 1970s television series *The Six Million Dollar Man* featured one of the most famous fictional cyborgs, Col. Steve Austin (Caidin, 1975).

However, the role cyborgs play in real life, according to some definitions of the term, is associated with the most basic metaphysical, physical attachments, humanity and technology. For example, a human fitted with a heart pacemaker or an insulin pump might be considered a cyborg, since these mechanical parts enhance the body's 'natural' mechanisms through synthetic feedback mechanisms. Some theorists cite such modifications as contact lenses, hearing aids or intraocular lenses as examples of fitting humans with technology to enhance their biological capabilities; however, these modifications are no more cybernetic than would be a pen or a wooden leg. Cochlear implants that combine mechanical modification with any kind of feedback response are more accurately cyborg enhancements (Menzel & D'Aluisio, 2009).

In modern medicine, the term 'cyborg' is used to refer to a man or woman with bionic, or robotic, implants. In current prosthetic applications, the C-Leg system developed by Otto Bock HealthCare is used to replace a human leg that has been amputated because of injury or illness. The use of sensors in the artificial C-Leg aids in walking significantly by attempting to replicate the user's natural gait, as it would be prior to amputation. Prostheses like the C-Leg and the more advanced iLimb are considered by some to be the first real steps towards the next generation of real-world cyborg applications. Additionally, cochlear implants and magnetic implants that provide people with a sense that they would not otherwise have had can additionally be thought of as creating cyborgs (Menzel & D'Aluisio, 2009).

In 2002, under the heading Project Cyborg, a British scientist, Kevin Warwick, had an array of 100 electrodes fired into his nervous system in order to link his nervous system into the internet. With this in place he successfully carried out a series of experiments including extending his nervous system over the internet to control a robotic hand, a form of extended sensory input and the first direct electronic communication between the nervous systems of two humans. Jesse Sullivan became the first person to operate a fully robotic limb through a nerve–muscle graft, enabling him a complex range of motions beyond that of previous prosthetics. By 2004, a fully functioning artificial heart was developed. The continued technological development of bionic and nanotechnologies begins to raise the question of enhancement, and of the future possibilities for cyborgs which surpass the original functionality of the biological model (Menzel & D'Aluisio, 2009).

The 'cyborg soldier' often refers to a soldier whose weapon and survival systems are integrated into the self, creating a human–machine interface. A notable example is the Pilot's Associate, first developed in 1985, which would use AI to assist a combat pilot. The push for further integration between pilot and aircraft would include the Pilot Associate's ability to 'initiate actions of its own when it deems it necessary, including firing weapons and even taking over the aircraft from the pilot'. This cyborg soldier is portrayed by Hollywood in the RoboCop series (Gray, 1995). Military organisations' research has recently focused on the utilisation of cyborg animals for interspecies relationships for the purposes of a supposed a tactical advantage. Defence Advanced Research Projects Agency (DARPA) has announced its interest in developing 'cyborg insects' to transmit data from sensors implanted into the insect during the pupa stage. The insect's motion would be controlled from a MEMS, or Micro-Electro-Mechanical System, and would conceivably survey an environment and detect explosives or gas. Similarly, DARPA is developing a neural implant to remotely control the movement of sharks. The shark's unique senses would be exploited to provide data feedback in relation to enemy ship movement and underwater explosives (Christensen, 2006).

Other proposals have integrated the mechanical into the intuitive abilities of the individual soldier. Researchers at the University of California, Berkeley have set out to 'create an exoskeleton that combines a human control system with robotic muscle' (Yang, 2004). The device is distinctly cyborgian in that it is self-powered and requires no conscious manipulation by the pilot soldier. The exoskeleton responds to the pilot, through constant computer calculations, to distribute and lessen weight exerted on the pilot, allowing hypothetically for soldiers to haul large amounts of medical supplies and carry injured soldiers to safety.

The cyborgisation of sports has come to the forefront of the national consciousness in recent years. Through the media, America has been exposed to the subject both with The Bay Area Laboratory Co-Operative (BALCO) scandal and the accusations of blood doping at the Tour de France levied against Lance Armstrong and Floyd Landis. But, there is more to the subject; steroids, blood doping, prosthesis, body modification and maybe in the future genetic modification are all topics that should be included within cyborgs in sports. As of now, prosthetic legs and feet are not advanced enough to give the athlete the edge, and people with these prosthetics are allowed to compete, possibly only because they are not actually competitive in the Ironman event, among other such -athlons. Prosthesis in track and field, however, is a budding issue. Prosthetic legs and feet may soon be better than their human counterparts. Some prosthetic legs and feet allow for runners to adjust the length of their stride that could potentially improve run times and actually allow a runner with prosthetic legs to be the fastest in the world. One model used for replacing a leg lost at the knee has actually improved runners' marathon times by as much as 30 min. The leg is shaped out of a long, flat piece of metal that extends backwards then curves under itself forming a U shape. This functions as a spring, allowing runners to be propelled forwards by just placing their weight on the limb. This is the only form that allows the wearer to sprint (Menzel & D'Aluisio, 2009). So, by 2050 cyborg players may become a reality just like in the RoboCop series.

Nurturing youth

James Watson (2004), the co-discoverer of the structure of DNA and author of the international bestseller *The Double Helix*, tells the story of the amazing molecule since its discovery 50 years ago, following modern genetics from his own Nobel prize-winning work in the 1950s to today's Dolly the sheep, designer babies and GM foods. Professor Watson introduces the science of modern genetics, along with its history and its implications, in this magnificent guide to one of the most triumphant achievements of human science.

So, could we nurture youth for the future? Are the prospects for designer athletes and rugby players possible? Dr Andy Miah (2004) discusses such a prospect in his book, *Genetically Modified Athletes*. Genetic engineering is the technique used where functioning genes are inserted into cells to correct a genetic error or introduce a new function. The application of genetic knowledge to sports tends to have been considered in relation to elite performers; however, genetic science in sport could be used in sport in the following ways:

- Genomics (using genetic technology to improve methods of performance enhancement by creating more effective drugs and training techniques).
- Somatic cell modification (altering the non-hereditary cells of the body, such as those specific to muscle modification and altering the hereditary cells of the body very early in life).
- Genetic pre-selection (using the information of a person's genotype to conclude suitability for sport either at embryonic stage or infantile stage).

This final category is the use of pre-selection of athletes where prospective athletes could be chosen on their predisposition for athlete capabilities, that is, designer babies. The University of Idaho has already used gene therapy in the cloning of racehorses (Galli *et al.*, 2003). Idaho Gem is a mule resulting from a cross between a female mare horse and a male donkey jack. The project is focused on enabling gelding champions to contribute their genotype to future generations, as well as opening up an opportunity to verify the reproducibility of traits such as character and sporting performance. If a Los Angeles fertility clinic in 2009 offered parents the choice of their children's sex, hair and eye colour (Keim, 2009), does this mean rugby nations and clubs will start the apprentice scheme in the science lab? Currently, it is only social ethics that are stopping this.

Concluding Remarks

New Zealand wins the Rugby World Cup in 2050 but by then the game will have changed. It may well be the result of evolution to singularity and a cyborg future in which the boundaries between human and non-human become blurred. The evolution towards this science fiction-type future is already occurring. The economic power of world sport and rugby – with being first and perfection as the key driving forces moving into the future – means it is likely that athletes will be at the cutting edge of body and mind modification.

Technology use and cost for future sporting events

The future is heavily influenced by the advance of technology; sports tourism is not an exception. The chapter provided a scenario where technology plays a vital part in every aspect of sports game from fans' experience, scoring, referee, the venue (i.e. artificial fields, automated roofs), control of weather, training and tracking of the athlete's progress and status. Thus, reflecting the vital role technology plays in presenting sporting games to an audience.

The future use of high-technology equipment and products to enhance sporting experiences and games will possibly increase the cost of managing or hosting sports events. If mega-events such as the Olympic Games, FIFA World Cup and Rugby World Cup all require the use of such high-technology equipment, not only will developing countries have problems bidding and hosting them, sports fans may also be hesitant in paying premium prices for tickets, thereby decreasing the demand for such events. In such a scenario, countries such as South Africa will probably not have the ability to host sporting events because they are unable to cope with the high costs in organising them.

The threat of the insperience economy

Besides the high costs of hosting and premium price tickets possibly deterring sports travel, the advancement of technology has decreased the distance between sport audience and games. The insperience economy comes about as technology allows sporting games to be presented in 3D, high-definition to an individual, all in the comfort of one's home. With that, the desire to travel for a sporting event will significantly decrease. This decrease in demand for travel to sporting events will ultimately have serious repercussions on hosting destinations, particularly accommodation sectors and food and beverage sectors.

Redefining sportsmanship

There are many reasons as to why people engage in sports. Sports can be a reflection of the desire of a healthy lifestyle, social interaction or even a symbol of personal achievement. Sports players and sports fans often look up to professional players as role models. This form of idolisation towards professional players is often related to their ability to achieve high standards in the sporting arena or their perseverance, motivation, teamwork and sportsmanship. Sports fans recognise professional players typically as people who are no different from them yet able to accomplish more, and therefore the sports fan feels motivated to work towards similar goals. However, with hi-tech equipment used to train flawless sports players, to measure the accuracy of a goal, and with future generations of professional athletes being combinations of hi-tech cyborg beings, the meaning of sports is likely to be altered to one where outcome outweighs process. This change – albeit not necessarily a positive one – is most likely going to have an impact on the mentality, behaviour and attitudes of current sports fans and future generations of sports supporters.

Resources

9 California and Metropolis Los Angeles 2050: Changing Landscapes, Cities and Climate Change

Learning points

- Today, Los Angeles and California have the optimal climate for tourism; however by 2050 because of warmer temperatures, rising sea levels, water shortages and peak oil these destinations will be unfavourable.
- California, once the lifestyle destination for wine tourism, will by 2050 have no wine industry.
- This chapter portrays the future akin to the science fiction film *Logan's Run*, where due to the harsh realities of climate change life is controlled and managed within a domed complex.

Introduction

By 2050, most regions of the world will be predominantly urban as 193,107 new city dwellers are added to the world's urban population every day. The urban drift translates to slightly more than two people every two seconds (UN-HABITAT, 2008) reflecting that the world's urban population will swell to almost 5 billion in 2030 and 6.4 by 2050.

Cities have long been the centre of tourist activity, from the early times of civilisation through to their highly developed state in the global economy. Cities hold a particular fascination for tourists, from the vast highly developed metropolitan cities such as Los Angeles to small historic cities such as Durham in the northeast of England. Professor Stephen Page of Stirling University argues (Page & Connell, 2006) that on a global scale urban tourism is arguably one of the most highly developed forms of tourism, in a post-industrial society and affluent society. According to Yeoman (2008), the growth of world tourism in the last decade has been due to inter-regional travel rather than inter-continental travel fuelled by inter-city short breaks and the budget airlines. Cities have become activity places for culture, sports and amusements as well as offering leisure settings with physical character-istics and socio-cultural features. Many planners have turned to tourism as a means of urban regeneration. For example, the redevelopment of the London Docklands in 1980s onwards has been marketed as an example of London's vibrant tourism economy. The urbanisation of tourism in Los Angeles has become a key component of the city's economy and integral part of the city's urban development. In recent years, IMAX screens, themed environments, mega stores, theatres, museums and sports venues have displaced marble-clad office towers. Los Angeles has become a sprawling metropolis of entertain-ment in the era of the experience economy. However, what is the future for the city of Los Angeles? According to studies by Scott *et al.* (2004), California and the cities of San Diego and Los Angeles could be classified as an optimal climate for tourism and all year round visitation. But what does the future hold given warmer climates, rising sea levels, water shortages, peak oil and the continuing urbanisation trend? Scott *et al.*'s (2004) study examined cli-mate change scenarios for tourism in US cities through 2030–2080 and found that Los Angeles tourism would be marginally better off in the winter months but overall would move from 'excellent' to 'marginal/unfavourable', as the climate would become unbearable for tourists. If so, how will the city of Los Angeles adapt and mitigate for such change given the certainty of climate change? Would Los Angeles in 2050 be something akin to *Logan's Run* (Nolan & Johnson, 1967) as portrayed in the classic science fiction film, where life is controlled and managed within a domed complex? This chapter takes a futur-istic perspective on what tourism in urban Los Angeles will look like includ-ing its relationship to California's hinterland in 2050.

California's Demography and Urbanisation

More than 70% of the population in the developed world lives in an urban environment. According to the United Nations, this urban population is expected to remain largely unchanged in the next two decades, increasing from nearly 900 million people in 2005 to nearly 1.1 billion by 2050; growth resulting from external in-migration rather than natural population growth. North American cities grew the fastest among all cities in the developed world between 1990 and 2000, particularly cities in the United States, which grew an average of 1% per annum. Las Vegas – the gambling and tourist resort in the state of Nevada – grew at the annual rate of 6.2%, and the city of Plano on the outskirts of Dallas, Texas, saw growth rates of 5.5% per year due to migration from other parts of the United States. As the US's most populous state, California increased from 30 million in 1990 to 36.5 million in 2004, growing on average 600,000 people per year. According to the California Department of Finance (Yeoman, 2008) the state's population is projected to exceed 48 million by 2030 and reach 60 million by 2050. These projections indicate that the majority of Californians will continue to reside in Southern California with Los Angeles remaining the most populous county in California. Los Angeles often abbreviated to LA and nicknamed *The City of Angels*, has an estimated population of 3.8 million and its metropolitan area with 12.9 million residents spans over 498.3 square miles (1290.6 km²) in Southern California.

Tourism in California

Tourists to California spent US$97.6 billion in 2008, supporting 924,000 jobs in the state, with international tourists representing 19% of all expenditure. Californians are the mainstay of tourism in the state, comprising 86% of domestic trips (visits by US citizens), whereas the top out-of-state domestic markets are Arizona, Nevada, Texas, Oregon and Washington. In Los Angeles, the economic value of tourism is US$13.8 billion or 14% of tourism expenditure in California and it is the second most visited city in the United States after New York for international tourists (Los Angeles Convention & Visitor Bureau, 2008). Los Angeles is an iconic tourism destination with many famous attractions in a relatively concentrated space; including Disneyland, Hollywood, Beverley Hills, the Museum of Contemporary Art and Malibu beach. The future of tourism in California and Los Angeles set out by the California Travel Tourism Commission *2007–2013 Strategic Marketing Plan* (CTTC, 2007) focuses on the key markets of greater California, the United Kingdom, Germany and Japan and tourism products of winter sports, food and wine tourism, culture and adventure tourism. Looking to 2050, markets and products will be different as envisaged in the forthcoming scenario.

Future Cities

Since the period of the Industrial Revolution, cities have often been blamed for causing environmental problems. Although the concentration of people, enterprises, motor vehicles and waste in cities is often seen as a 'problem', high densities and large population concentrations can also bring a variety of advantages for meeting human needs and for environmental management. Urbanisation offers an opportunity for the future. Dodman (2009) points out that the economies of scale, proximity and agglomeration mean that it is cheaper to provide the infrastructure and services needed to minimise environmental hazards; the concentration of enterprises means that it is less costly to enforce environmental legislation; and the relative proximity of homes and businesses can encourage walking, cycling and the use of mass transport in place of private motor vehicles.

From a tourism perspective, factors such as climate change, peak oil and future of natural resources could reflect a vision of a future city akin to the popular science fiction film *Logan's Run* (Nolan & Johnson, 1967). It depicts a dystopian future society in which population and the consumption of resources is managed and maintained in equilibrium by the simple expedient of demanding the death of everyone upon reaching a particular age, thus avoiding the issue of overpopulation. The story follows the actions of Logan, a Deep Sleep Operative or 'Sandman' charged with enforcing the rule, as he tracks down and kills citizens who 'run' from society's lethal demand only to himself ultimately 'run'. The author is not suggesting the death of everyone by the age of 30 as depicted in the film but a scenario of building closed self-sufficient cities which are sustainable.

Such a scenario is not beyond the imagination, as Hodson and Marvin (2009) conclude that cities have usually sought to guarantee their reproduction by seeking out resources and strategies for self-sufficient infrastructure. Cities are gaining increasing interest and prioritisation by a range of architects and engineers who are rapidly populating a socio-technical trajectory of urban development, 'the eco-city' or closed city. This is exemplified in New York's strategy of energy independence, the recent doubling of decentralised energy targets in London, San Francisco's strategy of water autonomy and Melbourne's development of renewable powered desalination, where cities are attempting to reduce reliance on external resources (de Graaf *et al.*, 2007).

New eco-city developments designed by engineers, planners and architects are seeking to reduce reliance on external infrastructure by building more autonomous urban development. For example, Arup, a global planning, engineering and design consultancy, has signed a contract with Shanghai Industrial Investment Corporation (SIIC) to plan the world's first sustainable eco-city city at Dongtan, in Shanghai, China (Arup, 2005). Dongtan is strategically located close to Shanghai and on the third largest island in China, situated at the mouth of the Yangtze river. As Hodson and Marvin point out:

> Dongtan aims to be the world's first purpose-built eco-city. The city is designed not only to be environmentally sustainable, but also socially, economically and culturally sustainable. Its goal is to be as close to carbon neutral as possible, with city vehicles that produce no carbon or particulate emissions and highly efficient water and energy systems. Dongtan will generate all of its energy needs from renewable source including bio-fuels, wind farms and photovoltaic panels. A majority of Dongtan's waste will be reused as bio fuel for additional energy production and organic waste will be composted. Even human sewage

will be composted and processed for energy and composting, greatly reducing or entirely eliminating landfill waste sites. (Hodson & Marvin, 2009: 202)

Future cities have an agenda in an era of resource scarcity and climate change of developing networks and coalitions that are defining the terms and shape of responses to finite resources and pollution (Hodson & Marvin, 2009). Cities are developing fixes that appear to be prioritising two scales of infrastructure connection: disengagement from national and regional infrastructure and the re-prioritising of city-based enclosed resources. It seeks to ensure continued intra- and inter-urban connections through new urban agglomerations of socio-technologies, Such strategies are wrapped within a wider issue of ensuring strategic protection and seeking to guarantee the sustainability of the city.

Urban Metropolis: Los Angeles in 2050

As a consequence of this drive for urbanisation and the impact of climate change, the following scenario is envisaged:

In this scenario, there is a realisation that the exponential growth of tourism as predicted by the UN World Tourism Organisation in 2012 was unsustainable. No longer was the resource consumption associated with holiday overindulgence morally justifiable. Although tourism is the world's largest industry and China is the world's leading destination, things have changed, as climate change policies are embedded in international trade agreements. It all started in 2015 when the government realised that emission reduction targets could not be met and Middle Eastern countries decided to stop selling oil to the West. So it was necessary to encourage people to travel less and this in turn required a public policy intervention to help households and individuals change their lifestyle. By 2025, we have seen a major attitudinal change towards travel and tourism.

In fact, transport is only allowed if it is green, clean and generates a low carbon footprint. For example, new cleaner technologies have made road-based car transport viable for a relatively short distance of up to 200 km. Car distances beyond that point are heavily taxed. Public transport – electric and low energy is efficient and widely used. This efficiency is typified in Metropolitan Los Angeles.

Visiting this metropolitan hub means hotels are sustainable, which includes self-contained power generation from solar panel cells. The hub has an excellent IT infrastructure needed for a striving financial services industry. Corporate meetings are now confined to virtual worlds ever since the introduction of telepresencing in 2028. Telepresencing combines video conferencing and virtual reality to create three-dimensional, high speed, fluid interaction across different geographical locations. Business people even have their own hologram to give that physical presence. The metropolitan hub has invested heavily in conference and exhibition space, combined with an efficient land-based transport system making this metropolitan hub an ideal association meeting's destination. In 2050, association meetings are still important for face-to-face situations. Not everything can be done by telepresencing.

Technology in this scenario lets the world deal with change and overcome many environmental and economic challenges. In this scenario, it is about transporting people from A to B in mass numbers, therefore reducing the need for individual journeys. Across the United States, urban hubs have organised themselves to minimise travel and carbon footprints. For example, Los Angeles is now a UNESCO tourism colony with award-winning features such as the skyscraper Botanical Gardens. The city's green credentials stretch from the connectivity of its ULRS (Urban Light Rail System), connecting the airport with the city's business and leisure districts, making the city centre a car-free zone, to the novel use of Segways for elderly and infirm tourists. Globally, competition is increasing between cities and not countries, and the winners in the competitive environment are those able to link high value-knowledge assets with a desirable workforce, good quality of life, and appropriate public assets such as cultural and educational resources. That is one of the reasons why cities are changing and Los Angeles Metropolitan hub is at the forefront.

However, cities have grown at the expense of rural communities. The rail network is practically non-existent outside Los Angeles. Many rural communities have become isolated and unsustainable due to the lack of tourists combined with immigration towards urban hubs. Some micro-climate rural communities do survive and position themselves as garden adventure playgrounds for urban day trippers. Over the last 40 years, there has been much change to California's tourism product. The Napa Valley, once the cornerstone of the state's wine and tourism industry is no more. Food tourism has virtually disappeared as Generic Modified and Replicator foodstuffs along with vitamin supplements have become the norm for today's Californians. The Channel Islands National Park survives as an exclusive destination for the mega rich who are searching for an authentic eco-tourism experience. Other islands such as Catalina Island had to be abandoned due to the high cost of transport and rising budget deficits. Walt Disney's theme park is still the icon for many

Californians as hedonism and fun are the key drivers in today's mass tourism market.

Air travel is relatively expensive as it is still dependent upon carbon fuels, heavily taxed at 80% GST and vulnerable to oil shocks. Plans to expand Los Angeles Airport were curtailed in 2020 with investment being switched to rail networks and urban hubs. Tourism in California is predominantly a city-based product with rural destinations offering an exclusive experience for those who can afford to travel to the islands and hinterland.

In this scenario, resource use is now a fundamental part of the tax system and people are more careful in their use of resources. So is this what it could look like?

Key Drivers of Change

The key drivers that will shape this scenario include:

Driver 1: Peak oil and affordability of air travel
Driver 2: Climate change and the eco system
Driver 3: Food supply
Driver 4: Environmental taxation
Driver 5: Budget deficit
Driver 6: Urban land transport systems
Driver 7: Urbanisation and immigration
Driver 8: Assault on pleasure
Driver 9: Preserving the rural environment through isolation and the drive for sustainable living
Driver 10: Green technologies

Driver 1: Peak oil and affordability of air travel

Peak oil is the point in time when the maximum rate of global petroleum extraction is reached, after which the rate of production enters terminal decline. The concept is based on the observed production rates of individual oil wells, and the combined production rate of a field of related oil wells. The aggregate production rate from an oil field over time usually grows exponentially until the rate peaks and then declines – sometimes rapidly – until the field is depleted. Optimistic estimations of peak production forecasts that global decline will begin by 2020 or later, and assume major investments in alternatives will occur before a crisis, without requiring major changes in the lifestyle of heavily oil-consuming nations. These models show the price of oil at first escalating and then retreating as other types of fuel and energy sources are used (IEA, 2007; Yeoman *et al.*, 2007). In 2005, the US Department of Energy published a report titled *Peaking of World Oil Production: Impacts, Mitigation, & Risk Management* (Hirsch *et al.*, 2005: 12) known as the Hirsch Report, it states:

> The peaking of world oil production presents the U.S. and the world with an unprecedented risk management problem. As peaking is approached, liquid fuel prices and price volatility will increase dramatically, and, without timely mitigation, the economic, social, and political costs will be unprecedented. Viable mitigation options exist on both the supply and demand sides, but to have substantial impact, they must be initiated more than a decade in advance of peaking. (Hirsch *et al.*, 2005)

The key points of Hirsch Report conclude:

- World oil peaking is going to happen.
- As a transition in energy usage, peak oil will be a unique challenge, in that it 'will be abrupt and revolutionary'.
- Oil peaking will adversely affect global economies, particularly those most dependent on oil.
- The problem is liquid fuels (growth in demand mainly from the transportation sector).
- Mitigation efforts will require substantial time.
- 20 years are required to transition without substantial impacts.

A 10-year rush transition with moderate impacts is possible with extraordinary efforts from governments, industry and consumers:

- It is a matter of risk management (mitigating action must come before the peak).
- Late initiation of mitigation strategies may result in severe consequences.
- Both supply and demand will require attention.
- Government intervention will be required.
- Economic upheaval is not inevitable ('given enough lead-time, the problems can be solved with existing technologies').
- More information is needed to more precisely determine the peak time frame.

Tourism by its very nature entails the movement of tourists from their source to the destination. Tourism industries are therefore very reliant on mobility, transport and oil as a fuel source. The majority of international travel entails the use of oil at some point, and could not be undertaken using alternative fuel sources, such as electricity derived from renewable power sources. Tourist destination managers should be concerned about oil for several reasons. Oil scarcity and lack of alternatives (e.g. for aviation) will lead to higher prices for travel and as a result lower demand. Oil prices will not only affect a tourist's destination decision making, but also how (extensively) they travel once at the destination. An extreme scenario of oil depletion means that oil would – at some stage – only be available for life-supporting industries and tourism travel will not be a priority in oil allocation. Destinations market composition is likely to change dramatically up to the extreme of no international tourism, but an increase in domestic tourism and local recreational activities that involves minimum mobility. Yeoman et al.'s (2007) study of tourism in Scotland, envisaged a near 40% reduction in international visitors as a result of peak oil over a 10-year period (see Chapter 12 for a wider discussion on the future of transport.)

Driver 2: Climate change and the eco system

Governor Schwarzenegger declared a state of emergency on 27th February 2009 due to drought conditions as state-wide reservoir storage was extremely low; snow pack water content was 39% below average (Department of Water Resources, 2009a). With water supply conditions dire, is this an example of the future? Projected climate change scenarios indicate more long-term and extreme droughts resulting in shortages, competition, poor quality and unreliability of water. Degraded water quality makes it difficult and costly to make drinkable; adversely affecting businesses and irrigated agriculture and rural communities dependent on water; straining ecosystems and risking sensitive and endangered plants, animals and habitats. As 25% of California's energy is hydroelectricity, power shortages occur due to disruption to flows and lack of water from the Colorado River. California's high dependence on reservoir storage and snowpack for water supply makes the state particularly vulnerable (Hayhoe et al., 2004).

Hayhoe et al.'s (2004) modelling of the impact of climate change and emission pathways observes increases in extreme heat in California. In particular, Los Angeles sees temperatures rising between 1.5 °C to 5 °C and 3.5 °C to 9 °C in different scenarios, causing the number of heat wave days and heat-related deaths to increase. Rising temperatures, exacerbated in some simulations by decreasing winter precipitation, produce substantial reductions in the snowpack on Sierra Nevada Mountains, consequentially shortening California's ski season and curtailing water-based activities due to dried river beds.

With wine and food tourism being an important cultural experience in California, reductions in water supply and extreme temperature change, things are most likely to change. Hayhoe et al. (2004) predict that excessive high temperatures will affect the quality of wines as ripening periods will be altered, leading to degraded quality. Higher temperatures also impact on life form mixes and vegetation types, particularly in reductions of alpine/ subalpine forests and the displacement of evergreen conifer forests and mixed evergreen forests. Changes in precipitation will result in higher frequencies of fires and more desertification of the region.

Scenarios constructed by the Department of Water Resources (Juricich, 2008) estimate 70 million people to be living in California in 2050; this means people will be moving into areas which were once rural and suscep- tible to flooding and fire. Irrigated crop land has decreased significantly while urban development and natural resource restoration have increased. Through a combination of advanced agricultural practices (e.g. multi- cropping) and technology, the agriculture industry has been able to increase the intensity of production with a shift to higher value permanent crops. California continues to face lawsuits to protect water quality and endan- gered species and the state has been held liable for billions of dollars in dam- ages from a series of flood events. The state legislature response towards these lawsuits on a case-by-case basis has created a lot of uncertainty for cities and water managers about future regulatory requirements.

The biggest impact is in the Delta where levees protect low-lying land, much of which was already below sea level. Impacts include increased air temperatures, variable precipitation patterns, significant loss of mountain snowpack, and peak river flows occurring earlier in spring. Global climate change has affected California's natural systems as rising sea levels disrupt ecosystems, coastal communities and ongoing tidal wetland restoration. A report by Medelin et al. (2006) for the Government of California indicates Los Angeles investment in sea water desalination. The largest desalination plant in the United States is currently being constructed near San Francisco which will filter 100 million gallons of seawater daily.

Driver 3: Food supply

If 11 million people live in Los Angeles in 2050, the impact on the food supply chain will be enormous. As such, food security – the potential to produce enough food so that people in California can lead healthy and pro- ductive lives – will be significantly stressed. The future status of agricultural production is especially critical, as vital resources like arable land, clean water, adequate energy and abundant biodiversity are rapidly depleted throughout California and the world. Of the 2.3 billion acres of land in the United States, only 460 million acres, or 20%, are considered suitable for agricultural production. California has a fair amount of that fertile land, and ranks first in agricultural production in the United States. However, a loss of agricultural land and subsequent decrease in production is imminent if cur- rent population trends continue. Essentially, the US population, including California's, is increasing geometrically while arable land per capita is simultaneously decreasing due to urbanisation, industrial spread, transportation systems, and erosions.

Agricultural production in California totals $20 billion each year. However, much of this income could easily be lost unless California's agricultural land base is protected from further population growth. Pimentel and Hart (2008) projects by 2050, per capita agricultural land will decrease to half of what it is today. With decreased supply and increased demand for food, food prices are expected to increase by three to five times of current prices. This change in the farming system will have a major impact on the economy and population of California. A growing population will cause California to lose a substantial amount of available farm land at a substantial economic loss, at the same time stressing other natural resources vital to agricultural production. If the current rate of land loss continues, in less than 33 years approximately half of California's cropland will no longer be available for production.

To summarise, California has a problem! So, what is the future? Maybe in 2050, the Replicator as seen on 'Star Trek: The Next Generation' will come true. The Replicator is used primarily to provide food and water on board starships, thus eliminating the need to stock most provisions. Any physical structure can be recreated as long as the desired molecular structure is on file, but it cannot create antimatter, dilithium, latinum or a living organism of any kind. Who knows?

Driver 4: Environmental taxation

Growing concern about climate change has brought environmental issues to the forefront of the policy agenda in many European countries. In addition to the substantial scientific literature assembled under the auspices of the Intergovernmental Panel on Climate Change, the October 2006 *Stern Review of the Economics of Climate Change* argued strongly for immediate and urgent action to mitigate the potential costs of global climate change. Taxes, charges, tradable permits and other economic instruments can play an important role in achieving cost-effective control of greenhouse gas emissions, but their potential scale and revenue contribution raise many wider economic and fiscal policy implications. The increasing use of environmental taxes, emissions trading and other economic instruments has been partly driven by recognition of the limitations of conventional environmental regulation. Fullerton *et al.* (2008) note that to make any serious impact on major environmental problems now facing policy-makers, environmental policies cannot be approached purely as a technical issue; to be resolved merely by requiring the use of specified abatement technologies, setting emissions limits and using taxation to curb demand. Examples of environmental taxes include the London congestion charge on motorists travelling within parts of London designated as the Congestion Charge Zone (CCZ), aimed to reduce congestion, and raise funds for investment in London's transport system. Many developing countries under balance of payments and foreign exchange pressure have targeted tourism as a means of development. However, no proper management strategies have been formulated to manage visitors and to minimise impact on natural resources, threatening the sustainability of many attractions such as Machu Picchu. Regulating the inflow of tourists and taxation are the two most popular tools used, or considered, to remedy the problem.

The United States imposes virtually no green taxes. Most programmes aimed to reduce pollution rely on mandatory standards such as the Clean Air Act's New Source Performance Standards (NSPS) for stationary polluters and the Corporate Average Fuel Economy (CAFE) standards for automobiles. Among the few green taxes imposed are the 'gas guzzler' tax on new cars that exceed fuel efficiency standards, a tax on ozone-depleting substances and miscellaneous taxes on fertilisers and pesticides used in agriculture. Gasoline taxes as a total of gasoline prices are 28% compared to 75% in the United Kingdom and 58% in New Zealand. It ranks second lowest after Mexico for gasoline as percentage of gasoline prices in the IEA (2005) according to a study by OECD. Globally, the United Kingdom imposes one of the highest environmental taxes for aviation passengers, up to £170 (US$280) for long haul passengers. Calculations by Yeoman et al. (2007) highlight environmental taxes would have to reach 40–60% of the total ticket price to change consumer purchasing decisions.

Driver 5: Budget deficit

The recent budget deficit in California (Goldenberg, 2009) meant that Governor Arnold Schwarzenegger's proposed closing up to 220 or 80% of state parks would save the state government US$70 million. This would leave the more popular tourist parks funded by entry and camping fees open to the public. The proposal which was defeated by the Californian state legislature raises the point of the purpose of national parks; are they seen as a cost or a benefit to society? As populations age, government revenue falls and questions will be asked about how California pays for a parks system given the further fiscal deficits. The scenario highlights the case of Catalina Island.

Driver 6: Urban land transport systems

Transport and communications are fundamental to development. The construction and maintenance of roads, ports and inter-urban railways determine, to a large extent, whether cities will succeed economically. According to the UN-HABITAT (2008), two-fifths of the world's fastest growing cities have benefited from diversification and improvement of regional transport systems. Investments in transport increase the overall productivity and reduce socio-economic disparities across space and people. Connectivity through transport infrastructure has been vital for the growth of cities in close proximity to larger urban centres by offering the amenities of urban life – proximity, convenience and diversity – without the disadvantages, such as air pollution, congestion and crime. It also effectively reduces the 'commuter territory' in many places, linking metropolitan and sub-regional spaces and interconnecting various urban settlements.

Between 1970 and 1990, the total area of the 100 largest urban areas in the United States increased by 82%. However, population growth accounted for only half of the increase in land area. This indicates that people are living further away from city centres and spending more time commuting. Car transport is a significant contributor to levels of CO_2 emissions in North American cities and UN-HABITAT (2008) reports that the number of miles driven by the average United States resident has increased by 25% in the last 10 years; the amount of time Americans spend in traffic though, has increased by 236%, costing roughly US$78 billion. As a consequence, urban mobility has become a key concern as it impacts the liveability of cities. Motorised urban transport, in particular, has become a hot topic among policymakers, planners and environmentalists who are seeking ways in which to minimise its negative effects, including greenhouse gas emissions, traffic congestion and air pollution.

Los Angeles has some of the worst congestion in the United States and the city's rapid transit systems have not kept pace with the city's growth. According to the US Census Bureau (Metro, 2008), the percentage of commuters who use public transportation in Los Angeles County is 7%, far lower than in other major American cities: 30% of San Franciscan workers use transit, 25% within Chicago and 54% in New York City. With the region's growing population, the city will not be able to support itself without future investments in transportation. Mobility, as stated by Roger Snoble, the Chief Executive Officer of the Los Angeles Metropolitan Transportation Authority (MTA), is a key aspect in determining the future economic success of a city. Currently, the Los Angeles Metro Rail only has 62 stations, supporting 10 million residents within the Los Angeles County. Funding problems and Los Angeles urban planning could curtail any growth plans, as its low-density sprawl sets difficulties to provide rapid transit service to every part of the city. In addition, the geographical spread-out sometimes requires riders to drive to kiss and ride stations to take the train. However, many once in the car, just decide to continue driving. Los Angeles' transport system will fail to deal with future population projections and is not in the same league as European cities or proposed urban transport systems in Shanghai or Hong Kong (Metro, 2008; UN-HABITAT, 2008).

Driver 7: Urbanisation and immigration

As earlier mentioned, the total urban population in the developed world is expected to remain largely unchanged in the next two decades, growing to nearly 1.1 billion by 2050. On average, 2.3 million people migrate into developed countries each year. This means that immigration – both legal and illegal – accounts for approximately one-third of urban growth in the developed world. Without immigration, the urban population of the developed world would likely decline or remain the same in the coming decades (Yeoman, 2010b). The Demography Research Unit for the California State Government projects California's population to reach 60 million people by 2050, with the 40 million mark being passed in 2012 and 50 million in 2032. Los Angeles will continue to be the largest county, topping 13 million by 2050. Los Angeles is the primary receiving county for immigrants to California, with approximately 300,000 legal immigrants from over 85 countries settling in Los Angeles in 2000.

Driver 8: Assault on pleasure

There is hardly any aspect of the modern world that does not attract some form of moral or political debate, one of which revolves around the relationship between state and the individual, where the former is increasingly regulating the social order and restricting the individual's choice of lifestyle. In a free society where the individual should have choice, the range of options is declining. Authorities are increasingly intervening to restrict options and to prohibit activities, such as smoking or gambling. From a consumer's perspective, political correctness has reached the point at which they always have to worry about what they do and how they behave.

Society appears to be worrying about all sorts of things and debating issues such as how much people drink, what gifts children should receive, whether flying should be allowed, what products should be advertised and the extent of our carbon footprint. To a certain extent, this phenomenon of excessive worrying is actually taking the fun out of pleasure in commercial activity as a result of regulations, resulting in tourism businesses being unable to operate viably. These issues lead to the new puritanical society and a trend which Yeoman (2008) refers to as the *Assault on Pleasure*, which – if followed to its natural conclusion – will result in the banning of tourism by 2050, because it will be deemed to be bad for the environment.

Driver 9: Preserving the rural environment through isolation and the drive for sustainable living

The Stern Report (2006: i) concludes that 'scientific evidence is now overwhelming: climate change presents very serious risks and it demands urgent global response', indicating the use of isolation as a strategy to conserve the environment for the future. Rivard *et al.* (2000) highlight that the natural isolation of Canada's national parks has resulted in species richness, extirpations and introductions as a consequence, conserving Canada's ecosystems. Isolation as a preserving mechanism for ecosystems seems the most effective tool in conservation management (Sanchez-Azofeifa *et al.*, 2002; Piessens *et al.*, 2005).

In 1964, the Congress of the United States enacted and the President signed 'An Act to establish a national wilderness preservation system for the permanent good of the whole people' – *The Wilderness Act*. The law states the national policy is 'to secure for the American people of present and future generations the benefits of an enduring resource of wilderness'. The goal is to assure that an increasing population, accompanied by expanding settlement and growing mechanisation, does not occupy and modify all areas within the United States and its possessions, leaving no lands designated for preservation and protection in their natural condition. In April 2001, a nationwide *Los Angeles Times* poll (reported in Pew, 2004) showed just how strongly the American shared the congressional purpose set forth in the Wilderness Act. This poll – like scores of others – documents the overwhelming consensus (91% to 7% in this poll) of people that preserving wilderness areas and open spaces is personally important to them. A majority (51%) says preserving wilderness and open spaces is extremely important, while only a tiny minority (7%) says it is not very important or not important at all. Since the first Earth Day in 1970, Americans have raised the health of the environment and protection of their public lands to the position of a major national issue. According to Pew (2004), the large majority of Americans support strong government regulations to protect public lands, natural resources and the environment, hence the feasibility of isolation and wilderness as a strategy.

Over the last 20 years, similar surveys by the Henley Centre (Yeoman, 2008) have asked people whether they believe that quality of life is better improved by looking after the community's interests 'rather than simply their own', or looking after themselves 'which ultimately raises the standards for everyone'. According to Michelle Harrison (2006) of the Henley Centre, for the first time in decades, their survey has recorded a majority of people suggesting that looking after themselves is the best way to improve the quality of life. This apparent rise in individualism manifests itself in a number of ways. People, for instance, accept their role in and responsibility for climate change. Harrison deduces that individual consumers are more 'at fault' for causing climate change than the service sector industries and therefore more 'responsible for tackling it', suggesting that consumers are starting to feel guilty about their environmental damage and want to do something about it.

As such, the world has seen a big rise in interest in the concept of sustainable living, referring to a lifestyle that attempts to reduce use of the Earth's natural resource. Practitioners of sustainable living attempt to reduce their carbon footprint by altering methods of transportation, energy consumption and diet. Proponents of sustainable living aim to conduct their lives in manners that are consistent with sustainability, in natural balance and respectful of humanity's symbiotic relationship with the Earth's natural ecology and cycles. The practice and general philosophy of ecological living are highly interrelated with the overall principles of sustainable development.

Driver 10: Green technologies

Green technology is the application of environmental science to conserve the natural environment and resources, and to curb the negative impacts of human involvement. Examples include the hybrid car, which has become the most common form of electric car, combining a gasoline power train with supplementary electric motors to run the car at idle and low speeds, making use of techniques such as regenerative braking to improve its efficiency over comparable gasoline cars. Other examples include wave power which is the transport and capture of energy by ocean surface waves to do useful work, that is, electricity regeneration, or water desalination. While wave power is a renewable energy source, it is currently not widely employed.

The Implications of Change on the Present

It seems that the world in 2050 will be different from that of 2012. The theme of reversal of fortunes occurs as tourism returns to a mass tourism experience for the middle classes and luxury as an ecotourism experiences is only available to the upper classes. For starters, tourism in California as seen in The California Travel and Tourism Commissions (CTTC, 2007) five year plan from 2007 to 2012 will be completely different compared to 2050. Overseas markets such as Japan, Germany, Korea and the United Kingdom would virtually disappear due to the high cost of air international travel and out-of-state travellers who normally fly from New York, Illinois and Texas would also decrease dramatically. Reasons for travelling to California such as 'change of scenery'; 'romance', 'escaping' and 'freedom' would no longer be valid as climate change would have fundamentally closed rural tourism to the middle classes of America. At the heart of the change would be the disappearance of California's unique lifestyle and culture which is focused on a causal, laid-back vibe of freedom of expression and an active outdoor focus. California as a brand *Find Yourself Here*© would no longer be relevant. Products such as winter sports and food and wine tourism would virtually disappear from the landscape as urban tourism becomes predominant. In strategic terms, tourism in California ceases to be a sustainable proposition after the oil shocks of 2015, resulting in an urban tourism experience shaped by the connectivity of transport structures and catchments.

Policy interventions by government drive this scenario, based upon a proposition of what sustainable transport should be and the consequences of over dependence on oil (Yeoman *et al.*, 2007). The resulting policy shift will see the demise of The California Travel and Tourism Commission and the strengthening of the Los Angeles Convention Bureau as urban centres become the economic powerhouses in 2050. Despite the end of rural tourism in California, conservation through isolation driven by policy changes will see existing rural tourism continued at a higher price. In this scenario, eco tourism is a luxury experience only accessible to those that can afford it.

This scenario implies that international tourism would disappear as a consequence of the decline and lack of accessibility to aviation. It would be expected that tourism in Africa and other developing countries would be deprived of access to developed markets such as the United Kingdom, Germany and the United States, suggesting that tourism can no longer be regarded as an economic engine of growth as their economies would not be able to trade, climate change would be disruptive and populations would starve. Scarcity of international aviation and dependence of land-based transport systems would characterise international tourism by regional travel rather than intercontinental travel.

One of the storylines in the scenario is a realisation that change is necessary: governments change the supply side structures of the tourism industry through legislation and conservation measures and consumers change their behaviours and attitudes towards the environment. As a consequence, tourism is no longer a right or privilege.

A reversal of fortunes occurs based upon the restrictions placed on tourist access. As a consequence we see the return of mass tourism and centralised control; a Marxist approach to society rather than individualism. In the scenario, tourism becomes a manufactured experience rather than an authentic one. The cultural experience of food and wine tourism changes considerably as the rural backdrop changes to be a Star Trek *Replicator* that generates food from a history bank of molecular structures. Food as culture moves from an authentic experience to a manufactured one. Tourism for the masses through Walt Disney in Los Angeles is a theme park of fun, dreams and fantasy; something that is not about 'time on your own', 'enrichment', 'reflection' and 'self actualisation'. It could be reasoned, that Los Angeles will just be another Las Vegas with lap dancers, retail therapy and gaming; a monoculture found in any city. In 2050, luxury tourism will be an ecotourism experience, maybe the only way the masses will access such an experience will be through the Star Trek *holodeck*.[1] Who knows!

The convention and meetings industries will evolve and adapt using technologies and video conferencing techniques such as telepresencing with a high value virtual reality dimension, supersede face-to-face meetings for ordinary transactions. However, it is noted that face-to-face meetings are still very important. But as seen in the scenario, Los Angeles is a super state with a high-density population, so business tourism would be about serving this community.

The role of Los Angeles as an urban tourism destination in 2050 would not be an urban gateway for international and domestic tourists anymore; rather it would be a contained city, focusing on the day tripper which will have negative implications for hotel accommodation and other related services. With local residents and commuters becoming main users of attractions and infrastructure, does this mean tourism is more defined as a leisure user as the blur between tourism and residents diminishes? Crime and safety becomes an issue with a large population concentration and scarce resources. How would residents (tourists) feel about their city and night-time activity? In the worse-case scenario, would Los Angeles become the new Johannesburg with a series of suburban fenced and gated ghettos (Sandton) and shanty towns (Soweto). Such a dark proposition is not favourable for a creative tourist destination.

In 2050, space is a premium; city planners will be under extreme pressures to protect green open spaces for urban development. Test cases and encroachment will become the norm. Urban zoos and performing circuses will probably have a reversal of fortune as tourists visit attractions they could not normally go to on holidays. Rising temperatures suggest that Los Angeles will construct a series of mega indoor attractions for tourists to reminisce on past experiences such as skiing and golf and an indoor water world similar to Seagaia Ocean Dome in Japan. It is envisioned (or hoped) that green technologies will mitigate the environmental cost of such constructions. However, tourism in 2050 is a manufactured experience.

This discussion does not mean that Los Angeles is a bad experience but one which faces many challenges. The role of planning must ensure that Los Angeles population density and economies of scale bring a major opportunity to reduce energy demand and minimise pressures on land and natural resources. Los Angeles is a creative city, with fantastic museums, and nightlife which are the envy of the world, a history associated with Hollywood and a celebrity destination. Therefore, a well-planned and well-regulated Los Angeles in this scenario could mitigate the consequences of climate change through technological innovation, the harmonisation of green spaces and the co-ordination of leisure activity. Combined with the use of green technologies, transport systems, icon cultures and urban parks, a sense of belonging and comfort needs to be created within a future Los Angeles.

Concluding Remarks

Urban cities are an integral component in many tourists' holiday plans today. The development of an urban area to increase economic value is at the heart of many political leaders vision; as a consequence tourism as an economic driver is focused on urban development. This scenario raises two key themes for the future for policy makers and political leaders to consider, first, *sustainability as the key concept for the future* and second, *price inflation*.

Sustainability as the key concept for the future

The impact of climate change on the development of urban cities is likely to take a turn towards sustainability. The expansion and development of urban areas resulting in negative outcomes such as the loss of rural areas, poor water quality, loss of snowcapped mountains and increased urban migration will ultimately affect tourism. As such, a sustainable urban design will eventually reduce the impact on the natural environment. The growing introduction of green designs and green technologies will allow urban destinations such as Los Angeles to undertake sustainable design initiatives. However, this may not come at a low price. Implementing sustainable design features may come with a cost much higher than that required to build normal urban facilities. This in turn suggests the possibility that the extra costs will be transferred on to the tourist, who will need to pay premium prices for tourism products like accommodation. With increased environmental consciousness among modern-day consumers, the likelihood of the tourist's willingness to pay a premium price for a more sustainable product is high. But, even if tourists are willing to pay premium prices, do they have the ability to do so?

Price inflation: The affordability of tourism

Increasing fuel prices and limited agricultural lands leading to food price inflation are some of the drivers indicating price inflation for the future of the tourism and travel industry. As climate change becomes a more pressing issue globally and urban populations start to suffer from climate change's effects such as hotter summers, shorter winter periods, floods or droughts, governments anxiously implement environmental taxations which ultimately increase the price of travelling.

Actions such as sustainable urban development and environmental taxations are likely to result in an exponential increase of travel costs. These increased costs might eventually decrease the demand for travel as people are unable to afford to go on holidays. The future scenario might revert back to the early centuries, where only the elite and rich have the ability to travel; similarly, future tourists may only encompass those who have the financial ability to engage in tourism and pay for sustainable products at premium prices.

And finally ...

Climate change is a strategic conversation taking place globally. The purpose of this chapter is to contribute towards the debate through 'shocking' the reader about the implications of change. Would you want to holiday in this world? Maybe *Metropolis Los Angeles* will be just like *Logan's Run:* a dystopian future society in which population and the consumption of resources is managed and maintained in equilibrium by the simple expedient of demanding the death of everyone upon reaching a particular age, thus avoiding the issue of overpopulation. This would be a world that does not have a rural experience (except for the exclusive few), no stories to tell about good food and wine, breathtaking views, iconic landscapes, special moments and mountains to ski down. Instead it would be a world of manufactured experiences rather than a natural wonderland.

This is a story about the future, not a forecast but is construction based upon likely trends, critical uncertainties and a creative imagination. A number of stresses or triggers named in the chapter, namely peak oil, urbanisation, immigration, climate change and food supply, if combined and taken to the extreme, lead to urban Metropolis Los Angeles in 2050 resulting in the death of tourism in California as it is known today.

The Future of Attractions

If the world in 2050 is too hot to go outside or travel is difficult and restricted, does this mean the construction of the kinds of mass manufactured indoor experiences we associate with destinations such as Dubai? Golf is one of the world's most popular games and associated with affluence and tourism development. However, the development of golf courses has a detrimental effect on the environment (Dodds, 2009). If this is the case, how about the world's largest indoor golf complex in the Netherlands (http://www.indoorgolfarena.eu/) with over a total of 34 bays and offer 14,000 square feet of synthetic grass practice facilities? It boasts a fantastic architectural design, shaped like a futuristic cocoon and features pure white frames and generous glass openings. Amenities include 20 state-of-the-art ProTee Golf Simulators, kids' training course, wellness and fitness facilities, comprehensive golf equipment shop, fine dining, bar and lounge areas, broad business services and, of course, a four-star hotel.

Owing to unbearable temperatures, will the great Californian surf move indoors? The Seagaia Ocean Dome was the world's largest indoor waterpark, located in Miyazaki, Japan. The Ocean Dome, which is a part of the Sheraton Seagaia Resort, measures 300 m in length and 100 m in width, and is listed on the *Guinness Book of World Records*. It opened in 1993, and visitor numbers peaked in 1995 at 1.25 million a year. The Ocean Dome was officially closed on 1st October 2007 as part of a renovation and partial re-branding of the resort. The Ocean Dome sported a fake flame-spitting volcano, artificial sand and the world's largest retractable roof, which provided a permanently blue sky even on a rainy day. The air temperature was always held at around 30 °C and the water at around 28 °C. Entrance cost was ¥2600 per adult and ¥1600 for children, depending on the season.

Will Dubai host the winter Olympic Games in 2050 due to climate change? Such is the pace of development in Dubai that Ski Dubai is to be one of the largest indoor ski resorts in the world, with 22,500 m² of indoor ski area. It is a part of the Mall of the Emirates, which is one of the largest shopping malls in the world. Will the world in 2050 have no natural snow?

Note

(1) The holodeck is a simulated reality facility located on starships and starbases in the fiction *Star Trek Universe*. An episode of *Star Trek: The Animated Series*, 'The Practical Joker', formed the groundwork for the idea in the 1970s by portraying a recreation room capable of holographic simulations. The holodeck was first seen in the pilot episode of *Star Trek: The Next Generation*, 'Encounter at Farpoint'.

10 Seoul 2050: The Future of Food Tourism

Learning points

- Food tourism today is a representation of cultural capital, differentiation and the experience economy.
- The societal significance of food, its consumption, advancement in science, food inflation and urbanisation are some of the drivers that will shape future of food tourism. This chapter demonstrates the significance of these drivers and their implications for the future of food tourism.
- In this chapter, a *Soylent Green* science fiction future is portrayed, where food is only for the elite in society as they are the only ones who can afford real food.

Introduction

Soylent Green is a dystopian story of the future:

Where demand for food outstrips supply and food riots occur. The film is set in New York City of 2022, a crowded urban nightmare in which creature comforts, employment and anything beyond basic necessities are virtually nonexistent. The basic foodstuffs – crackers called Soylents Red, Yellow and Green – are produced and distributed by the Soylent Corporation, a monopoly that controls all agricultural lands. Soylent Green, a high-protein item is in great demand. Sold only on special days, it often runs out rather quickly, leading to riots by the unemployed and hungry masses. Amongst them, Detective Robert Thorn (Charleton Heston) shares a small apartment with his 'police book', Sol Roth (Edward G. Robinson). Roth seeks out the intelligence Thorn needs to pursue his cases. Occasionally, Thorn manages to buy or pilfer things and foods that are no longer available on the street, making life a little less unpleasant. For the most part, life in 2022 is pretty miserable. A very small group of wealthy men who control the Soylent Corporation live in large, comfortable apartments with ample supplies of water, soft beds, air conditioning and beautiful women (called 'furniture', providing sexual services). They have all the food, liquor and other luxuries they desire and also privy to the knowledge that the oceans are dying, which means no more plankton and greater food shortages. Soylent Green is the solution to this crisis and it is a threat to reveal the secret of Soylent Green leading the men to order the murder of one of their number, William Simonson. Fundamentally Simonson holds a secret that the Soylent Corporation has over harvested the world's oceans and as a consequence, created an euthanasia food chain for human remains. Robert Tom is the detective assigned to the case and pursuit of the murdered, against a background plot of how he and Roth deal with the discovery of the euthanasia food chain, Soylent Green. (Lipschutz, 2006: 573)

So, imagine a world in 2050, the world is overcrowded and poor production systems have failed. In order to feed this world, mass-produced synthetic food is the norm everywhere except Seoul.
Picture this ...

In 2050, 100 million people live in Seoul mostly in housing that is dilapidated and overcrowded, and the homeless fill the street and line the fire escapes and stairways of the buildings. This is a dystopian city suffering the effects of climate change pollution, overpopulation, depleted resources, poverty, dying oceans and a hot climate. Food is a rare and expensive commodity. Most of the city survives on the rations produced by the Korean Soylent Corporation, including Soylent Red and Soylent Green which are advertised as 'high-energy concentrate which as produced from a combination of high-energy plankton and the euthanasia food chain'. Soylent Green is much more nutritious and palatable than the red and yellow varieties, but it is, like most other food, in short supply, which often leads to food riots. Seoul is a city of inequalities; the masses survive on Soylent Green whereas the elite have access to real food.

This is the story of Kenny Jeong-Keun Oh and 'Liu', who live in a gated community apartment complex in the suburb of Apgujeong. The community is self-sufficient in some foodstuffs due to a vertical farming system. For those that have money, real food and the cultural history of ancestors are luxury experiences. Kenny has booked an overnight stay in a traditional Korean guesthouse owned by the Yoo family in the city. This is a place where the elite of society can escape, live like their ancestors did and learn how to make kimchi, a salted napa cabbage dish stuffed with radishes, green onions and cucumbers and bound with a chilli paste.

Upon arrival at the guesthouse, Kenny and Lui are shown to simple accommodation, a room constructed from rare Korean hanji paper water-proofed by special nanotechnology oils, which act like a natural air-conditioning system. Having settled into the guesthouse, they spend the afternoon dressing up in a Hanbook, a traditional Korean costume followed by instruction from Park Yoo, the 135 year old grandmother chef in ancient gastronomy of kimchi making and royal court cuisine. Kenny and Liu were so pleased to be able to learn ancient crafts and consume such luxury.

Food Tourism

Food at a philosophical level is 'the thesaurus of all moods and all the sensations' (Ellmann, 1993: 112). It is not only an important signifier of culture and symbolic order, but also plays a vital role in our sense of self (Mulcahy, 2009). Eagleton (1997) observes that genuine eating combines pleasure, utility and sociality. These perspectives show that food is not only fuel, but also a foil for philosophy, socialising and a means for simultaneously enriching experiences, expressing personal identities and adding to a quality of life. As a tourist, all these characteristics come into play when seeking new experiences through new cultures and new tastes (Yeoman, 2008). Food is unique and personal as it is the only cultural activity that is ingested. Regardless of its variety, tourists consistently make food choices aligned with their class identity, which reflects socio-economic hierarchies of power and control. This relationship between tourists and food is quite distinctive as their selection and consumption of food becomes a marker of identity and difference. Food is also integral to a destination's cultural heritage through providing its own unique character and authenticity.

Gastronomy can be traced back to Archestratus who perceived it as 'the pleasure of taste according code or set of rules' and wrote what might be considered the world's first eating guide called *Gastronomia – Literally, Rules for the Stomach* (Santich, 1996). The modern champion of gastronomy, Jean-Anthelme Brillat-Savarin, defined gastronomy in 1825 as the 'reasoned knowledge of everything pertaining to man, insofar as he nourishes himself'. Fundamentally, gastronomy is the heart of human life by satisfying primal needs and facilitating cultural adaptation and reflection; it acts as a highly sensitive marker for much more broader social, political and economic changes in society. Peoples' food preferences and ability to discriminate aesthetically is deeply ingrained and socially embedded so that it seems natural, although it has been learned rather than being innate. As gastronomy is an ingested experience, it has become a representation of identity and culture used in many tourism policies and marketing campaigns (Yeoman, 2008).

In the 6th and 7th centuries, the Silk Road connected Korea and Arabia. Arabic travellers influenced Koreans' socially and in culinary terms by placing food at the centre of conservation and social life. The most famous side dish is kimchi also spelled gimchi, kimchee or kim chee, is a traditional fermented dish made of vegetables with varied seasoning.

Korean cuisine has regional distinctions and has undergone historical transformation – including the effects of wartime food shortages and preparation techniques. Today, food is extremely important in the Korean society and is the centre of a national and cultural identity played out by tourism. According to the Korean Tourism Organisation, the Yoo family is one of the most famous and popular food tourism experiences in Korea;

> Boasting over 600 years of history, Yoo's Family is situated inside Bukchon Hanok Village, between the Gyeongbokgung Palace, Changdeokgung Palace, and Jongmyo. The region resonates with a traditional atmosphere as the cosy venue sits nestled amongst traditional Korean hanok houses flush in the middle of Seoul's two main palaces.
>
> Yoo's Family is a Hanok family managed by Yoos, offering traditional culture experiences for foreigners interested in Korean living cultures and traditions. Most classes are short-term courses and reservations can be made up to one day in advance. Reservations are only available for groups of 2 or more and groups of 10 or more may even choose their own times to hold classes. Translation in English and Japanese are available for all courses as well. (Korea Tourism Organisation, 2010)

But ...

The absence of wealth puts food as a necessity, rather than a form of luxury in life. Food pervades our lives from almost any perspective we care to consider; it is a primary feature of everyday life – we must find, purchase or prepare food and eat every day to stay healthy and alive; food permeates our relationships – we eat with others, and in particular and symbolic ways; food infiltrates our language – the images and metaphors of food surround us (I'm fed up with you, you make me sick, etc.); food reflects our position and status – whether we eat minced mutton, rabbit ragout or pasta primavera; food pervades popular culture – evidenced by the large number of cooking programmes on television and the ubiquitous cooking recipes and restaurant reviews. Food is a critical contributor to a human's physical well-being, a major source of pleasure, worry and stress and the 'single greatest category of expenditure'.

So, what is the future? The scenario in the chapter represents a bipolar society of economic divide in which a reversal of fortunes has occurred. Food is the most important component in people's daily lives, to many it is a fight for survival and necessity whereas to the few, real food is the ultimate luxury experience.

Key Drivers

Imagine a future of tourism in Korea akin to something more like North Korea rather than South Korea, where the common man is dying from starvation and only the rich have access to food. What if? This was the future. The drivers that would shape this scenario are:

Driver 1: The corporation controlling the food supply chain
Driver 2: The role of food in society
Driver 3: Climate change in Korea
Driver 4: The South Korean diet
Driver 5: Food inflation: A world problem
Driver 6: Wealth distribution: Haves and have nots
Driver 7: Urbanisation
Driver 8: The scramble for food
Driver 9: The role of food supplements and a healthy lifestyle
Driver 10: The advancement of science

Driver 1: The corporation controlling the food supply chain

This is a growing trend in Korea's retail food industry which for a long time has being dominated by a large number of small-scale food retailers as major sales outlets such as small-scale grocery stores and 'mom and pop' (Steigert & Kim, 2009). However, in recent years, modernised supermarkets and discount stores have developed as major retail groups, such as Shinsegae and Lotte participating in the discount store business, and major global retailers, such as Carrefour, Tesco and WalMart entering the Korean market. This entrance of foreign distributors with discount store formats has contributed to the rapid development of discount stores and large-scale retailers significantly affecting consumers, producers and the overall food marketing system. As the market shares of major supermarkets and discount store chains increased sharply in recent years, food handlers and farmers have been concerned about market power exercised by dominant food retailers. Although market power exercised by large-scale food retailers is not significant in fresh fruits and vegetables where distribution channels are diverse, it may have a greater influence on rice prices between large retailers and local rice millers where direct marketing is a major distribution channel, resulting in a price squeeze (Steigert & Kim, 2009).

In 1973, Soylent Green portrayed control of the food supply as a conspiracy between government and food producers. Taking globalisation into account, will governments still be part of the equation in 2050? If not, who will be regulating the food supply? Currently, there exist huge disparities between the economies of the producers and consumers of food. Coffee farmers are paid a few cents per kilo while we buy a single cup with dollars. Patel (2007) depicts this disparity in the shape of an hourglass showing the concentration of power in the hands of the corporations who bring the products to market. Figure 10.1 shows the aggregated data from Netherlands, Germany, France, the United Kingdom, Austria and Belgium.

The second hourglass in Figure 10.1 shows similar but not entirely comparable data from the United States. Patel argues that the world has ended up with few corporate buyers and sellers as the process of shipping, processing and trucking food across distances demands a great deal of capital. As Patel says:

> This means that the bigger a company is, the more transport and logistics it does, the cheaper it is for that company to be in the business. .....
> The small fish have being devoured by the Leviathans of distribution and supply. And when the number of companies controlling the gateways from farmers to consumers is small, this gives them market power both over the people and who grow the food and the people who eat it. (Patel, 2007: 12)

To summarise, with farmers at the top, consumers at the bottom and the five or six corporations that control 50% of the market in the middle.

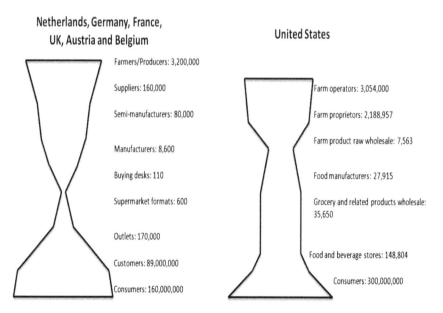

Netherlands, Germany, France, UK, Austria and Belgium

Farmers/Producers: 3,200,000
Suppliers: 160,000
Semi-manufacturers: 80,000
Manufacturers: 8,600
Buying desks: 110
Supermarket formats: 600
Outlets: 170,000
Customers: 89,000,000
Consumers: 160,000,000

United States

Farm operators: 3,054,000
Farm proprietors: 2,188,957
Farm product raw wholesale: 7,563
Food manufacturers: 27,915
Grocery and related products wholesale: 35,650
Food and beverage stores: 148,804
Consumers: 300,000,000

Figure 10.1 Food channel
(*Source:* Patel, 2007)

Driver 2: The role of food in society

In 1977, Dr William David Hopper, founding president of the International Development Research Centre and former vice president of the World Bank, suggested that the politics of food involves more than economic development, economic growth and the interaction between rich and poor nations. Food is a commodity charged with emotional symbolism as well as material substance (Patel, 2007). It is not surprising then that sociologists have plenty to say on the subject. However, when it comes to food tourism, social science is strangely silent. The sociology of food literature intersects with this chapter in a number of different ways. On the one hand, there are ethical and social justice issues to do with production and distribution; and on the other hand, there are the social and psychological aspects of food consumption. Ethical issues related to this chapter include biotechnology, agribusiness, economic change and the social construction of eating, obesity and starvation. According to Patel, there is no lack of food in the world today. Obesity and starvation are part of the same problem, linked through chains of production that bring the food to our plate (Patel, 2007).

Overeating is a prominent social problem as governments worldwide look for ways to curb obesity. Campaigns and interventions often target children, the next generation of overeaters, yet;

> Governments appear yet to find a way to effectively intervene to reduce obesity prevalence among children. (Crowle & Turner, 2010: 89)

Bourdieu (Swartz, 1998), famous for his work on economic, symbolic and cultural capital to reveal the dynamics of power relations in social life, argues for the structuring nature of life experiences specifically using food tastes as a metaphor for social class divisions. Cultural capital is also often associated to socially valued forms of art, music, literature, fashion and cuisine, in other words 'class' or 'good taste' (Swartz, 1998). Food plays a central role in the display and sharing of cultural capital (Counihan & Van Esterik, 2007). It is here, in the midst of display and sharing knowledge, experience and good taste in food that the cultural capital gained by the food tourist in eating out comes into play.

Although often taken for granted,

> the public dining room, where anyone with sufficient funds could go to eat, in the presence of others is a creation of the late nineteenth century ... and it is the gradual evolution of eating out into a leisure activity that characterises the last 100 years. (Warde & Martens, 2000: 23)

As Bourdieu distinguishes, food has cultural capital in society and real food is portrayed as the ultimate luxury experience. Particularly with increased pressure on the Earth as a finite resource, demand is created for the food tourism experience as a cultural identification, reflected through by Kenny Jeong-Keun's search for cultural identity in a post-modernist world. This experience is a social process undertaken in the context of changing historical conditions reflecting culture as a social practice, and not something that individuals possess.

Berry (1994) premises that luxuries are remnents of basic human needs such as food, shelter and health care. Maslow's (1970) hierarchy of needs shows how basic physiological needs such as hunger lead up to needs of self-actualisation through satisfying lower-level needs, suggesting a possible way in which different activities, or different goods that are used in different activities, could be ordered on a necessity–luxury continuum.

Jelliffe gives the following definition of luxury or prestige foods:

> All cultures have prestige foods, which are mainly reserved for important occasions or, even more, for the illustrious of the community ... even in vegetarian societies, these are usually protein, frequently of animal origin. They are usually difficult to obtain, so that they are expensive and relatively rare. In the western world they may have been hunted wild, as opposed to distant regions. (Jelliffe, 1967: 279–281)

Food is a form of differentiation, where the powerful distinguished themselves from their inferiors by the sheer quantity they ate: 'those who could, gorged themselves; those who couldn't, aimed to' (Mennell, 1997: 324). Similarly, Veen (2003) argues that in the 18th and 19th centuries, East Polynesia staple foods were elevated in status, the diversity of forms in which they were served or the sheer abundance of display. This includes the quantity of food, preparation effort and importance of formal communal dining and feasting in Goa, West Africa and in Bahrain.

As Veen says:

> in highly complex societies, the emphasis is on quality and style: the focus is on expensive, rare and exotic foods, on the complexity of the meal and its ingredients, table manners and expensive porcelain, with knowledge of correct cuisines and etiquette written down in cookbooks and manuals. Here the emphasis is on exclusivity: the wealthy convert their economic capital into cultural capital with the purpose of creating distance. This distinction between the emphasis on quantity and cohesion or quality and exclusivity is significant as it reveals the hidden meaning behind consumption events and a society's structure. This distinction lives on in many modern societies today, with the former characterizing the feasting among the lower classes, and the latter the dining of the higher classes. (Veen, 2003: 420)

Driver 3: Climate change in Korea

The impact of climate change in South Korea will be profound, with recent research (Parry *et al.*, 2007) suggesting greater warming and damage than other regions. Korean Peninsula temperatures have over the past hundred years, increased 1.7 °C, more than double the increase in the Earth's temperature. This is causing a sub-tropical climate to appear on Jeju Island and some southern regions of the peninsula. In addition, South Korea is increasingly assailed by unusually harsh storms with recurrence increasing from about 24 days in the 1950s up to 40 days per year by 2010. The winter season has also been shortened by one month.

Driver 4: The South Korean diet

South Koreans are one of the healthiest nationals in world, with the lowest obesity ranking in the OECD. According to Lee *et al.* (2002), the traditional Korean diet is a low-fat and high-vegetable diet. Therefore, nutrition specialists are initiating numerous efforts to advertise and educate the public on the advantages of a traditional diet versus that of a Western one, and reviving the traditional diet to Koreans using a contemporary approach. Reasons for the low-fat intake in South Korea include a relatively high level of carbohydrate intake, the style of cooking and, most importantly, the various movements to retain the traditional diet. Contrasting to the low level of fat intake, vegetable consumption in South Korea is among the highest in Asia; kimchi is the main subsidiary food in the Korean diet and is the most typical processed vegetable food.

According to Lee *et al.* (2002), the low-fat intake and high vegetable consumption level is the result of South Korea's vegetable-centred traditional dietary culture. Despite having gone through vast changes in the consumption of clothing, food and housing due to industrialisation, the Korean's conservative attitude towards food has prompted their dietary habits to remain relatively intact. There has also been a recent boom in the demand for traditional restaurants in South Korea. Restaurants called 'Country dining table' that serve mostly vegetable side dishes, 'Raw vegetable house' where people use assorted vegetables to wrap their own food, and 'Native local food restaurants' and 'Buddhist temple restaurants' where meats are excluded, are gaining popularity, even among modernised people. The trend of pursuing healthy foods had already begun in the mid-1980s when chronic illnesses became a major health concern in South Korea, which reflects efforts to solve health problems by improving the diet.

Driver 5: Food inflation: A world problem

According to Evans (2008), the main drivers for food inflation are: the rising costs of agricultural inputs and energy, water scarcity, decreased land availability and climate change.

Today's global agricultural system is predicated on the availability of cheap, readily available energy, for use in every part of the value chain: both directly (e.g. cultivation, processing, refrigeration, shipping, distribution) and indirectly (e.g. manufacture of fertilisers, pesticides). World oil prices peaked in 2008 and will remain relatively high in the long term as the world has passed the point of peak oil. In addition, since food can now be converted into fuel, there is effectively an arbitrage relationship between the two, implying an ongoing linkage between food and fuel prices. Water scarcity is also likely to become a more pressing issue. Global demand for water has tripled in the past 50 years; 500 million people live in countries chronically short of water, a number likely to rise to 4 billion by 2050.

There is also the issue of land availability. Some commodity analysts argue that although historical increases in demand have been met through increasing yields, the future would require an expansion of acreage. However, this will be expensive, given the infrastructure investment involved; there may also be diminishing returns, since much of the best land is already cultivated. Above all, there is simply increasing competition for available land, including food, feed, fibre (e.g. timber, paper), fuel, forest conservation, carbon sequestration and urbanisation, on top of high rates of soil loss to erosion and desertification. The Food and Agricultural Organisation (FAO) of the United Nations estimates that there is at most 12% more land available that is not already forested or subject to erosion or desertification, and that 16% of arable land is already degraded.

The final and perhaps most fundamental factor is climate change. The International Panel on Climate Change (Parry et al., 2007) projects that global food production could rise if local average temperatures increase between 1 °C and 3 °C, but could decrease above this range. This projection is before extreme weather events are taken into account; and the IPCC judges state that extreme weather, rather than temperature, is likely to make the biggest difference to food security. It estimates that glacial melting will affect agriculture and many Himalayan glaciers could disappear by 2035, bringing catastrophic outcomes for Chinese and Indian agriculture industries. It assesses that 'climate change increases the number of people at risk of hunger', and will lead to an increase of the number of undernourished people to between 40 million and 170 million.

Driver 6: Wealth distribution: Haves and have nots

A noticeable factor in the Soylent Green scenario is the divide between the wealthy and poor. Maybe in 2050, Seoul will be more akin to present day North Korea rather than the advanced economy of South Korea. North Korea has a GDP per capita of US$1900 compared to South Korea's US$28,100 and a life expectancy of 64 years of age compared to South Korea's 79 years of age (CIA, 2010). North Korea's society is divided disproportionately between the political elite and the mass classes. This is represented by Christian Caryl's (2007) story in *Newsweek* titled *Even Hermits Can Get Rich*:

> Even amid the grandeur of North Korea's Myohyang Mountain tourist area, where few Westerners have ever been allowed to visit, it's impossible not to gawk at him: a middle-aged North Korean sightseer decked out in a crisp Kim Jong Il-style suit, sunglasses and implausible upswept hairdo. But the most striking thing isn't his Dear Leader-wannabe getup; it's the device he's holding. In one of the most desperately poor countries on earth, it's worth half a year's pay for most of his fellow inhabitants: a sleek little Japanese digital video Handycam. Everyone has heard that North Korea is a country that can't feed itself – as underlined earlier this year by the United Nations World Food Program, which warned once again of the danger of impending famine in the Hermit Kingdom. Less well known, though, is that some people in North Korea are actually getting rich. Reliable statistics are hard to come by, of course, given the obsessive secrecy of the North Korean state. Still, when a South Korean university polled 500 defectors from the North in 2005, 58 percent of them said that the biggest change in their home country over the previous three years was the widening gap between rich and poor; another 28 percent cited the increase in personal wealth. Last year the South Korean aid organization Good Friends, which boasts a broad range of sources in the North, published a revealing study of its own. It concluded that North Korea's wealthy now spend 10 times as much on food as those less privileged, live in homes equipped with modern conveniences like refrigerators and washing machines (largely unknown to their countrymen), and can even afford maids and private tutors for their children. (Caryl, 2007)

Driver 7: Urbanisation

The world's population reached 6 billion people just before 2000 and will increase by another 4.8 billion by 2050. Most of this increase will be in less/least-developed regions of the world, where populations are projected to rise from 6.5 billion now to 9.5 billion by 2050 (Yeoman *et al.*, 2010). South Korea experienced rapid growth of urban areas due to rural migration. Today, Seoul's population stands at 9.7 million, which will fall to 9.3 million by 2025. However, Greater Seoul has a population of over 25 million people and will continue to grow. South Korea is one of the world's most densely populated countries, with an estimated 489 people per square kilometre in 2010. Its population density is almost twice as concentrated as New York and eight times greater than Rome according to the United Nations State of Worlds Cities Report (2010).

Driver 8: The scramble for food

Food security is a complex topic, standing at the intersection of many disciplines. Food security refers to the availability of food and one's access to it. It exists when all people, at all times, have physical, social and economic access to sufficient, safe and nutritious food to meet their dietary needs and food preferences for an active and healthy life. According to Evans (2009), global per capita food production has been increasing substantially for the past several decades.

It is becoming increasingly difficult to maintain food security in a world beset by a confluence of 'peak' phenomena, namely peak oil, peak water, peak phosphorus, peak grain and peak fish. More than half of the planet's population of 3.3 billion people lives in urban areas as of November 2007. Any disruption to farm supplies may precipitate a uniquely urban food crisis in a relatively short time. Therefore, as seen in Soylent Green, the future is a world of food insecurity.

Food insecurity will mean a period of pronounced turbulence. Evans (2009) predicts an increased prevalence of *shocks*: sudden onset crises, such as extreme weather events driven by climate change, or sharp spikes in the price of energy. There will be *stresses*: slower onset impacts such as land degradation or gradual price inflation that risk being overlooked by short-term policy or investment planning. Then there is the risk caused by human action through *ignorance or accident*: think of the positive feedback loop caused by one set of countries suspending exports while another attempts to build up imports. Finally, the food system could be disrupted by *malicious action*, for example during conflicts or through intentional systems disruption by terrorists or insurgent groups. As such the food supply chain is threatened.

Driver 9: The role of food supplements and a healthy lifestyle

The consequence of consumers' awareness of ageing has brought about a trend called the 'smart food revolution'; a new science-based trend towards using what we eat to fight disease, slow ageing and improve our minds. To many, this is about taking food substitutes, vitamins or dietary supplements to keep old age at bay or the promise of improved memory. The trend probably started when technology interceded in food production and advances in science and technology has since changed consumers understanding towards the dimensions of food. Eating practices have changed around the world; Warde and Hetherington (1994) report that 34% of households in the United Kingdom buy takeaway meals at least once a week, and 12% dine out at restaurants once a week. Guthrie *et al.* (2002) report that in the United States between 1977–1978 and 1994–1996 the proportion of calories obtained from outside food increased from 18% to 32% as it simply contains higher total and saturated fat with less dietary fibre. Widespread availability of ready-made meals is changing household food production and eating practices. A large survey in Britain in 1995 (cited in Bell & Valentine, 1997) found that one-quarter of respondents almost always ate their evening meal in front of television, or mealtimes were constructed around the timing of television programmes. Surrounding all this is the salience of health. Crawford (1980) identified 'healthism' as a feature of modern society in the 1980s which has since continued to be a major preoccupation to many. Since food is salient for health, and vice versa, it is not surprising that food and health have become elided to a considerable degree in contemporary society.

An increasing number of people have begun to engage in dietary supplementation, most commonly with vitamins and minerals, and frequently for health reasons. Rates of dietary supplementation are surprisingly high, with findings showing that 35–55% of US adults aged 30 years or older report supplement use within the last month (Ervin *et al.*, 1999). The linkage of food and medicine is obvious as these products are commonly presented in drug-like form, for example, pills and tablets, complete with dosage instructions and notes on contraindications. Vitamin and mineral combinations are readily available in this form, alongside a huge range of special 'treatments' for various 'conditions', such as specific formulations for strengthening the immune system, for the prevention of prostrate conditions in men or for the alleviation of menopausal symptoms for women. Other dietary-related products offer supplements for lifestyle reasons, such as the various electrolytic replacement drinks for the exercising middle classes (the marketing of 'Sweat' in Japan, using the English word as the product name, provides one interesting example), or supplements marketed specifically to bodybuilders and body-sculptors, many of whom have diets considerably removed from the ordinary. Most of these products are becoming more easily available through supermarkets and are no longer limited to pharmacies and specialist health food shops.

Driver 10: The advancement of science

The original idea of Soylent Green is based upon Chlorella, a very popular nutritional supplement in Japan with possible effects on metabolic rate. The name *Chlorella* is taken from the Greek word *chloros* meaning 'green' and the Latin diminutive suffix *ella* meaning 'small'. Although many people believed *Chlorella* could serve as a potential source of food and energy because of its high photosynthetic efficiency and high nutritional value, *Chlorella* was not as cheaply or easily harvested as technicians predicted it would be 40 years earlier because it is a single-celled alga and the fact that humans and animals cannot digest *Chlorella* due to the tough cell walls encapsulating the nutrients.

Rozema and Flowers (2008) suggest that the cultivation of salt-tolerant crops can help address the threats of irreversible global salinisation of fresh water and soils. Currently, humans use about half of the fresh water readily available to them to support a growing world population. Agriculture has to compete with domestic and industrial uses of fresh water which is rapidly becoming a limited and expensive resource. In addition, competition for fresh water and the irreversible spread of salinisation is increasingly affecting fresh water and soil, particularly in arid and semiarid climatic zones. Although only about 1% of the water on Earth is fresh, there is an equivalent supply of brackish water (1%) and a vast quantity of seawater (98%), calling for the need to explore the agronomic use of these resources.

GM foods are foods derived from genetically modified organisms where specific changes are introduced into their DNA by genetic engineering techniques, involving the insertion or deletion of genes. It provides a realistic alternative to feeding the world's population in 2050 (Chamberlain, 2004) as it is able to increase crop productivity and therefore the ability to feed more. Future envisaged applications of GM are diverse and include bananas that produce human vaccines against infectious diseases, metabolically engineered fish that mature more quickly, or fruit and nut trees that yield years earlier.

The concept of vertical farming involves large-scale agriculture in urban high-rises or 'farmscrapers'. According to Desponier (2010), using advanced greenhouse technology and methods such as hydroponics, these buildings would be able to produce year-round food and significantly alleviate climate change produced by excess atmospheric carbon through reduced energy needed to transport food to consumers. Unlike traditional farming, indoor farming multiplies the productivity of farmed surface by a factor of 4 to 6 depending on the crop. Furthermore, the sales of crops in the same infrastructures in which they are grown decreases the need for transportation, resulting in less spoilage, infestations and energy required. The protection of crops from weather is increasingly important with global climate change. Vertical farming provides a controlled environment which allows it to be independent of weather and extreme weather events, apart from earthquakes and tornadoes.

Alternatively, as seen in *Star Trek Replicator,* the replicator can create any inanimate matter repeatedly as long as the desired molecular structure is on file. This works by rearranging subatomic particles to form molecules and arrange those molecules to form the object (Drum & Gordon, 2003). For example, to create a steak and French fries dinner, the replicator would first form atoms of carbon, hydrogen, nitrogen and so on, then arrange them into amino acids, proteins and cells, and put it all together into the form of a steak and French fries meal.

A Reversal of Fortunes

Food as a luxury experience

What if, we had a reversal of fortunes, where food tourism is only available to the elite in society rather than mass middle classes? In *Tomorrow's*

Tourist (Yeoman, 2008), the key drivers of food tourism are described based upon growing affluence, which has had a profound impact on consumer spending. Food expenditure used to be staple. However, with increased discretionary income, changing demographics, falling food prices, individualism, time pressures and an experience economy that was diverted to durable consumer goods and services. But with the combination of decreased discretionary income with food inflation and scarcity, it could be a reversal of fortunes into the Soylent Green scenario.

Food tourism in this scenario becomes a luxury experience only available to the elite in society, akin to a masculine experience reversing the trend of feminisation of luxury found in much of the luxury literature (Berry, 1994). Soylent Green is a male preserve and for Kenny Jeong-Keun Oh, food is his new passion and cultural identification.

Masculinity

In Anthony Giddens (1991) works *Modernity and Self Identity*, men construct their identity for themselves using leisure and other signifiers in a post-traditional modernity without having to conform. They become passionate about food and cooking, not for the provision of sustenance, but rather for who they are and what they do. Food helps men to form part of their identity like work, politics and sport. Yeoman (2010a) observes (see website www.tomorrowstourist.com):

> Don't think for one moment that tomorrow's male will be metro sexual or someone that has found his feminine side. The new wave of celebrity chefs are visibly laddish, macho or just plain angry when cooking. They assert their aggression in the kitchen – just like footballers on their field. If you have watched 'Hell's Kitchen' you will know what I mean.

> Micro trends are based upon the idea that the most powerful forces in our society are the emerging, counterintuitive trends that are shaping tomorrow before us. Therefore moving into the future, tomorrow's food tourist will be the upwardly mobile male, aged 26–44 who will see cultural capital and social cachet in America's food experiences. In general, men are becoming more interested in food. This means more connectivity between food and wine, whether it is as an incentive product for those involved in business tourism or just more men taking food tours. Deluxe kitchen manufacturers will probably offer cookery lessons with the celebrity chefs in a wonderful location so you can learn how use all those gadgets. Cookery schools with probably offer 'Man Food' courses for those that want to know how to 'cook a decent curry' for those on urban weekends. Restaurants will be taken over by budding Gordon Ramsays, who will fight it out just like 'Hell's Kitchen'. Those budding celebrity chefs will

pay for the privilege for doing so and they will invite their friends and relatives to consume that food (which you will charge for) and you will then sell them a DVD of the experience. (Yeoman, 2010a)

Cultural identity or erosion

Globalisation has led to a higher percentage of people born and bred in a country different from their ethnicity or ancestral roots. Since food is an important component in the reflection of one's culture and identity, this trend may result in individuals travelling in search of their own identity and culture through food tourism.

However, with decreasing availability of food and agriculture activities and possible introduction of genetically modified foods, food in the display of one's culture may eventually be eroded. This may be due to the unavailability of ingredients needed to prepare an authentic cultural food item. Even in substitution, a genetically modified cabbage may not result in a taste similar to that of those used to make authentic kimchi. Diminishing food ingredients will hence lead to a possible erosion of culture in the context of food and even affecting the experience of food tourists in search of authentic cultural foods.

Back to basics

Recent consumer trends indicate the desire to return to 'basics', where consumers are demanding things more natural and green. The more conscious consumer is also more paranoid towards health scares. As such, although genetically modified foods may provide an alternative to food, consumers may not be willing – or in fact wary – to accept it. The perception that these foods are not grown 'naturally' may be a barrier to the acceptance of such 'new foods'.

Therefore the social implications are . . .

Increased urbanisation will see an influx of farmers into cities when agriculture and farming has become too expensive for them. This influx of farmers, particularly for developing countries such as China and India where rural literacy levels are low, will ultimately lead to a series of social problems, placing pressure on urban areas and possibly affecting the image of destination cities. Rural-to-urban migration will eventually increase the disparity between the rich and the poor as they are not able to find jobs that promise substantial pay. Even for educated farmers, moving into urban cities could result in overpopulation, increase depletion of resources and increase competition for jobs. Although advancement of science and technology presents more opportunities for high-tech farming, the cost of such agriculture will increase exponentially, ousting rural farmers and increasing the price of foods. Such a scenario will worsen the situation of unequal wealth distribution. By then, even if people were willing to try genetically modified foods, they will not have the ability to do so. The situation where the rich will live in luxury with ample food and the poor without food security will become more pronounced.

The trend towards a healthy lifestyle and a more environmentally conscious consumer may slow down the bleak outlook towards a dystopian food future. The choice of food by such consumers will decrease the demand for luxury, or rare foods as they increase their intake on more greens, thereby slowing the process of climate change and depletion of resources. Despite this, such a trend may not take place consistently worldwide. Countries such as China, whose definition of luxury, particularly in the context of food, often use rare and expensive ingredients such as sharks fin, crocodile meat and so forth. Many of this culture's authentic cultural dishes also require the use of such ingredients. Destinations who wish to incorporate the culture of food tourism into their destination product may be indirectly causing an increase in demand for these ingredients. Food tourists increase this demand due to their search for authentic experiences, bringing a conflict towards resource depletion and cultural erosion.

The experience of a food tourist at a destination is highly influenced by the quality, authenticity and the availability of cultural foods. Implications of a bleak future outlook of food have a direct impact on the ability of destinations to provide an authentic experience. In an extreme scenario, hostilities may arise from host communities who are unable to afford basic food necessities, towards food tourists being able to pay premium prices for cultural foods.

Concluding Remarks

Changing lifestyles

Hall *et al.* (2003) demonstrate how growing interest in food tourism is a reflection of changing lifestyles; food has become a status symbol and signifier of identity. As the world evolves into an experience economy, food tourism becomes a central part, with many destinations using food tourism as a driver of economic development. Food is unique and is a representation of regional identity; whether it is Scottish haggis or Korean kimchi, food has become an attraction in its own right. Food tourism, defined as visitation to primary and secondary food producers, food festivals, restaurants and specific locations for which food tasting and/or experiencing the attributes of specialist food production regions are the primary motivating factor for travel has become important feature of the tourism economy. Horng and Tsai (2009) examine food tourism in Asia and confirmed Hall's findings that food and cuisine played an

important role in the culture of Asian culture through differentiation and identification of places. Food is playing an important part in tourism experiences
and is being leveraged as marketing driver for destination.

Food as a point of differentiation

However, the role of food changes; no longer is it a mass tourism experience but one only available to the elite in society. The ingestion of food has
economic and social power with all the attributes of a class system. Showing
off your culinary prowess brings recognition and honour. The social elite are
consuming a product that is scarce and inaccessible to the masses. The food
of choice is associated with Korean royal court cuisine, a style of cookery
within Korean cuisine traditionally consumed at the court of the Joseon
Dynasty. The reference to royalty is about opulence and conspicuous
consumption.

Without doubt, food tourism will be an luxury experience based upon
scarcity, as food demand increases with the inability of supplies to feed the
global population (Yeoman *et al.*, 2010). The world's agricultural system will
go through a number of pressure points as food competes with oil for land
and water shortages shrink accessible farming land. All of this acts as a catalyst for wealth disparity, and a reversal of fortune akin to North Korea rather
than South Korea. In 2050, the world would become an urban jungle, while
demand for rural products is increasing. Tied to time and enrichment as
luxury, space and tranquillity will be at a premium. In the scenario, simplicity and authenticity are important connections to historical links and cultural identity. Food becomes a material luxury in highly complex societies;
with the focus on expensive, rare and exotic food. Kimchi is that exotic food,
surrounded by a cultural etiquette, passed down through an oral history,
exclusive and scarce.

The forthcoming scarcity of fresh authentic foods can be of benefit to
some destinations. Such experiences will be wrapped up in local identity
and culture. Here, food becomes an escape from the urban world. However,
the disappearing middle classes scenario will not benefit tourism as they
have been the driving force of economic growth in many destinations. From
a policy perspective, securing a sustainable food chain and tourism experience is extremely important for tourism and mankind in general. The only
thing I know, is that Soylent Green is not what I want to experience on
holiday in 2050.

11 Shanghai 2050: The Future of Hotels

Learning points

- This chapter highlights the key drivers of change that will shape hotels of the future in Shanghai including but not limited to the price of land, sustainable architecture and technologies of bedroom design.
- Hotels of the future will embrace customer-orientated innovations becoming living laboratories to constantly enhance service.
- Futuristic concepts such as claytronics and nanotech-fabrics have the potential to bring about a paradigm shift in bedroom design.

Introduction: Shanghai Today

Shanghai is the first place for everything that is modern about China, first motor car, first train tracks, first cinema and first modern sewers. It is the intellectual and cultural capital of Chinese writers, including the socialist writers of critical realism such as Lu Xun or Nien Cheng or the more bourgeois romantic and aesthetically inclined writers such as Shi Zhecum or Eileen Chang. Shanghai is the commercial and financial centre of mainland China. It was the largest and most prosperous city in the Far East during the 1930s, and rapid redevelopment began in the 1990s. This is exemplified by the Pudong District, which became a pilot area for integrated economic reforms. Today, Shanghai is again one of the most galvanic cities in the world. Its cosmopolitan character, sophisticated and affluent consumers, and highly educated skilled labour force make it highly attractive to overseas investors. Shanghai has recorded double-digit growth for 15 consecutive years since 1992 to become the centre of finance and trade in new China (Horwath, 2010b). The city is China's creative hub of hedonism and bohemian culture captured by the tone of postmodernism and a futuristic outlook. Basically, Shanghai is 'the' place to be in China. However, what is the future of the city? Given the exponential growth in tourism what will the hotel look like in the future considering the price of land, climate change and the drive towards sustainability? The purpose of this chapter is to picture what a futuristic hotel in Shanghai would look like in 2050, demonstrating the key drivers of change.

Over the last decade, China's tourism industry has gained much international recognition in terms of its huge source of outbound tourism potential and a unique inbound destination. With a history of more than 5000 years China's reemergence onto the global stage has been driven by a strong fundamental desire to be a world leader. The country has experienced dramatic economic and social transformation since 1978 when it embarked on a series of strategic economic reforms to modernise the economy. These initial reforms gained significant momentum in the 1990s envisioning a socialist market economy. With trade and investment opened to the global marketplace, China's economy has maintained breathtaking expansion over the last 20 years. Growing at an annual compound growth rate (CAGR) of approximately 17% between 1991 and 2009, China's economy stood as the second largest in the world after that of the United States when measured on purchasing power parity (HVS, 2011) with a GDP of US$8.8 trillion (2009).

In line with the country's economic success, both domestic and international tourist arrivals have grown at an impressive rate. Domestic tourist arrivals quadrupled between 1993 and 2009 from 0.4 billion to over 1.9 billion tourists. This represents a CAGR of 10.1%. The rising affluence of Chinese consumers as a result of sustained economic progress has been the main driving force for domestic tourism. With the increasing level of disposal incomes, travel and tourism is fast becoming a lifestyle requirement. Similarly, international tourist arrivals have grown fivefold from 27 million tourists in 1990 to 126 million visitors in 2009, reflecting a CAGR of 8.4%.

As one of the first places where international tourism was initiated, Shanghai plays a critical role to the development of China's tourism industry. In the early 1920s and 1930s, a world-famous travel company, Thomas Cook and Sons, opened offices in Shanghai and Beijing, and the first Chinese travel agency – China Travel Service – was established by the Shanghai Commercial Savings Bank in Shanghai (Zhang et al., 2005). Following the establishment of the People's Republic of China in 1949, trade reforms and economic liberalisation, the influx of Western culture greatly influenced Shanghai to become a melting pot for cultures from both East and West, significantly shaping its unique landscape. As a central hub for finance and trade, modern Shanghai is a significant destination for both leisure and business travellers. Unlike other destinations in China which are distinct in historical heritage or natural wonders, Shanghai is more renowned for its cosmopolitan reputation with business, nightlife and shopping central to its tourism product. In 2009, Shanghai recorded 6.3 million international arrivals and 124 million domestic visitors. In the same year, international tourism contributed approximately USD$4.8 billion in foreign exchange while domestic travel expenditure accumulated to RMB191.3 billion (Shanghai Municipal Statistics Bureau, 2010). Tourism has been put in the city's economic limelight, expecting to contribute 9% to the city's GDP in 2010 with the hosting of the World Expo (Qian, 2009).

Shanghai's long-term goal to develop into a global economic, finance, trade and transport hub will see the continual urban development of the city (Shanghai Municipal Statistics Bureau, 2006). According to the China National Tourism Administration classified hotel rooms grew from 46,256 in 2000 to 61,169 in 2009, translating to a CAGR of 3%. This modest increase in absolute numbers was accompanied by profound changes in the supply structure. In 2009, there were a total of 298 star-rated accommodations within Shanghai, of which 38 are five-star hotels, 58 are four-star, 122 are three-star, 76 are two-star and four are one-star accommodations with room supply of five- and four-star hotels significantly increasing at CAGR of 10% and 7%, respectively. On the other hand, the supply of one-star and two-star-graded hotel rooms declined by 8% annually.

The drive to become a global business hub will increase the demand for good quality, short-stay accommodations, as exemplified by the recent Shanghai World Expo 2010, which saw a surge in developments and renovations within the hospitality sector. For example, URBN Hotel (http://www.urbnhotels.com) which is the first carbon neutral hotel in Shanghai/China was architecturally designed to be sustainable and the newly refurbished Fairmont Peace Hotel Shanghai which incorporates both futuristic and modern amenities with the preservation of old styles, signifying a trend of retro-futurism. The increase in accommodation operators will mean increasing attempts to differentiate developments based on location, service packages or even architectural styles.

Shanghai's rapid urbanisation has resulted in negative environmental impacts such as pollution. Coupled with external factors such as climate change, competition for urban land space and decreasing availability of clean water, Shanghai's urban development plan requires a sustainable design for the future. The notion of future sustainable living has also been acknowledged and reflected in the 2010 Shanghai World Expo, as the city strives to develop an 'eco-friendly society and maintain the sustainable development of human beings' (Shanghai World Expo, 2010).

So, This is a Story about Sean ...

Zhong Nai (Sean) is flying into Shanghai from Kunming, staying at the Green Hotel, an ecofriendly boutique hotel in the city's suburbs for one night. The reasons for staying at the hotel include his company's sustainable only policy, colleagues' recommendations, contemporary feel, value for money and ubiquitous technology. Prior to arrival, the hotel sent him a text with a unique barcode which will act as his security key upon arrival. For extra security he has registered his retina eye scan with the hotel.

Each bedroom has an intelligent agent accessible with an interface in the bedroom's mirror which does everything from recommending a personal menu, ordering room service, planning journeys and setting the mood of the room including temperature, colour and ambience. The room's stunning outlook across the city can also change to modern paintings of landscapes or Art Nouveau. The room has all the latest innovations in technology including holographic TV and programmable bed which can change shape and offer different degrees of comfort. The hotel offers excellent value for money due to automated room attendants and self-cleaning glass. Sean spends a comfortable 12 hours in the hotel before heading into the city for business.

Futurism, Architecture and Design

The modernity of hotel design has a foundation in futurism, which is a reactionary movement which started during the 19th century, under the influence of Filippo Tommaso Marinetti (Berghaus, 2009) who began the futurist movement through the publication of his *Futurist Manifesto* in 1909. The concept of futurism stems from an opposing view of the past, characterised as a dynamic, energetic and radical new movement that wholeheartedly embraced the modern amd fought against the foppish sentimentalism of the romantic era. Futurism embraced originality, science and modernism against sentimentalism and history; it offered a new freedom in expression by allowing a wider spatial thought for design.

Futurism was applied to a variety of art media such as film, sculptures, graphic design and even architecture. Futuristic architecture seeks to transform futurist visions into bold urban forms and is characterised as anti-historical as it aims to create something detached from the shadows of the past. This concept will shape modern architecture and design in a wholly different manner as it allows bold imaginations to create and embrace ideas of science, technology and modernity. The concepts of modernity and futurism fit closely with architecture and technology, which reflect the modernity of future Shanghai. In an era of diminishing resources, climate change and advancing of technology, modern architectures will be more inclined to incorporate futuristic concepts and ideas to embrace these elements. The inclusion of science, technology, modernity and other futuristic elements not only aim to improve design efficiency, but also play a critical role in the aesthetic quality of the building. Hence, futuristic architecture will revolve around both operational and aesthetic design.

Evolving Trends in the Hospitality Industry: Hotels 2020

A report conducted by Amadeus (Talwar, 2010a) revealed findings on the future of hotels, indicating the need to embrace customer-oriented innovations and create a more personalised hotel experience for future travellers as they become 'living laboratories' to constantly enhance their service. This is acknowledged with more than 90% of respondents reflecting expectations on personalisation of their hotel experience. The evolving hospitality industry is influenced by a series of drivers including evolving global trends, changes in attitudes and behaviours of the future traveller, the innovation of strategies used within the sector and the question of how future technology will potentially interact with the guests' experience.

Political changes, diminishing energy resources, potential natural disasters, evolvement of new forms of travel such as space tourism and the uneven global pattern of investments are some key global trends influencing the industry's future. The global shift in powers from West to East will see the increase in price-sensitive middle-class travellers that will drive hotel prices down. Sustainability will continue to be a key factor in the design and operations of hotels, with 83% agreeing that by 2020, environmental considerations will play an influential role in consumers' choice of hotels.

Findings reveal that traditional segmentation methods would fail to identify future market segments as identities become more fluid. Future hotels will strive to steer away from a 'producer-led segmentation' to a 'consumer-driven choice' by providing a wider variety of choice for a personalised experience. The increasingly popular use of social media would enable hotels to gather important guest data to ensure a satisfied experience; but on the other hand, increase in the demand for connectivity – particularly amongst Generation X onwards – and convenience. By 2020, 24/7 connectivity will no longer be an expectation, but rather a demand. Technologies will have a large influence on the guest–hotel experience interaction as factors such as speed and convenience will come into play.

By 2020, innovative strategies will be undertaken by hotels in order to stay competitive in a saturated hospitality industry. By embracing open innovation, collaborative design and engaging in service innovation, the sector is looking at creative strategies to stay competitive. This includes embracing mobile technology, fast media and collaborating with technology companies such as Apple to create easier and more convenient service channels. In all, 95% of respondents in the Amadeus (2010) survey agreed that hotels will increasingly look to new technologies such as nanotechnology to increase efficiency, reduce cost, personalise the customer experience and improve service.

The potential change within the hospitality sector would spur experimentations of new sorts of business models such as invitation-only hotels.

It proposes that hotels which undertake horizon scanning, anticipate and respond with rapid implementation of appropriate strategies will be successful in the future. The demand for a personalised guest service coupled with increasingly fragmented customer segments will require hotels to switch towards a customer-centred strategy as they strive to differentiate themselves through unique architectures and innovative service strategies.

Main Drivers Shaping the Future of Hotels

The scenario about Scan and self-making beds, mood settings, ubiquitous computing and robotic room attendant; may sound science fiction. However, the scenario has a substantive foundation found in the following nine drivers shaping the future hotel in Shanghai.

Driver 1: Sustainable architecture
Driver 2: Land as a limited resource in Shanghai
Driver 3: Changing consumer tastes: Generations Y and Z
Driver 4: The unimaginable futuristic changes
Driver 5: New personal technologies
Driver 6: Technologies of bedroom design
Driver 7: The future room attendant
Driver 8: Trends in hotel design
Driver 9: Return on investment

Driver 1: Sustainable architecture

Sustainable architecture is a general term that describes environmentally conscious design techniques in the field of architecture. Sustainable architecture is framed by the larger discussion of sustainability and the pressing economic and political issues of our world. In a broad context, sustainable architecture seeks to minimise the negative environmental impact of buildings by enhancing efficiency and moderation in the use of materials, energy and development space. Most simply, the idea of sustainability, or ecological design, is to ensure that our actions and decisions today do not inhibit the opportunities of future generations. This term can be used to describe an energy and ecologically conscious approach to the design of the built environment.

In the hotel industry, sustainable architecture is central to H2Otel (www.h2otel.nl), which introduces a new hotel typology as its environmentally friendly architecture design using water in oxy-hydrogen generators to provide a source of energy for heating, cooling, cooking and electricity. Situated along the Amstel River, operations will have a carbon neutral design with modern technologies that harness solar passive design to minimise heat gain in rooms. H2O also utilises a creative arrangement of wooden lamellas which prevent overheating and creates a unique ambience (Meinhold, 2010a). The technologised hotel space and emphasis on connectivity, for example, will see better services for people with hearing and sight disabilities. Darcy (2010) suggests the likelihood of an increase in inclusive practices and a more enabling accommodation sector that will contribute to the economic and social sustainability of the enterprise.

Another example of award-winning architecture can be found in the Songjiang district, near the city of Shanghai. In this place, a set of hotels called Songjiang, is proposed to be designed and built into the side of a quarry; it will run on geothermal energy, use sustainable materials and will use resources efficiently (Amadeus, 2010) (Figure 11.1).

Examples of sustainable architecture include the incorporation of efficient heating, ventilation and air conditioning (HVAC) systems in a well-insulated building (Syed, 2011). A more efficient building requires less heat generating or dissipating power, but may require more ventilation capacity to expel polluted indoor air. Passive solar building design allows buildings to harness the energy of the sun efficiently without the use of any active solar mechanisms such as photovoltaic cells or solar hot water panels. Typical passive solar building designs incorporate materials with high thermal mass

Figure 11.1 Songjiang Shimao Intercontinental Hotel
(*Source:* http://www.atkinsglobal.com/showcase/index.aspx)

that retain heat effectively and strong insulation that works to prevent heat escape. Low-energy designs also require the use of solar shading, by means of awnings, blinds or shutters, to relieve the solar heat gain in summer and to reduce the need for artificial cooling. In addition, low-energy buildings typically have a very low surface area-to-volume ratio to minimise heat loss. Sustainable building materials that may be used include recycled denim or blown-in fibre glass insulation, sustainably harvested wood, Trass, Linoleum, sheep's wool, concrete (both high and ultra-high-performance Roman self-healing concrete), panels made from paper flakes, baked earth, rammed earth, clay, vermiculite, flax linen, sisal, seagrass, cork, expanded clay grains, coconut, wood fibre plates and calcium sandstone. All in all, sustainability is now the cornerstone of everyday architecture (Syed, 2011).

Driver 2: Land as a limited resource in Shanghai

Urbanisation has delivered substantial economic growth and radically reduced poverty in countries such as China (McKinsey & Company, 2011). The economic progress of modern Shanghai is to a large extent due to its massive urbanisation. The development of the city into an urban area attracted foreign investors and business, which contributed greatly to the city's economic growth. According to the Hong Kong Trade Development Council (HKTDC), the top three largest industries in Shanghai were financial services, retail and wholesale and real estates (HKTDC, 2010). In 2008, investment in Shanghai's real estate industry totalled to RMB136.69 billion, an increase on 4.5% since 2007. In the same year, 22.96 million square metres of newly built commercial housing were sold, reflecting the huge demand for properties (Office of Shanghai Chronicles, 2009).

Land sale is a major source of government revenue, raising about US$234 billion in 2009 and as a result, surges in urban development have put a strain on the availability of land. Despite this, property investments continue to pour into the city leading to a boom in property prices; Shanghai's property prices have risen more than 150% since 2003, pushing the price of a typical 1100 square foot apartment up to $200,000 (Barboza, 2010). This surge in property prices is driven by an inadequate supply of land parcels designed for housing development as home sales outpaced land supply since 2006 (East Day, 2010). In response, the Chinese Government implemented actions such as property taxes to adjust the demand and supply chain, curb property speculation and squeeze the housing bubble (China Business Times, 2011) in the hope of cooling the property market and ensuring the sustainability of the local government's revenue with its years of dependence on land sales.

As space becomes scarce and expensive, the design of hotels will have to be ergonomically functional. One example of this change is the award-winning Citizen M Hotel room (http://www.citizenm.com/) which has redefined the hotel bedroom. Measuring 14 square metres, the design removed the hotel bathroom and incorporated the design into the bedroom therefore minimising the space required. The room features a wall-to-wall window, liquid crystal display (LCD) television with free film channels, an extra large king-sized bed, free Wi-Fi and a Philip's designed touch screen mood pad which allows the guest to control everything in the room from television, window blinds, temperature, coloured lighting and wake-up alarm theme. Expect to see more ergonomically designed hotels in Shanghai in the future (Figure 11.2).

In the long term, Shanghai will continue to face pressing problems with land availability. High property prices may eventually be transferred to the final consumer such as hotel guests. Shanghai's growing financial hub will continue to expand its tourism market but at the same time, decreasing land

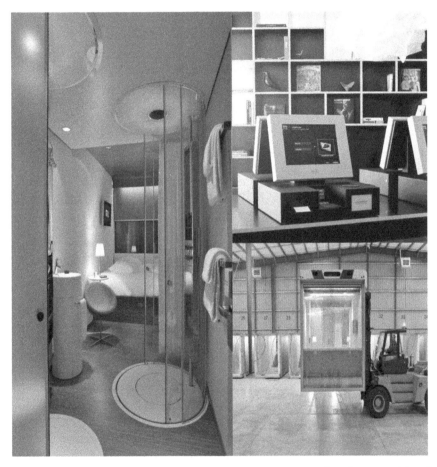

Figure 11.2 Citizen M Hotel: Automated check-in, bedroom pod at factory and hotel bedroom (viewing clockwise)
(*Source:* www.citizenm.com)

availability means that the city will need to construct new models of hotels, such as airborne accommodations in order to ensure demand meets supply.

Driver 3: Changing consumer tastes: Generations Y and Z

Social and demographic trends have a bearing on behavioural shifts within different market segments. Generation cohorts are seen as a future consumer indicator, as marketers shift their strategies accordingly to each generation's change in values, attitudes and consumption patterns. Generation Y (Gen-Y) typically refers to the generation born between 1977–1994 and Generation Z (Gen-Z) to those born between 1995–2009. Both generations have been recognised as being different from their predecessors as they are more technology-dependent, multi-taskers and bigger spenders (Spire, 2010). Research indicates that travel is an important element to the future of Generation Y (Moscardo et al., 2011), reflecting the integration of travel into their life. As future consumers of tourism products, these changes are indicators of demand that drives new product innovations.

Technology is at the heart of the Green Hotel in the scenario because technology is a key driver in influencing how these generations approach travel and tourism. Gen-Y has witnessed the advent of personal computers, digital cameras, game consoles and the internet. With the pace of development, Gen-Z has learnt to harness and exploit the uses of more sophisticated devices such as palmtop computers, WAP, text messaging and broadband, reflecting their level of comfort when interacting with technology. This means that they are unlikely to rate highly a holiday where they are left disconnected from their normal modes of connectivity. Besides that, these generations show an increasing concern for the world and the environment, as well as a higher tolerance for diversity and flexibility (Moscardo et al., 2011), indicating that environmentally sustainable factors will be taken into consideration in the future purchase of hotel rooms.

It is argued that the study of generations encompasses a cross-cultural element (Moscardo & Benckendorff, 2010), particularly in the Chinese context. Research conducted by Spire (2010) notes that the Chinese Gen-Y (born between 1980–1989) as products of China's one-child policy differ in some aspects from people of other generations in their consumption patterns. Spire characterises those living in cities as optimistic, highly indulgent shoppers, with high technology and information literacy. They have increasing drives, hopes and demands, and are open to Western ideas and products, but still proudly supportive of their own culture. In particular, Chinese urban consumers prefer modern retail formats and shopping for leisure and entertainment. However, rural youths appear to be less comfortable with information technology, preferring outdoor advertisement, local brands and word-of-mouth recommendations (McEwen et al., 2006). The Chinese Gen-Yers modernise, but do not Westernise. In many aspects, beneath the pursuit of superficial modernity, this generation remains deeply rooted in their Chinese values and perceptions, for example, by placing priority on family and relationships, upholding harmony, endurance and sacrifice and reflecting traits of collectivism rather than the individualism in the Western world (Lynton & Thogersen, 2010). These trends reflect how Chinese Gen-Y pursues Western modernity and desires to remain culturally connected to their roots at the same time.

Future segments of hotel users, Generations of X, Y and Z are generations which grew up among computers and technology. They are comfortable when interacting with technology and to a certain extent, demand it. A survey conducted by Travolution (2009) revealed that 65% of Generation Z (children born between early 1990s and 2000s) prefers to book their holidays online. Findings also reveal that 45% take their iPod/MP3s with them on holidays, 42.5% take their handheld games and 41% take their mobile phones. In addition, almost 55% of this generation utilise technologies such as SMS and social media to keep in contact with friends. These generations demand a high level of connectivity, expecting its presence in all stages of the future hotel experience from information search, booking, purchase, check-in/out, actual accommodation nights, payment and event feedback channels. *e|merse* is an example of a future hotel which targets this market, delivering an authentic urban experience by meshing a hotel with its surroundings. It links urban businesses with interactive maps equipped with global position systems (GPS) to allow guests to explore their site and activity preferences. Guests can complete a user profile prior to arrival, which will then be used to find local amenities that suit their tastes, network with other guests, provide feedback on the attractions and activities they have done (WATG, 2011a). The hotel industry is becoming one of the fast-paced technology adopters and the incorporation of technologies is likely to see an increase guest satisfaction and hotel efficiency.

Driver 4: The unimaginable futuristic changes

The current pace of technology advancement means that there can be bold ideas for future infrastructure designs and architectures. In the scenario, the Green Hotel's bed can change shape and alter the degree of comfort. This is achieved because of claytronics or programmable matter. The concept of claytronics combines nanoscale robotics and computer science to integrate sight, sound and feel into original ideas, allowing users to interact with the idea physically in 3D form. It will enable objects to be scaled to life-size, larger or smaller and capable of continuous 3D motion such that it provides end users with an impression of the object in reality (Claytronics, 2011). With claytronics, future hotel designs and architectures can be viewed in 3D reality even prior to actual construction. This provides a platform beneficial for all stakeholders such as hotel developers, investors and end users as they would be able to interact with the idea in reality and provide feedback that may prove useful to the development. The applications of claytronics represents the reconfiguration of everything, so just imagine the future hotel bed that could change its degree of comfort from a hard to a soft mattress without too much effort, the possibilities are endless.

Driver 5: New personal technologies

Hotels function as a liminal space in which anything is possible and multiple (Giddens, 1991). Shaped by discourses of anonymity, romance and adventure, hotels are places 'out-of-time' and 'out-of-place' where outpourings of excess and challenging norms may take place (Pritchard & Morgan, 2006). The fluidity of an individual's identity means that the modern hotel room acts as a platform between the everyday and the new, allowing the transgression of boundaries of self. As the needs and wants of individuals expand greatly into a wider spectrum, the emergence of personalised service spectrums will be evident as hotels work to provide a more personalised hotel experience. At the centre of the luminal space is the blurring between technology and reality.

As the scenario portrays, future generations become increasingly comfortable with technology, and congruently the interaction between humans and technologies may become integrated on a single platform. The concept of ubiquitous computing is the opposite of virtual reality, where technology interacts with humanity out in the open rather than the user connecting with the computer; it is the interaction of one user with many interfaces. The possibility of a ubiquitous computing future is depicted in science fiction films such as *Minority Report*, which suggest that computer technology would be so integrated that our everyday realities are paved with unimaginable volumes of passive technological interaction. One of the technologies seen in *Minority Report* is gestural interfaces with the goal of interpreting human gestures via mathematical algorithms. Gestures can originate from any bodily motion or state but commonly originate from the face or hand. Current focuses in the field include emotion recognition from the face and hand gesture recognition. The principle of gestural interfaces is simple, based on an array of sensors behind the screen (similar to those in digital cameras) which receive light when LCD pixels switch off and act like a lens. Every sensor from the array can 'see' you hard and because there are a few hundred pictures of your position at one time, each differing slightly from the one captured by sensors in proximity, depth of field can be computed, thus the gestural display will have a 3D image of your hand. For example, games like the Kinect, a controller-free entertainment experience that incorporates a 'natural user interface' with advance body recognition software including gesture, facial and voice recognition. It then uses these data to track and interpret the user's movement. Similarly, Playstation Move is designed with a wand controller and a light-emitting diode (LED) sphere that has the ability to track 3D movements.

The internet in its current stage is a transition into the future of ubiquitous computing, where technology slowly recedes into the background of our daily lives. The growth in the increasing popularity of multifunctional mobile devices has prompted the emergence of mobile spatial interaction. The incorporation of inertial sensing components into mobile devices will create a different platform to allow users to interact with data in a rich and natural manner. This proposed system, takes the form of a highly interactive 'push-pull' system, with more emphasis on 'pull', where the user decides when to present information on their device and directly interact in an 'eyes-free' manner with the hybrid physical/virtual environment (Strachan & Murray-Smith, 2009). As technologies integrate into our everyday environments, they may turn into a source of distress and annoyance as they increasingly require too much attention, or bring too much information for the user to digest. The notion of 'calm technology' then comes into play, suggesting the ability of technology to bring calm and comfort into everyday lives. Calm technology engages both the centres and the periphery of our attention, and moves back and forth between the two. Examples of calm technology, such as inner office windows, work on the basis of providing awareness of the surroundings to the user yet at the same time do not require the user's attention. In this case, the user – rather than the environment – chooses where their attention should be placed (Weiser & Brown, 1996).

Driver 6: Technologies of bedroom design

The scenario portrays the future hotel bedroom would be one infused with technology to enhance the visitor's experience, providing convenience, luxury and entertainment all within a single bedroom. Beds have long been a central component in the hotel experience. Most hotels now have all-white beds after the Westin Hotels and Resorts started the 'Heavenly Bed' concept in 1999. With increasing attention being put on hotel beds, a variety of designs have since surfaced, particularly high-technology ones. For example, the HiCan High Fidelity Canopy combines relaxation with entertainment, featuring a central control system for all features in the room, a state-of-the-art sound system, reading lights, built-in PC and full multimedia components with game and entertainment console, all connected to a projector for high-definition film enjoyment. The Somnus-Neu, designed by Grier Govorko is a media-rich oasis with motorised curtains, retractable video screen, Wi-Fi, a docking station for electronics, a five-point audio system and three zones of LED lighting – reading, ambient and floor – all to enhance guests' rest experience (McKeough, 2009). These beds provide enjoyment, entertainment and convenience.

Nanotechnology has a significant impact on developments in design. By incorporating nanotechnology, designs can be improved without sacrificing the original state of the object. Project PASTA (Integrating Platform for Advanced Smart Textile Applications), undertaken by IMEC and its project partners explores a bed linen application with an integrated sensor to monitor humidity and signal excessive humidity due to bed-wetting (Nanotechnology Now, 2010). Incorporating nanotechnology into fabric enables it to conduct electricity and heat, eliminate pests, have hygienic surfaces and provide self-cleaning coatings. For example, including nano-whiskers into fabric will produce a lightweight water and stain-repellent material; and, textiles impregnated with silver nanoparticles will have the ability to deactivate harmful bacteria and viruses (Denman, 2010).

Nanotechnology designs are more cost-effective, energy-efficient and more in-tune with the environment, influencing the overall design–development–construction process. Chemical engineers discovered that the use of titanium dioxide (TiO_2) can help to keep buildings free of discolouring pollution and have since applied it to buildings such as the Marunouchi Building in Tokyo. The chemical breaks down organic molecules found in grime and pollution when exposed to light and water, and then releases them into the air. Although the chemical currently only reacts to the sun's ultra-violet rays, there is a possibility of altering the chemical to react to a normal bathroom light bulb. In the future, sustainable bathroom designs may be incorporated with self-cleaning surfaces, reducing the necessity for bathroom cleaning (Todras-Whitehill, 2006).

Technology spurs innovation in product design. The Cybertecture Mirror for example, is a reflective window to a digital life as it elegantly displays and monitors the time, temperature, local traffic, news, television, energy consumption and health data via a wireless connection. Guests can get the latest information with a touch of the mirror (HFTP, 2010). Consumers' desire for soft and natural designs saw hotels such as the Four Season Residences in Denver incorporate natural light into the bathroom setting (Drillinger, 2010). This combination of design and technology means that guests can look to enjoy a much connected and relaxed bathroom experience.

Driver 7: The future room attendant

The room attendant as we know today may become a thing of the past. New innovations like cleaning robots act as labour substitutes as they provide faster and smarter ways to get jobs done. In the scenario, robots are used as a labour substitute in a world where labour is scarce. Robots as cleaning devices are not new to the market; irobot.com offers a large variety of robots for cleaning including vacuuming and washing floors, sweeping the garage and cleaning the pool and gutters (Yoshimi et al., 2004). The University of Stanford's STAIR (http://stair.stanford.edu) robot project has since its birth in 1956, set out to develop an AI system that exhibits broad-spectrum competence and intelligence. In the STAIR (Stanford AI Robot) project, the university has built a robot that can navigate home and office environments, pick up and interact with objects and tools, and intelligently converse with and help people in these environments. The single robot platform integrates methods drawn from all areas of AI, including machine learning, vision, navigation, manipulation, planning, reasoning and speech/natural language processing. This is in distinct contrast to the 30-year trend of working on fragmented AI sub-fields, and will be a vehicle for driving research towards true integrated AI. As a consequence, prototype models can deliver items around the home or office, tidy up a room including picking up and throwing away rubbish, and using the dishwasher, prepare meals using a normal kitchen or use tools to assemble a bookshelf. A robot capable of these tasks will revolutionise home and office automation, and will have important applications ranging from home assistants to elderly care.

Another example is the Toshiba ApriAlpha-V3 robot, with an omni-directional auditory process that allows the robot to recognise the direction of the user as it extracts a sound stream and recognises the content of the speech (Koga *et al.*, 2007). The robot has the ability to evolve into a 'life support partner' with the ability to deliver human-centric technologies that provide assistance and support to the elderly and young children. ApriAlpha-V3 is also able to interact with the user by responding to a repertoire of commands, registering a user and following him/her even among others (TOSHIBA, 2005).

As robots continue to take on more caring roles, it will not be surprising if hotels decide to replace human staff to run hotel operations. In the long run, robots may be a cost-effective solution as they do not require recruitment, training, monthly wages and other considerations related to people management. For the hotel industry, the human room attendant would be no more in 2050.

Driver 8: Trends of hotel designs

With the movement away from the provision of kitchens in homes, and an increasing frequency of fast food and prepared meals, trends towards hotel designs are evolving. McDonalds, for example, have diversified their brand and offerings by providing catered wedding dinners and the launch of their first hotels – The Golden Arches – in Zurich, Switzerland. The hotel offers travellers the McDonalds philosophy of reliability, convenience and service where check-in and check-outs are done by simply swiping a credit card. The design incorporates modernity and technology, allowing travellers to surf the internet, collect mail from the television and operate room lightings with a card (Chen & Richardson, 2010).

Hotels in 2050 will be driven by technological advances. For example, 'Bucket List Lodging' is a mobile luxury accommodation which allows users to move from one location to another without the hassle of switching hotels. Inspired from the film *The Bucket List*, this design aims to provide travellers with the solution to visit 'must-see' places, typically in remote areas where little accommodation is available. Designed as a modular kit big enough to fit into the cargo hold or shipping container, the hotel maintains the natural beauty of the environment that the traveller chooses, leaving no trace when the season ends. Another new future hotel model is the Aeroscraft, which is an airborne cruise ship. This new revolution in transport infrastructure will carry leisure travellers and cargos to remote locations, thus rivalling luxury cruises (Aeros, 2006; WATG, 2011b). Improvements in technologies, evolving segments of hotel users and diminishing resources are some of the main drivers that shape revolutionary changes in hotel design and architecture today.

Consumers today, are three times more price sensitive than they were 20 years ago (Yeoman, 2008). This indicates that future travellers are most likely attracted to products which are budget, or relatively affordable with stylish designs. The concept of pod hotels stemmed from the Japanese innovation of capsule hotels, where guests were provided similar amenities in a hotel at a very small space at approximately 3 feet × 4 feet × 6 feet (Mishima, 2011). Lookotels recognises the demand of future travellers for the simple, yet modern, basic and sustainable with no compromise of the products' quality. Its design of a modular capsule, which varies from 9.7 square metres to 12.1 square metres, incorporates sustainability and technology into the original pod concept, offering energy-efficient designs and self-sufficient rooms with a sofa bed, television, chair, Wi-Fi access, telephone, air-conditioning, bathroom and automated controls. Technology comes into play, with automated self check-in kiosks and vending machines for food and beverages (Lookotels, 2011; Meinhold, 2010b). The progress of technology will continue to act as a catalyst for the development of futuristic hotels. At present, futuristic hotel projects such as the Space Resort – a low Earth orbit and the Hydropolis (www.hydropolis.com) – an underwater luxury hotel in Dubai, are in the process of design and construction. Changing consumer attitudes and trends will continue to influence and drive changes in the designs of future hotels as operators attempt to stay more competitive.

Driver 9: Investments in hotels

The growth of Shanghai as a financial and trade hub have had a positive impact on the growth of visitor arrivals, increasing the demand for short stay, good quality accommodation. Investments in the contemporary hotel market only started in 1985 with the entrance of the Sheraton Huating as the first international hotel chain. Since then, another 15 international chains including InterContinental, Accor, Marriott and Starwood have entered the Shanghai market. Between 2002 and 2008, four- and five-star hotels increased 54.8%, where five-star hotels accounted for 26.4% of the total. Hotel investments increased significantly in Shanghai, particularly in 2009–2010 as the city geared up for the World Expo 2010, opening 16 five-star hotels during this period (Savills, 2009). According to HVI (2011), the average value per room in Shanghai surpassed RMB1,000,000 in 2007, being the culminating point of a six-year growth. The four-star segment registered the most significant increase in room values at a CAGR of 3.8% between 2001 and 2009, equating to RMB300,000.

The growth in four- and five-star hotels notwithstanding, research has found that prior to 2010, the gross operating profit (GOP) levels of the five-star hotel sector in China have fallen to the lowest in the eight years that the China Hotel Industry Study has been publishing. In Shanghai, the GOP level for 2009 was RMB119,645. This decline is attributed to the oversupply of hotels in these markets (Horwath, 2010a). Statistics rebounded in 2010 with positive impacts from the World Expo, as market-wide occupancy level peaked about 70%, recording a 39% increase over the same quarter in 2009. As a result, market-wide RevPAR recorded an exceptional growth of 80% over the third quarter 2009, which was an increase of 63% compared to the same period in 2008 (Horwath, 2010b).

Concluding Remarks

How change is already occurring

The scenario of Sean's stay promotes a future world of contemporary design, sustainability and technological innovations as the foundation of the future hotel. This is already happening.

The sustainability agenda is becoming the increasingly important priority for countries around the world, as Matteo Theo says:

> The term sustainability could almost be defined as the buzz word of the early 21st century. Sustainability is the talk of the town, not only in the economy or in politics, but also in the construction industry. Considering everything closely however, only one aspect of sustainability catches the industry's attention, the ecological perspective. In this respect, the use of different resources throughout a building's complete lifecycle is balanced. This ecological balance corresponds to the materials used from production to demolition and even the essential resource needs for building management throughout the whole usage period. The two other aspects of sustainability are often forgotten, the economic and socio-cultural points. The building should maximise its potential to

reduce maintenance costs, if possible even generate profits and should lose very little in value. On the other hand, it should also cater to the user's wellbeing in regard to health and comfort aspects as well as be aesthetically pleasing. (Putz-Willems, 2009: 67)

Architecture is important for offsetting the negative aspects of hotel buildings by enhancing efficiency of resources as well as making the design aesthetically pleasing. Futuristic architecture and sustainable design provide an opportunity for pushing out barriers and thinking beyond the known. Future innovation in architecture moves us to a liminal space where reality and science fiction are blurred, new ideas and concepts are emerging that shift the concept of a hotel bedroom are constantly emerging. Science fiction films often have their basis in emerging technologies. Therefore, what we now think of as science fiction, in fact comes true. Gestural interfaces (as seen in the sci-fi film *Minority Report*), self-cleaning devices, mood zones and claytronics may well be an everyday reality in 2050. Technology is integral to new modern hotels for two main reasons: to improve the efficiency of hotel operations and to cater better to the evolving new segments of hotel users. The future hotel will become a technologised space, shifting from its original labour-intensive nature. This trend is driven by changes in demography and technological innovation. Inventions such as nanotechnologies in self-cleaning devices, robot room attendants, high-technology wall-mounted toilets, lighting, ambience and furniture that allow guests to recreate their personal space to suit their moods are all possible.

As a report by Amadeus (2010) points out, at the core of any hotel stay, guests will want to exercise most choice when it comes to the location and contents of their room. The range of options would need to include the floor, corridor positioning, view, room dimensions, shape, number of windows, size of bathroom and the type, amount and layout of furniture. By 2020 (Talwar, 2010a), modular, intelligent furniture with built-in memory will remember a guest's preferred settings and adapt to changes in body posture. Taking this concept one stage further, claytronics will allow furniture to re-configure itself based upon programmable matter.

At the heart of a hotel room, customers want to choose from a range of different beds, pillows, linens and amenities at different quality levels and price points. Some will require transparency of the environmental footprint of the supply chain of everything that goes into their room. Guests want the ability to control environmental factors such as temperature, lighting and even the colour of the walls. Choice could also be extended to the type of artwork displayed on the walls or for the provision of digital photo frames to display the guest's own choices. As technology advances and intelligent wallpapers emerge, so guests may be able to configure the room décor on arrival or download their preferred design beforehand. The Citizen M Hotels (www.citizenm.com/) in Amsterdam combine innovations in room technologies to provide the guest with a chic, and due to the small size, affordable experience. The pod-like size requires an innovative approach to space management; for example, there is no room to move around the bed to change the sheets. Citizen M has applied to patent a system whereby the whole mattress can be pulled up to the front of the bed vertically. The used sheets fall off and the clean sheets can be hung up on the two upper corners.

Technology advancement

The rate of advance in technology and the likely emergence of high-bandwidth mobile devices mean guests may want a room with no technology (just to get away from everything). Others may simply be looking for a display screen or surface to project a larger image holographic TV from their own device. A guarantee of the chance to try out the latest gadgets may become a brand differentiator and attract a particular type of customer. Some guests may want to book the opportunity to test out a new product or schedule a session with a technology advisor to help them master what they already have. Trump Soho in Manhattan (www.trumpsohohotel.com) is an exemplar of the trend towards individualism and life with technology. Central to its guestrooms and suites is the energy saving 'Control4 Suite System' that enables guests to control ambient temperature, lighting, curtain drapes and entertainment options with a remote device. Guests can set their own room preferences using the Green feature button. This offering is augmented by flat-screen televisions, a home iPhone/iPod and docking station as well as optional in-room computers and personalised stationery. The offering is completed with a Nespresso coffee maker in each guestroom and suite. Moving into the future, technology will play and even more important part in the hotel bedroom, the use of gestural interfaces will change room control panels. 3D hologram TVs will become the norm. The application of technologies is probably unimaginable and occurring very fast. One example is the medical mirrors designed by MIT researcher Ming-Zher Poh (Chandler, 2010), which will advise consumers of health requirements, how they feel and what they can order off the room service menu. The system:

> measures slight variations in brightness produced by the flow of blood through blood vessels in the face. Public-domain software is used to identify the position of the face in the image, and then the digital information from this area is broken down into the separate red, green and blue portions of the video image. (Chandler, 2010)

With the price of land at a record high in Shanghai, reaching a record US$2000 per square metre in the city's' Chongming Island in February 2011 (Ying, 2011), space becomes a premium commodity. Prices will drive investors to push average yields up in order to recoup investment, hence the growth will be in four- and five-star hotels in Shanghai rather than the lower end of the market. Futurism will influence the 21st century hotel industry given China's emphasis on modernity, youth, speed, power and technology which will break from tradition and the past. Shanghai in 2050 will be an exemplar of a modern hotel industry against an environment of sustainable living and scarcity of resources. Change is already taking place.

So, what is your opinion? Technology, sustainability and contemporary innovation are the keywords that describe Sean's stay at the Green Hotel. This is what the future could look like, where science fiction meets reality and where futurism is the expectation of change.

12 2050: The Future of Transport

Learning points

- The critical short-term issues influencing the future of transport are peak oil and climate change.
- Peak oil and climate change will drive innovative technological solutions for the future of transport, including the electric car, fuel cells and hypersonic travel.
- The future of tourism is dependent on the future of transport.

Introduction: Why Transport and Tourism Go Together

Transportation is an integral part of the tourism industry; in fact expansion in the industry is largely due to improvements in transportation. In Switzerland, the World Economic Forum (2007) found Switzerland to have the most competitive travel and tourism sector, a key contributing factor for this recognition was transport. The public transport network is one of the most efficient in the world, stretching 25,612 km with 27,300 stopping points. The network is integrated with timetables coordinated to the extent that postal-bus services arrive prior to the departure of the next train. Transport can also be a key form of innovation for tourism development as the example of British Columbia's seaplanes shows. British Columbia's seaplanes are both a tourism product and necessary passenger transport.

Transportation has also been vitally important to Morocco's tourism industry. Tourism policy in Morocco has been driven by increases in international visitation, with a target set at 10 million (Page *et al.*, 2009). To achieve this, the government has an open skies policy, which saw 23 new routes established from the United Kingdom, France and Spain in 2006, and a modern rail network described as the best in Africa. The Moroccan example illustrates how a destination invests in its transport infrastructure to develop a competitive destination. Transport is not a panacea for the future development of a country's tourism industry by itself, but rather a key enabling factor when seeking to attract visitors in a competitive environment.

To enable travel, transport must be efficient and effective. The legacy of the intrepid traveller of old, invulnerable to fear and prepared for any eventuality, lives on in the allocentric tourist (Plog, 1974). However, the allocentric tourist is not renowned for exploring the same place twice and most destination plans aim to attract repeat visitors. The rise in middle-class travel and the legacy of 9/11 means that most travellers expect to be transported in a degree of comfort without undue worries about mishaps (Page et al., 2010). Safe and efficient transport enables tourism, while as the EU's ban on Indonesian airlines demonstrates, its absence acts as a barrier (Page et al., 2010).

We are at the point of peak oil (or thereabouts) according to Becken (2008), in which the maximum rate of global petroleum extraction is reached, after which the rate of production enters terminal decline. At the same time the world is increasingly paying attention to environmentalism and this has the potential to impinge upon tourism in a major way. No transport means no tourism and climate affects tourism destination products such as skiing in the French Alps or sunbathing in Hawaii. The environment is part of the consumer psyche and consumers are today taking action against climate change. As the environment becomes increasingly important countries such as China, Brazil and India are taking the issue seriously. However, Pavan Sukhdev (2010) suggests that the greening of economies is not a burden on growth but rather a new engine for growth, employment and the reduction of persistent poverty.

Improvement in transport opens up opportunities to travel. However, transportation is seldom considered in the destination planning process, resulting in a number of biodiversity-rich areas being destroyed (Page et al., 2010). At present, tourism is dependent on the availability of oil and is comparatively oil-intensive (Becken, 2008). So, change is coming. With increasing pressure caused by the surge in demand for transportation of people and products, will alternative fuels and green economy initiatives develop to the point that transportation will continue to underpin the expansion in tourism? Is investment in transport infrastructure money wisely spent? Or will oil be the flip point in a sclerosis of travel? Is there an alternative to oil? Futurist literature discusses bullet trains, hypersonic travel, fourth-generation biofuels and even teleportation. As the price of oil increases, opportunities for alternatives may open up. This chapter looks at the critical issues pertaining to transport and tourism, examining what transport might be in 2050. So, in the words of Captain Kirk, *Beam me up Scotty.*

Our Transport System

Globalisation, for better or worse, is a dominant feature of our world. As barriers between continents, countries and cities have diminished with urbanising populations, economic growth and prosperity have become inextricably linked to accessibility; accessibility to markets, production materials, services, food and culture. Accessibility is therefore dependent on an efficient and intricate global network of air, rail, road and water links between and within our population centres of cities and megacities.

According to the recent UN World Urbanization Prospects' report (Smith, 2010), only 13% of the world's population lived in cities in 1900, growing to 29% in 1950, and 49% in 2005. Due to urban migration, cities are also expanding in size. In 1950, there were 83 urban areas with more than 1 million people living in them. Today, in 2010, 476 of them are spread around the world. Parallel with this global urbanisation trend and need for long-distance transportation networks, a complementary trend toward 'suburbanisation' began: urban centres grew outwards into suburbs, and further still into exurbs, where ring roads encapsulate the urban areas, and highways and commuter rail systems provide connectivity between them. Cities and megacities are the organs of the global economy, and intercity travel and transport is the lifeblood. Urban centres are the nexus nodes binding the world together. Global economic command centres such as Tokyo, New York, Los Angeles, London, Chicago, Paris, Mexico City, Hong Kong and Buenos Aires, constitute a substantial portion of national economies. As a consequence, the world is witnessing rapid growth in transportation usage.

Globally, the number of road vehicles will grow from 800 million now to 1.1 billion in the next 15 years (Frost & Suillvan, 2009). The industrial world's addiction to cars is costly and will become more so as the Texas Transportation Institute reveals that in the United States alone, 2.3 billion gallons of gas is wasted each year in traffic jams (Smith, 2010) with a usage of 21 million barrels of oil each day.

Over the last 25 years, a huge increase in private car ownership is evident in China, India and a number of other Asian countries where rapid economic growth has taken place. China is now the fourth largest motor vehicle producer and the third largest consumer in the world (Smith, 2010). According to the National Bureau of Statistics of China (Smith, 2010), the total number of civilian-use motor vehicles reached 64.67 million in 2008, and private vehicle ownership increased by 18.1% between 2004 and 2008.

India is another growth economy experiencing a dramatic increase in the automobile industry. Economic liberalisation policies post-1991, have seen the blossoming of the automobile manufacturing sector in terms of production, export and innovation. By 2050, India is expected to top the world in car volumes as its automobile industry becomes an outsourcing hub for automobile companies worldwide.

According to Boeing (2010), the Global Financial Crisis had a significant impact on airline profitability and traffic. In 2009, air traffic declined by about 2% as the world's worst economic recession drove economies into a period of stagnation. However, Boeing predicts passenger traffic to grow at 6% per annum between 2011 and 2014 with the delivery of 30,900 new airplanes by 2029. The foundation of this growth is the rapidly expanding air service within China and other emerging economies and the spread of low-cost carrier (LCC) business models throughout the world. Half of the world's new traffic added during the next 20 years will be to, from or within the Asia Pacific region which will grow at 6.8% per year. Driven by economic development and the increasing accessibility of air transport services, traffic within the region will grow faster than traffic to and from other regions. High fuel costs are compelling airlines to accelerate replacement of older airplanes. Therefore, the increased capabilities of the latest long-range, twin-aisle airplanes create opportunities for operators to take advantage of the ongoing liberalisation of air transport markets to open new non-stop routes.

The cruise sector has grown phenomenally since the emergence of leisure cruising some 40 years ago. Passenger numbers in North America more than doubled between 1970 and 1980: from 600,000 to 1.4 million and increased fivefold from 1980 to 2000 to 7 million. Between 2000 and 2008, passenger numbers grew another 89% to 13.2 million (CLIA, 2008). This pattern of growth in the cruise sector is expected to continue. From 2008 through to 2011, new constructions will add 38 new ships with more than 100,000 berths (Klein, 2011), resulting in approximately 5 million additional passengers worldwide.

According to Klein:

> The size of ships has also increased dramatically. In their early days, ships could accommodate 750–1,000 passengers, but new purpose-built cruise ships are increasingly taking on larger proportions. By the late 1990s, new ships launched by Carnival and Royal Caribbean were accommodating more than 3,300 passengers. These were soon eclipsed in 2006 by Royal Caribbean's 160,000-ton Freedom of the Seas with the capacity for 4,370 passengers and over 5,700 people in total including crew. More recently this was overtaken by Royal Caribbean's Oasis of the Seas introduced in December 2009, weighing 220,000 tons and accommodating more than 7,000 passengers (at capacity) and carrying a complement of close to 2,000 crew members. It is staggering to compare this to the ships Royal Caribbean and Carnival started with – Song of Norway at 18,000 tons and 724 passengers, and Mardi Gras at 27,300 tons and 1,024 passengers. (Klein, 2011: 114)

Critical Issues: Peak Oil and Climate Change

Critical issues of climate change and oil dominate global conversations as it depletes slowly despite societal dependence on fossil fuels. Climate change or global warming is related to the increase in world temperatures as a result of carbon emissions and their effects. Peak oil, on the other hand, has to do with coming shortfalls in the supply of fuels that society has become overwhelmingly dependent on, leading to higher prices for oil and its many products, and perhaps to massive economic disruption and more oil wars. Thus, the first has more directly to do with the environment, the second with human society and its dependencies and vulnerabilities.

The impact of tourism on climate change is dominated by the emissions of tourism transport (Peeters, 2010), which accounts for about 75% of all emissions. It has become clear that the growth of tourism contribution to climate change has mainly been caused by growth in tourism transport, particularly in long-haul travel. In 2005, 40% of all tourist kilometres were by air, 41% by private car and the remainder by train, coach, ferries and cruise ships. Yeoman *et al.* (2007) observe that the majority of international tourism trips entail the use of oil at some point, which could not be undertaken with other fuel sources. However, in the event of extreme oil price hikes, there are means for tourists to switch away from oil. Over the next 20 years, there may be increased use of non-oil-based transport systems such as electric railways and cars and non-oil-based electricity generation. Tourists may travel shorter distances, using lower cost transport that may, for example, be more time consuming. Despite the possibility of shifting demand away from oil-based transport, it would however be inevitable that higher oil prices would feed through, making tourism more expensive and overall, reducing global tourism demand.

Peak oil

Peak oil is the point in time when the maximum rate of global petroleum extraction is reached, after which the rate of production enters terminal decline. This concept is based on the observed production rates of individual oil wells, and the combined production rate of a field of related oil wells. The aggregate production rate from an oil field over time usually grows exponentially until the rate peaks and then declines – sometimes rapidly – until the field is depleted. According to Becken (2010), the world is now in the period of peak as majority of the studies about peak oil suggest a point between now and 2022 (Figure 12.1).

A point of peak oil signifies a period of oil depletion and exponential decline with the end of oil predicted to be pessimistically 2054 and optimistically 2094.

What we can learn from Hitler?

Many futurists are arguing that peak oil really is not a problem as alternatives are available. The Fischer–Tropsch (F–T) process, which is a set of chemical reactions that convert a mixture of carbon monoxide and hydrogen into liquid hydrocarbons. The process, a key component of gas to liquids technology, produces a petroleum substitute, typically from coal, natural gas or biomass for use as synthetic lubrication oil and as synthetic fuel. The F–T process has received intermittent attention as a source of low-sulphur diesel fuel and to address the supply or cost of petroleum-derived hydrocarbons, hence possibility of synthetic oil. Hitler championed the cause of F–T process during the Second World War to produce synthetic fuels. It is estimated that the F–T production accounted for an estimated 9% of German war production of fuels and 25% of automobile fuel (Steynberg & Dry, 2004).

Syntroleum, a publicly traded US company, has produced over 400,000 gallons of diesel and jet fuel from the F–T process using natural gas and coal. Using natural gas as a feedstock, the ultra-clean, low-sulphur fuel has been tested extensively by the US Department of Energy and the US Department of Transportation. Most recently, Syntroleum has been working with the US Air Force to develop a synthetic jet fuel blend that will help the Air Force to reduce its dependence on imported petroleum. The Air Force, which is the US military's largest user of fuel, began exploring alternative fuel sources in 1999. On 15th December 2006, a B-52 took off from Edwards AFB, California for the first time powered solely by a 50–50 blend of JP-8 and Syntroleum's FT fuel. The seven-hour flight test was considered a success. The goal of the flight test programme is to qualify the fuel blend for fleet use on the service's B-52s, and then flight test and qualification on other aircraft. The test program concluded in 2007. This programme is part of the Department of Defense Assured Fuel Initiative, an effort to develop secure domestic sources for the military energy needs.

The US Department of Energy (DoE) calls oil 'the lifeblood of modern civilisation' (Hirsch et al., 2005: ii). Around 86 million barrels (13.7 billion litres) are consumed each day. Oil supplies 37% of the world's energy demand and powers nearly all of the world's transportation. Without it, production and trade would grind to a halt. Studies have shown that GDP growth is very strongly related to increased use of oil (Smith, 2010). When the price of oil increases, the cost of nearly all economic activity rises. This often induces recessions. High oil prices have been associated with three major periods of economic recession in the past 40 years, including the lead-up to the recent global economic crisis. The world's oil production capacity may not be sufficient to match growing demand in coming years. When that happens, a price spike may be triggered, with major detrimental effects on economies, especially economies dependent on tourism (Yeoman et al., 2007).

According to Smith (2010), not all the oil that is thought to be in the ground has been found. The key measure of discovered oil is 'proven reserves' (or 'proved reserves'), which is the amount of oil in a given field that the

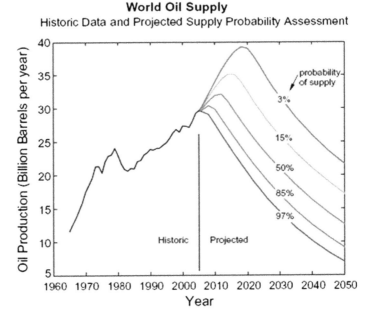

Figure 12.1 Probability of peak oil (Becken, 2010)

owner is 90% confident is present and can be extracted with existing technology. As of 2009, the official total of proven reserves worldwide, including non-conventional reserves, stood at 1.25 trillion barrels of conventional oil and 150 billion barrels of Canadian oil sands. The United States Energy Information Agency (EIA, 2009) forecasts that proven reserves would be sufficient to meet world demand for another 25–32 years, providing that oil production capacity can continue to expand.

Few big oil reserves have been found in recent decades. Between 1963 and 1980, 15,000 wells found nearly 1.5 trillion barrels of oil. But between 1980 and 2002, 60,000 more wells found half as much new oil. It now takes approximately 10 wildcat wells on average to discover the same quantity of reserves as a single wildcat well would discover 50 years ago (Smith, 2010).

Newly discovered oil is rarely cheap to extract as it is typically in deep offshore reserves or unconventional deposits, requiring additional inputs and special equipment. Refining oil from tar sands, for example, requires huge amounts of water and land, while deep-sea drilling requires rigs worth over half-a-billion dollars each. Additionally, extraction of unconventional oil deposits is often very carbon intensive, resulting in greater costs as countries introduce carbon pricing schemes. By keeping some of the cheapest oil off the market with its quotas, OPEC forces more expensive reserves to be used to meet demand, increasing the price of oil and their profit. The price of oil will continue to rise as the world is forced to turn to more expensive sources of oil for the marginal supply even if demand remains constant as low-cost reserves are exhausted and more expensive sources replace them.

Demand is rising particularly fast with former exporters like China, Indonesia and the United Kingdom now being net importers of oil. The supply of oil available to satisfy demand from countries that are dependent on oil imports is being squeezed by domestic demand in oil-producing nations. Between 2007 and 2009, oil exports fell 4.8% while world consumption fell only 1.8%.

Oil demand is relatively inelastic, – that is, consumers cannot quickly find alternatives to oil that allow them to carry on routines as usual (Becken, 2010). As such, consumers have little alternative but to keep consuming, resulting in reduction on other expenditures. It is also highly inflationary; consumers pay more for both oil and products that use oil for their manufacture and transportation. Falling consumer demand and higher prices may lead to recession. Between 2004 and 2008, oil prices rose dramatically to USD$147 a barrel; over twice the previous record of USD$70 a barrel set during the Hurricane Katrina disaster in 2005, itself a 30% increase on the previous high of USD$55 a barrel set in late 2004. The price of oil and the financial crisis hampered economic activity to the point that the world economy entered recession. It was only when the recession caused demand for oil to ease that the supply crunch ended and the price fell. This may have been the first in a cycle of supply crunches and recessions following the same pattern: as demand rises faster than production capacity, the world's oil supply buffer is whittled away. The supply crunch raises the price which tips into recession once reaching a certain level. Demand is lowered, recreating the supply buffer, and resulting in a lower price. This enables economies to recover, which increases their oil demand and decreases the supply buffer. Once production capacity starts to fall, rising demand will eat up the supply buffer at lower and lower levels. Once maximum world oil production is reached, that level will be approximately maintained for several years thereafter, creating an undulating plateau. After which, production will experience a decline.

Oil writer David Strahen describes the economic ramifications:

> What will almost certainly follow is a period of extreme oil price volatility, as demand repeatedly hits the ceiling of production capacity, whether that is determined by short term events above ground or the fundamental geology. This is likely to set off recurrent economic slow-downs or recessions, which in turn could have the effect of smearing out what would otherwise be a relatively sharp oil production peak into a more extended corrugated plateau. Paradoxically, the very worst short-term outcome might be not a sudden shock, but a milder recession. If this were to create some spare oil production capacity by depressing demand, the economists would claim it was all back to normal. (Strahen, 2008: 52)

The future of the oil market appears bleak as production capacity is not expected to keep up with demand, leading to severe economic consequences. To meet demands, oil companies are forced to extract oil in more difficult and expensive conditions (deep-water, oil sands, lignite to liquids) from smaller, less favourable reserves. The marginal (price-setting) barrel of oil costs around US$75–$85 a barrel to produce. This will continue to rise with higher demand and exhaustion of reserves.

Climate change and global warming

Climate change is about the increase in the average temperature of Earth's near-surface air and oceans. According to the 2007 Fourth Assessment Report by the Intergovernmental Panel on Climate Change (Parry *et al.*, 2007), global surface temperature increased by 0.74 ± 0.18 °C (1.33 ± 0.32 °F) during the 20th century, largely due to increasing concentrations of green house gases (GHG), resulting from human activity such as the burning of fossil fuel and deforestation.

The latest IPCC (2007) report projected that global surface temperature is likely to rise a further 1.1–6.4 °C (2.0–11.5 °F) during the 21st century. This will cause sea levels to rise, change the amount and pattern of precipitation, expand subtropical deserts and cause melting in the Arctic. It also increases the frequency and intensity of extreme weather events, species extinctions and changes in agricultural yields.

One important attribute of global warming is the GHG effect, which is the process by which absorption and emission of infrared radiation by gasses in the atmosphere warm a planet's lower atmosphere and surface. The question is how the strength of the presumed greenhouse effect changes when human activity increases the concentrations of GHG in the atmosphere.

Since the Industrial Revolution, human activity has increased the amount of greenhouse gasses in the atmosphere; concentrations of CO_2 and methane have increased by 36% and 148%, respectively, since 1750. Fossil fuel burning has produced about three-quarters of the increase in CO_2 from human activity over the past 20 years, mostly due to land-use change, particularly deforestation.

The transport sector plays a crucial role in world energy use and emissions of GHG. In 2004, transport energy use amounted to 26% of total world energy use and the transport sector was responsible for about 23% of world energy-related GHG emissions (IEA, 2009). The 1990–2002 growth rate of energy consumption in the transport sector was highest among all the end-use sectors. Table 12.1 indicates that light-duty vehicles and freight trucks consume the highest amount of energy within the transport sector, and that virtually all transport energy comes from oil-based fuels.

Table 12.1 World transport energy use in 2000, by mode

Mode	Energy use (EJ)	Share (%)
Light-duty vehicles (LDVs)	34.2	44.5
2-wheelers	1.2	1.6
Heavy freight trucks	12.48	16.2
Medium freight trucks	6.77	8.8
Buses	4.76	6.2
Rail	1.19	1.5
Air	8.95	11.6
Shipping	7.32	9.5
Total	76.87	100

Source: IPCC (2007)

Growing international investments and reduced trade restrictions are driving the increase in migration and the demand for intercity and international recreational travel. In the United States, intercity travel accounts for about one-fifth of total travel and is dominated by auto and air transport. European and Japanese intercity travel combines auto and air travel with fast rail travel. Contrastingly, intercity travel in developing worlds is dominated by bus and conventional rail travel, though air travel is growing rapidly both regionally and globally.

The Short-Term Future of Transport

There seems little doubt that short of worldwide economic collapse, transport activity will continue to grow at a rapid pace for the foreseeable future. However, the shape of that demand and the means by which it will be satisfied depend on several factors. First, transport can be fuelled by multiple alternative sources, beginning with liquid fuels from unconventional oil, natural gas or coal, or biomass. Other alternatives include gaseous fuels such as natural gas or hydrogen and electricity, with both hydrogen and electricity capable of being produced from a variety of feedstocks. However, all these alternatives are costly, and several – especially liquids from fossil resources – can increase GHG emissions significantly without carbon sequestration. Second, the growth rate and shape of economic development that drives transport demand is uncertain. If China, India and other Asian countries continue to rapidly industrialise, and if Latin America and Africa fulfil much of their economic potential, transport demand will grow with extreme rapidity over the next several decades. Even in the most conservative economic scenarios, considerable growth in travel is likely.

Third, transport technology has been evolving rapidly. The energy efficiency of the different modes, vehicle technologies and fuels, as well as their cost and desirability, will be strongly affected by future technology developments. For example, although hybrid electric drive trains have made a strong early showing in the Japanese and US markets, their ultimate degree of market penetration will depend strongly on further cost reductions. Longer-term opportunities requiring more advanced technology include new biomass fuels beyond those made from sugar cane in Brazil and corn in the United States, fuel cells running on hydrogen and battery-powered electric vehicles.

Fourth, growing income from developing nations will spur investments in transport infrastructures. Current trends point towards growing dependence on private cars, although other alternatives exist, such as Curitiba and Bogota with their rapid bus transit systems. Taking into account differences in income, car ownership varies widely around the world, resulting in different countries making different choices as they develop. The future choices made by both governments and travellers will have huge implications for future transport energy demand and CO_2 emissions in these countries.

A Further Longer-Term and Futuristic Perspective on Transport

Beam me up Scotty!

Teleportation is the transfer of matter almost instantaneously from one point to another. It became very popular with the 1966 television series 'Star Trek' with Captain Kirk's famous catchphrase 'Beam me up Scotty'. Teleporting human beings will probably never be realistic or safe, but is it possible to teleport simple materials reducing the need for cargo ships and trucks? In 2008, the Defense Advanced Projects Research Agency (DARPA) issued a request for proposals to learn more about quantum entanglement, among the strangest phenomena known to science. Albert Einstein referred to this area of quantum mechanics as 'spooky action at a distance'. In quantum teleportation, particles can become 'entangled' into a single entity, and a change in one instantaneously changes the other even if it is far away (Cetron, 2008). The project called Quantum Entanglement Science and Technology (QuEST) works with quantum teleportation, tiny units of computer information called quantum bits. The technology the DARPA is interested in has applications crucial for quantum computing and quantum cryptology. Key examples are the exponential speed-up of critical computations such as with Shor's prime factoring quantum algorithm and secure quantum communication protocols leading to unbreakable codes and unbelievably fast computer technology. Scientists are now able to relocate, on an instant basis, atoms and photons (hence the name quantum teleportation).

The technology is called teleportation because the information moved behaves more like an object than normal information (Cetron, 2008). Teleportation technology is a giant leap in forward communication and computing. But in 2009, researchers at the University of Michigan, Maryland, are only recording a success rate of one in every 100 million teleportation attempts (Brumfiel, 2009). We are now only beginning to plumb the depths of the human mind and the potential of psychic abilities and according to scientists at Magriteck, the reality seems unlikely (see http://www.darpa. mil/mto/programs/quest/, accessed 10 September 2010).

Hypersonic transportation and space travel

You think about hypersonic travel and history tells us the story of Concorde. The Aérospatiale-BAC Concorde is a turbojet-powered supersonic (not hypersonic) passenger airliner, which flew at Mach 2 or twice the speed of sound. It was a product of an Anglo-French government treaty, combining the manufacturing efforts of Aerospatiale and the British Aircraft Corporation. First flown in 1969, Concorde entered service in 1976 and continued commercial flights for 27 years. It eventually failed due to the high costs, lack of routes and noise pollution. More recently, futurists have being discussing hypersonic flight travelling at speeds above Mach 5.5. For example, the A2 plane developed by Reaction engines is:

designed to carry 300 passengers at a top speed of almost 4000 mph (6400 kmh), five times the speed of sound, engineers who designed the hypersonic jet said on Tuesday, Feb. 5. Part of an EU project to expand the boundaries of air travel and partially funded by the European Space Agency, the LAPCAT (Long-Term Advanced Propulsion Concepts and Technologies) project could see the plane operating within 25 years, the firm's boss Alan Bond told the Guardian newspaper. The A2 is designed to leave Brussels international airport, fly quietly and subsonically out into the north Atlantic at mach 0.9 before reaching mach 5 across the North Pole and heading over the Pacific to Australia. The plane, which at 143 metres (469 feet) long would be about twice the size of the biggest current jets, could fly non-stop for up to 12,500 miles (20,000 km).' It would be lighter than current intercontinental planes and designed to operate on liquid hydrogen, which is seen as more ecologically friendly than the carbon emitted by today's planes. [The A2] The A2 produces only water vapour and a little bit of nitrous oxide as exhaust,' Richard Varvill, technical director of Reaction Engines. 'And although a hypersonic jet loaded with liquid hydrogen might sound dangerous, hydrogen fuel is actually no more explosive than normal jet fuel.' Passengers would, however, have to live without a view of passing over the North Pole and Pacific as heat produced by the jet's high speed makes windows impracticable. Flat screen monitors instead would substitute for an actual look outside the jet. Bond said he could imagine about 10% of air travel taking place on hypersonic jets by 2033. The noise associated with supersonic speeds would prevent the jet from flying over heavily populated areas. Fares for the four-hour and 40-minute flight to Australia would be comparable with current first-class tickets on standard flights, of around 3,500 pounds (4,700 euros), researchers said. Flights from Europe to Australia now take about 22 hours. 'It sounds incredible by today's standards but I don't see why future generations can't make day trips to Australasia,' he said. 'Our work shows that it is possible technically; now it's up to the world to decide if it wants it.' (DW-World, 2008) (Figure 12.2).

Yeoman (2008) propositioned that in 2030 Gleneagles Lunar Space Station will be the world's most exclusive resort. Catching the Virgin Galactic from Auchterarder, space tourists will fasten their seat belts, hear the rockets roar and feel a sudden power acceleration of 4G. As the spaceship reaches the stratosphere, tourists gaze down on planet Earth for the most exclusive view of the world. Sound a bit far fetched? It is not. Virgin Galactic is a real proposition starting a regular passenger service from New Mexico in 2012 with celebrities and the mega-rich initially paying US$200,000 for the privilege. The experience is a 3 hour flight including 7 minutes of floatation

Figure 12.2 A2 hypersonic plane
(*Source:* Reaction Engines)

time. For US$20,000,000 Space Adventures offers tourists the experience of visiting Mir, the orbiting space station operated by the Federal Space Agency of the Russian Federation. Dennis Tito, an American businessman became their first space tourist having undergone a 5-month training course for a 10-day stay on the space station.

The future of cars

According to Horn and Docksai (2010), the US economy has continued to depend on the gasoline-fuelled, internal combustion engine for powering cars and trucks. This method is inefficient, as for every $1 that spent on gas, 85¢ is wasted in heating the engine block and the surrounding air (the reason it needs both an oil and water pump to cool it); only 15¢ goes into moving the car down the road. Electric cars have the potential of significantly reducing city pollution by having zero tail pipe emissions. Using an electric car would result in a 30% reduction in carbon dioxide emissions in the United States, 40% in the United Kingdom, 19% in China and as little as 1% in Germany, depending on the country's energy mix. Electric cars will have a major impact in the auto industry given advantages in city pollution and less dependence on oil. World governments are pledging billions to fund development of electric vehicles and their components; the United States has pledged US$2.4 billion in federal grants and China announced it will provide US$15 billion to initiate an electric car industry. Nissan CEO Carlos Ghosn has predicted that one in 10 cars globally will run on battery power alone by 2020 (Figure 12.3).

Futurists have always talked about the flying car, whether it is Chitty Chitty Bang Bang or something out of the Jetsons, but the *Terrafugia* (http://www.terrafugia.com/) is licensed by the Federal Aviation Authority as a Light Sports Aircraft and also complies with the Federal Motor Vehicle Safety Standards. Basically, it is the world's only flying car. A hydrogen vehicle is an alternative fuel vehicle that uses hydrogen as a form of fuel. The term may refer to a personal transportation vehicle, such as an automobile, or any other vehicle that uses hydrogen in a similar fashion, such as an aircraft. The power plants of such vehicles convert the chemical energy of hydrogen to mechanical energy either by burning hydrogen in an internal combustion engine, or by reacting hydrogen with oxygen in a fuel cell to run electric motors.

The future of cruise ships

Does this mean the future of cruise liners is more akin to aircraft carriers? Designed with a length of 4500 feet, a width of 750 feet and a height of 350 feet, *Freedom Ship* would be more than four times longer than the HMS Queen Mary. The design concepts include a mobile modern city featuring luxurious living, an extensive duty-free international shopping mall and a full 1.7 million square foot floor set aside for various companies

Figure 12.3 Tesla Roadster
(*Source:* Tesla)

to showcase their products. *Freedom Ship* would not be a cruise ship, but rather a unique place to live, work, retire, holiday or visit. The proposed voyage would continuously circle the globe, covering most of the world's coastal regions. Its large fleet of commuter aircraft and hydrofoils would ferry residents and visitors to and from shore. The airport on the ship's top deck would serve private and small commercial aircraft (up to about 40 passengers each). The proposed vessel's superstructure, rising 25 stories above its broad main deck, would house residential space, a library, schools and a first-class hospital in addition to retail and wholesale shops, banks, hotels, restaurants, entertainment facilities, casinos, offices, warehouses and light manufacturing and assembly enterprises. Finally, this concept would include a wide array of recreational and athletic facilities, worthy of a world-class resort, making *Freedom Ship* a veritable 'Community on the Sea' (Figure 12.4).

The bullet train

The *Shinkansen*, also known as *the bullet train*, is a network of high-speed railway lines in Japan operated by four Japan Railways Group companies.

Figure 12.4 The Freedom Ship
(*Source:* The Freedom Ship)

Starting with the *The Tōkaidō Shinkansen* in 1964, the now 2459 km (1528 miles) long network has expanded to link most major cities on the islands of Honshu and Kyushu at speeds up to 300 kmh (186 mph). Test runs have reached 443 kmh (275 mph) for conventional rail in 1996 and up to a world record of 581 kmh (361 mph) for Maglev train sets in 2003. As the world's busiest high-speed rail line, it carries 151 million passengers a year (March 2008), and has transported more passengers than any other high-speed line in the world. Between Tokyo and Osaka, the two largest metropolises in Japan, up to 10 trains per hour with 16 cars each (1300 seats capacity) run in each direction with a minimum headway of three minutes between trains, serving commuters who travel to work in metropolitan areas from outlying cities.

Given the future price of oil, bullet trains are proposed in many countries as an alternative to air transport, including a number of cluster projects in the United States; a high-speed rail link connecting Vietnam's capital, Hanoi and the southern commercial hub of Ho Chi Minh City; and linking Brazil's cities of Rio de Janeiro, Sao Paulo and Campinas.

Transrapid is a German high-speed monorail train using magnetic levitation. The superspeed Maglev system has no wheels, axles, transmissions or pantographs. It hovers using the attractive magnetic force between the two linear arrays of electromagnetic coils – one side in the vehicle, the other in the guideway – that function as a magnetic dipole. In China, the *Shanghai Maglev* connects Pudong International Airport to Shanghai via an electromagnetic reaction created between the cars and the tracks.

Concluding Thoughts

A dependency relationship

Transport and tourism are interlinked in the context of the travel industry, and are significantly affected by the availability of fuel and by climate change. The predicted decline in fuel and possible increase in fuel prices will increase the costs of travel and tourism, ultimately causing fluctuations in the future demand for tourism. Technology advancement and innovation of new forms of transport may contribute to a range of new attractions and activities for tourism. As mentioned, some forms of transport are used to engage tourists in activities, such as scenic flights. The evolvement of new technology may see transport becoming an attraction in itself, rather than the sole purpose of transport. This may include new advancements in submarines, hot-air balloons or even rockets. These transport modes may even replace current modes, such as aircrafts, to allow travel between two destinations.

Is the future oil or something else

Passenger vehicle technology is expected to remain dependent on petroleum fuels and internal combustion engines (ICE) for the foreseeable future. Enhancement of ICEs through clean diesels, hybrids and new combustion techniques will ensure increased efficiency. Alternative fuels will also increase steadily in penetration, with second-generation biofuels such as synthetic biomass-to-liquid (BTL) significantly by 2035 and synthetic gasto-liquid (GTL) already expected to grow strongly in the coming decade (Hirsch *et al.*, 2005). Hydrogen fuel and fuel cell vehicles are expected to gain a market foothold by 2035 and grow towards 2050. By 2050, gasoline and diesel fuels will still play a major role, but their biofuel portion will be significant. Electric power utilisation in transport will also increase, particularly in OECD and richer developing countries. This will be manifested as increased hybridisation with a potentially significant element of pure electric vehicles powered by batteries and/or fuel cells. Commercial vehicles comprise over 40% of land transportation energy consumption. Improvements will likely remain based on the diesel engine, with innovations such as variable valve timing and new combustion techniques. In aviation, engine and materials technologies and flight management measures will potentially be available, improving aircraft efficiency by over 30%. However, set against the expected 200% growth in air travel by 2050, efficiency improvements can serve only to dampen the increase in consumption. Aviation fuel presents a particular opportunity for alternative fuels, since aviation fuel (kerosene) can be, and is already made using the synthetic F–T process, which can use gas, coal or biomass as a feedstock.

With substantial projected economic growth over the next 43 years, improvement in transport energy sustainability is required and break-throughs in technology will be necessary by 2050. For example, hydrogen fuel cells and battery electric vehicles can contribute significantly only if high costs and consumer's performance demands are met. Air travel is pro-jected to grow significantly faster than all other personal travel modes between 2000 and 2050, at 3.3% per annum in passenger/km terms. Its pro-portion of global transportation energy consumption is predicted to rise from 12% to 18% indicating that any effort taken to reduce either total transport energy growth or the total transport energy consumption must take aviation into account. However, these technical solutions appear able only to dampen the growth in aviation energy demand as only technologies that are economically viable will be implemented, a factor highly influenced by petroleum prices. Oil is the critical issue for the future of tourism.

How we travel

With concerns over the environmental impact of air travel or the lack of an alternative to oil in the aviation sector, there are concerns that the future of tourism will be based more on land transport than air transport. So, does this mean the demise of intercontinental travel or the reversal in fortunes when only the rich (or super rich) could afford to holiday in far-away places such as Kenya, Hawaii or Patagonia? On the road to 2050, will the individual be given a personal carbon or travel allowance in which they could swap, trade or save up for that once in a lifetime intercontinental holiday? As the importance of sustainability grows in consumers' lives, is there a realisation that the collective good overrides individual's right to travel? Yeoman (2008) suggests that the critical issue of environment is changing behaviour, whether it is the rise of the slow travel movement, penalties for inefficiencies, congestion charges or the surge in the use of bicycles in many cities.

Afterword 1

Travel and Tourism in 2050

Examining the landscape of travel and tourism in 2050 is in many respects an exploration of the possibilities and scenarios for how the world itself may develop. Indeed, we cannot envisage the future of travel without thinking about the changes that we could see in terms of the map of the world, the shape of the economy, the impact of globalisation, the evolution of financial systems and personal finances, developments in societal values and expectations and advances in technology.

When we think about a 40-year horizon we have to consider the possibility that national boundaries may have changed, states may have merged and new political groupings emerged on the world stage. There are also many scenarios for how the global economy itself may have evolved. For example, could we see a single electronic global currency, would future financial disasters lead to radical reshaping of banking systems and how will the philosophies of the new power brokers from the east influence the shape of global financial institutions?

One question we might ask is whether the forces of globalisation will have eliminated the differences between destinations, raising the question 'how is anywhere different from here?' While tourism has become more accessible, it is still dependent on the individual traveller having the income and wealth to finance their aspirations. Hence, we have to ask how the nature of work, incomes and personal finances may have evolved over the next four decades. Will poverty have been eradicated – making travel accessible to all? In which case how will we cope with the impact of 9 billion wanting to travel; what would be the demand on our environmental resources, could our infrastructures cope and how would the citizenry of the most popular destinations cope with such an influx? Alternatively, if income disparities have grown and there is a major gap between the haves and have nots – will travel be seen as a luxury only for the wealthiest?

We also have to ask the question of how the societal role of vacations will change. Will environmental factors lead us to ostracise those who travel and thus consume more than their fair share of resources and contribute to greenhouse gas emissions? Alternatively will those who travel and gain a range of life experiences be valued more by society? Could environmental pressures lead to travel itself being rationed – with destinations limiting the number of visitors and only allowing access to the highest spenders?

Technology will also play a huge influencing role in shaping the future of travel. Some colleagues in the futures world believe that by 2050 we will have reached the point where human have been 'enhanced' with technology enabling our brains to interact directly with the internet. If this happens, could environmentally driven travel restrictions mean that the majority of us can only access new destinations by downloading someone else's experiences?

Finally, we have to think about travel technology itself and how it might have evolved. Will hypersonic flight have moved from the military to the commercial domain – enabling us to fly from Auckland to London in 3–4 hours? How will the notion of hotels have evolved? Will 'pop up' hotels become more common; erected and dismantled quickly for the holiday season and then rotated between destinations as their popularity waxes and wanes?

One could go on highlighting the scenarios, questions and possibilities that could shape the future of travel. There are clearly multiple drivers, complex issues and intricate inter-relationships shaping that future. Rather than throw our hands up in the air and say it is all too complicated, I am delighted that Ian Yeoman has taken on the challenge of acting as our tour guide on an exploration of how the travel landscape could evolve out to 2050.

Rohit Talwar
CEO
Fast Future Research
London

Afterword 2

Anticipating the Future of Tourism

According to Joel Arthur Barker, there are three keys to the future of any organisation: anticipation, innovation and excellence. Excellence is at the end of this list as it is the necessary price of entry. Innovation is the way to gain competitive edge. Anticipation provides the information that allows a business or organisation with its excellent and innovative product to be in the right time at the right place (Barker, 1993).

One of the options for a tourism organisation to deal with the future is to *react* to currently ongoing developments and the changes that they generate. As the post-war baby boom generation is gradually retiring, about 120,000 people will leave the labour market each year in the Netherlands, according to Johan Kasper, scenario planner at the European Tourism Futures Institute in a study he is currently working on. This will have major consequences. Do we have to fill the vacancies with migrant labourers? Or do we have to invest to combat the consequences of such a development? The ageing of the population in the north of the Netherlands will cause significant shifts in the consumer market. How should the zoo in Emmen react to a change from young families with children to elderly coming by e-bike or rollator? The fringes of the North Netherlands begin to experience the first signals of population decline. Many facilities are in the red zone. How should the region deal with such changes? Are investments needed to maintain the quality of life in the villages, or should the attention be focused to the major towns and cities? The increase of shopping on the internet has an enormous impact on the number of visitors of inner cities. Last year, some cities in the Netherlands saw a decline of about 40%! How should such towns deal with these developments? How can a city like Leeuwarden maintain its social and economic function? These are some of the key issues and drivers that will impact on the future of leisure and tourism in the north of the Netherlands, investigated by the European Tourism Futures Institute.

However, there are also developments that cannot be foreseen, are not foreshadowed by trends and we cannot react upon. These developments have to be anticipated *pro-actively*. Such anticipations are affected by three major concerns. Firstly, we have to realise that we live in exponential times (Fisch *et al.*, 2005). Wubbo Ockels shares his expectations about the exponential growth of solar energy production: 'although in 2010 0.003% of the energy generated on earth was produced by solar panels, the production is expected to double each year. If it does, the first years the production increase will hardly be noticeable, but within 10 years time the production will have passed the level of 100%' (Ockels, 2011). Secondly, we also have to take into account the unexpected. Events such as the attack on the Twin Towers, by the man who put himself on fire in Tunisia, and the earthquake and tsunami in Japan make us realise that we also have to face discontinuity in the developments that have given us comfort and security. Last but not least, we have to realise that we are imprisoned in our paradigms, which prevents us from seeing new opportunities.

To be able to anticipate changes and developments, whether they can be predicted based on early warning signals or not, will be a matter of continuous monitoring of what is happening in the world around us. But we also need to stimulate our creativity to image ourselves possible futures of leisure and tourism and to invent or develop new leisure, service, business or regional concepts that are based on these pictures. As humans beings we have learned to use only a minor fraction of our brains. Our innate creativity has been reduced by our parents and teachers from 100% at birth to 95% during infant school to 10% among adults! (Buzan, 2010).

Creativity and imagination can be stimulated in networks, communities of practice and meshworks (Center for Human Emergence Netherlands, 2010) in which actors in the tourism business or tourism organisation can interact to exchange information, cooperate and learn from each other. Such platforms are the breeding places for innovation and excellence anticipating the future. Here, Ian Yeoman's book *2050: Tomorrow's Tourism* and his seminal book *Tomorrow's Tourist* (2008) mean a significant contribution to imagining, discussing and debating the possible futures of tourism.

Albert Postma
Professor Scenario Planning
European Tourism Futures Institute
(www.etfi.eu)

References

Aeros (2006) Worldwide Aeros selects Wimberly Allison Tong & Goo (WATG) for interior design of airborne cruise ships. 20 January. Accessed 20th September 2011 at www.dexigner.com/news/6764

Anderson, C. (2007) *The Long Tail: Why the Future of Business Is Selling Less of More*. London: Random House.

Anderson, C. (2008) *Long Tail: The Revised and Updated Edition: Why the Future of Business is Selling Less of More*. London: Hyperion.

Anderson, P. and Kumar, R. (2006) Emotions, trust and relationship development in business relationships: A conceptual model of buyer–seller dyads. *Industrial Marketing Management* 35, 522–535.

Arup (2005) *Arup unveils plans for the world's first sustainable city in Dongtan, China*. Press Release 24 August 2005, accessed 22 June 2009. http://www.arup.com/arup/news item.cfm?pageid=7009

Ashby, A. (2010) *Dreams Uses Augmented Reality in Santander Visitor's Centre Installation*. 15 November.

Ashworth, G.J. and Tunbridge, J.E. (2000) *Retrospect and Prospect on the Tourist Historic City*. Oxford: Elsevier.

Asthana, A. (2007) *Amsterdam closes a window on its red-light tourist trade. Observer*, accessed 26 September 2007. http://www.guardian.co.uk/travel/2007/sep/23/travelnews.amsterdam

Audi, T. (2009) Government meetings: Stay away from sin city. *USA Today*, accessed 12 February 2010. http://online.wsj.com/article/SB124822843228670879.html

Australian Interactive Media Industry Association (2009) *Australian Mobile Phone Lifestyle Index* (5th edn). Sydney: Australian Interactive Media Industry Association (AIMIA).

Avila, G. and Hinestroza, P. (2008) Tough cotton. *Nature Nanotechnology* 3, 458–459.

Balassa, B. (1964) The purchasing power parity doctrine: An reappraisal. *Journal of Political Economy* 72, 584–596.

Bapat, S. (2009) Modern trends in medical education: A critical appraisal. *Kathmandu University Medical Journal* 7, 330–330.

Barber, T. (2004) A pleasure prophecy: Predictions for the sex tourist of the future. In D. Waskul (ed.) *Net.SeXXX: Readings on Sex, Pornography and the Internet* (Chapter 15, pp. 323–336). New York: Peter Lang Publishers.

Barboza, D. (2010) *Market Defies Fear of Real Estate Bubble in China*. 4 March. Accessed 4th April 2011 at www.nytimes.com.

BBC (2004) *Hourglass fertily link*, accessed 24 September 2004. http://news.bbc.co.uk/2/hi/health/3682657.stm

Becken, S. (2008) Developing indicators for managing tourism in the face of peak oil. *Tourism Management* 29, 695–705.

Becken, S. (2010) *The Future of Oil*. Victoria Management School Seminar Series, Wellington, 28 July.

Bell, D. and Valentine, G. (1997) *Consuming Geographies: We Are Where We Eat*. London: Routledge.

Benotsch, E., Somlai, A.M., Pinkerton, D., Kelly, J.A., Ostrovski, D., Gore-Felton, C. and Kozlov, A.P. (2004) Drug use and sexual risk behaviors among female Russian IDUs who exchange sex for money or drugs. *International Journal of STD and AIDS* 15, 343 – 347.

Beresford (2006) *Use of online social media*, accessed 10 August 2011. http://www.beresfordresearch.com

Berghaus, G. (2009) *Futurism and Technological Imagination*. Amsterdam: Rodopi.

Bergman, A., Karlsson, J. and Axelsson, J. (2010) Truth claims and explanatory claims – An ontological typology of future studies. *Futures* 42, 857–865.

Berry, C.J. (1994) *The Idea of Luxury: A Conceptual and Historical Investigation*. Cambridge, MA: Cambridge University Press.

Bjorkman, I. and Kock, S. (1995) Social relationships and business networks: The case of Western companies in China. *International Business Review* 4, 519–535.

Blackman, C. (1994) From forecasting to informed choices. *Futures* 26, 3.

Blanco, A. (2010) *The Future of Biometrics*, accessed 23 February 2011. http://www.securityworldnews.com/2010/02/07/the-future-of-biometrics/

Bloom, D. (2011) 7 Billion and counting. *Science* 333, 562–569.

Bluhm, H. and Siegmann, H.C. (2009) Surface science with aerosols. *Surface Science* 603, 1969–1987.

Boeing (2010) *Market outlook, 2009–2029*, accessed 10 December 2011. http://www.boeing.com/commercial/cmo/

Bonsor, K. (2009) *How augmented reality really works*, accessed on 21 February 2011. http://computer.howstuffworks.com/augmented-reality1.htm

Bourdieu, P. and Nice, R. (1987) *Distinction: A Social Critique of the Judgement of Taste*. Boston: Harvard Business Press.

Brand, S. (2010) *Whole Earth Discipline: Why Dense Cities, Nuclear Power, Transgenic Crops, Restored Wildlands, and Geoengineering Are Necessary*. London: Penguin Books.

Brants, C. (1998) The fine art of regulated tolerance: Prostitution in Amsterdam. *Journal of Law and Society* 25, 621–635.

Breazal, C. (2004) Function meets style: Insights from emotion theory applied to HRI. *IEEE Transaction on Machine, Cybernetics and Systems* 34, 135–142.

Brents, B. and Hausbeck, K. (2007) Marketing sex: US legal brothels and late capitalist consumption. *Sexualities* 10, 425–439.

Brock, A. (2006) *Understanding Moore's Law*. New York: Chemical Heritage Foundation.

Brumfiel, G. (2009) *Atom takes a Quantum leap*, accessed 10 December 2010. http://www.nature.com/news/2009/090122/full/news.2009.50.html

Bryant, C. (1982) *Sexual Deviancy and Social Proscription*. New York: Human Sciences Press.

Buhalis, D. (2009) Personal communication on owner-trinet-l@HAWAII.EDU discussion board.

Caidin, M. (1975) *The Six Million Dollar Man*. New York: Star Books.

Caryl, C. (2007) Even hermits can get rich. *Newsweek*, accessed 15 October 2010. http://www.newsweek.com/2007/11/10/even-hermits-can-get-rich.html

Campbell, R. (1998) Invisible men: Making visible male clients of female prostitutes. In J. Elais, V. Bullough, V. Elias and G. Brewer (eds) *Prostitution: On Whores, Hustlers and Johns*. New York: Prometheus Books.

CapGemini & Merrill Lynch (2009) *World wealth report*, accessed 20 September 2009. http://www.capgemini.com/resources/thought_leadership/2009_world_wealth_report/

Cetron, M. (2008) *Vision: Teleportation; beam me up, DARPA*, accessed 10 December 2010. http://www.allbusiness.com/science-technology/experimentation-research-defense/11580911-1.htm

Chamberlain, K. (2004) Food and health: Expanding the agenda for health psychology. *Journal of Health Psychology* 9, 467–481.

Chand, K. and Jaeger, A. (1996) Ageing populations and public pension schemes. *IMF Occasional Paper 147*, accessed 26 September 2011. http://www.imf.org/external/pubs/nft/op/147/index.htm

Chandler, T. (2010) *Your vital signs on camera*, accessed 27 Febraury 2011. http://web.mit.edu/newsoffice/2010/pulse-camera-1004.html

Channel News Asia (2001) *Being there even when you are not.* 6 February. Accessed on 4th April 2011 at www.channelnewasia.com

Channel News Asia (2011) Tablets, smartphones to outsell PCs: Deloitte. 10 February. Accessed on 5th April 2011 at www.reuters.com

Chen, G. and Richardson, A. (2010) Fast food giant McDonald's Corp is finding a new role for itself in Hong Kong – As a wedding planner. 16 October.

China Business Times (2011) Property tax aims to squeeze real estate bubble. 5 January.

Christensen, B. (2006) Military cyborg sharks. *LiveScience*, accessed 7 June 2009. http://www.livescience.com/technology/060307_shark_implant.html

CIA (2010) *World fact book*, accessed 5 November 2010. https://www.cia.gov/library/publications/the-world-factbook/

citizenM (2011) *Company Info*, accessed 10 February 2011. http://www.citizenm.com/about-hotel-group.php

Claytronics (2011) *About claytronics*, accessed 2 February 2011. http://www.cs.cmu.edu/~claytronics/claytronics/index.html

CLIA (2008) *Cruise market profile*, accessed 20 December 2010. http://www.cruising.org/vacation/node/251

Clift, S. and Carter, S. (2000) *Tourism and Sex: Culture, Commerce and Coercion*. Oxford: Pinter.

Clynes, M. and Klines, N. (1960) Cyborgs and space. *Astronautics* Sept, 26–27 and 74–75.

Cohen, J. (2003) Human population: The next half century. *Science* 302, 1172–1175.

Coleman, J. (2009) Speech to Victoria University Tourism Management students. 15th March 2009. New Zealand Parliament, Wellington. Jonathon Coleman is the Associate Minister for Tourism in the New Zealand government.

Connell, R. (2004) *Rent-a-doll hooker market wide open*, accessed 28 September 2009. http://whoeverfightsmonsters-nhuthnance.blogspot.com/2007/07/man-made-woman.html

Consumers International (2007) *Drugs, Doctors and Dinners*, accessed 12 December 2007. http://www.marketingoverdose.org/documents/ci_pharma_2007.pdf

Cosmetic Surgery Review (2008) *1 in 5 Americans will receive aesthetic cosmetic procedures in 2015*, accessed 14 September 2009. http://cosmeticsurgerytoday.wordpress.com/2008/06/26/1-in-5-americans-will-receive-aesthetic-cosmetic-procedures-in-2015/

Counihan, C. and Van Esterik, P. (2007) *Food and Culture: A Reader*. London: Routledge.

Crawford, A. (1998) Rugby in contemporary New Zealand. *Journal of Sport and Social Issues* 12, 108–120.

Crawford, R. (1980) Healthism and the medicalisation of everyday life. *International Journal of Health Services* 10, 365–388.

Crowle, J. and Turner, E. (2010) *Childhood obesity. Australian government productivity commission: Canberra*, accessed 1 November 2010. http://www.pc.gov.au/_data/assets/pdf_file/0016/103309/01-preliminaries.pdf

CTTC (2007) *Strategic marketing plan. California travel and tourism commission, Sacramento*, accessed 22 July 2009. http://tourism.visitcalifornia.com/b2b/PDF/5YEARPLAN.pdf

Darcy, S. (2010) Inherent complexity: Disability, accessible tourism and accommodation information preferences. *Tourism Management* 31, 816–826.

Davies, K. (1937) The sociology of prostitution. *American Sociological Review* 2, 744–755.

de Graaf, R.E., van de Gieson, F. and van de Ven, F. (2007) The closed city as a strategy to reduce vulnerability of urban areas for climate change. *Water Science & Technology* 56, 165–173.

DeLamater, J. (1989) The social control of human sexuality. In K. McKinney and S. Sprecher (eds) *Human Sexuality: The Societal and Interpersonal Context* (pp. 30–62). Norwood: Ablex.

Denman, S. (2010) The nano man. 17 February. Accessed 5th April 2011 at www.constructionweekonline.com/article-7592-the-nano-man

Department of Water Resources (2009a) *California Water Draft*, accessed 28 June 2009. http://www.waterplan.water.ca.gov/cwpu2009/index.cfm#volume1

Department of Water Resources (2009b) *California's Drought: Water Conditions & Strategies to Reduce Impacts*. Report to the Governor. 30 March

Desponier, D. (2010) *The vertical farm: Reducing the impact of agriculture on ecosystem functions and services*, accessed on 10 November 2010. http://www.verticalfarm.com/more?essay1

Dodds, R. (2009) *The Future of Sustainable Tourism*. 25 May. Video Conferencing Lecture, Victoria University of Wellington. http://mdsweb.vuw.ac.nz/Mediasite/Viewer/Viewers/ViewerVideoOnly.aspx?mode=Default&peid=0089b586-d9b5-458f-9ce2-9392167cc842&pid=e969d88d-96e9-4947-a64c-1511c4b576a9&playerType=WM7

Dodman, D. (2009) Blaming cities for climate change? An analysis of urban greenhouse gas. *Environment and Urbanisation* 21,193–215.

Drillinger, M. (2010) Comfort, not modernity, is the new wave. 1 October. Accessed 5th April 2011 at www.hotelmanagement.net/bath/comfort-not-modernate-new-wave.

Drum, R. and Gordon, R. (2003) Star trek replicators and diatom nanotechnology. *Trends in Biotechnology* 21, 325–328.

Drummond, K. (2009) Pentagon preps soldier telepathy push. 14 May. Accessed 5th April 2011 at www.wired.com/dangerroom/2009/05/pentagon-preps-soldier-telepathy-push/

DW-World (2008) *Hypersonic travel*, accessed 30 December 2010. http://www.dw-world.de/dw/article/0,3109529,00.html

Eagleton, T. (1997) Edible Ecriture. *The Times Higher Education Supplement* 24 October, No. 1303.

East Day (2010) *Land price for homes climb 50%*, accessed 10 February 2011. http://english.eastday.com/e/101225/u1a5630479.html

Economist (2012) Wolfgangs woes. *Economist* 20 February 2012, accessed 22 February 2012. http://www.economist.com

Elliot, A. (2008) *Making the Cut: How Cosmetic Surgery Is Transforming Our Lives*. London: Reaktion Books.

Elliott, M. (2009) *Sport: An untapped asset. World Economic Forum*, accessed 7 June 2009. http://www.weforum.org/en/knowledge/Events/2009/AnnualMeeting/KN_SESS_SUMM_27356?url=/en/knowledge/Events/2009/AnnualMeeting/KN_SESS_SUMM_27356

Ellmann, M. (1993) *The Hunger Artists: Starving, Writing and Imprisonment*. Cambridge: Harvard University Press.

Ervin, R., Wright, J. and Kennedy-Stevenson, J. (1999) Use of dietary supplements in the United States, 1988–94. *Vital Health Statistics* 244, 1–14.

European Travel Commission (2007) *ETC Market Insights: India*, March 2007, accessed 10 December 2007. http://www.etccorporate.org/resources/uploads/ETCProfile_India_6_07.pdf

Evans, A. (2008) *Rising Food Prices*. London: Chatham House, accessed 5 November 2010. www.chatham.org.uk

Evans, A. (2009) *The Feeding of Nine Billion: Food Security for the 21st Century*. London: Chatham House, accessed 10 October 2010. www.chathouse.org.uk

Faruque, H. and Mühleisen, M. (2003) Population ageing in Japan: Demographic shock and fiscal sustainability. *Japan and the World Economy* 15, 185–210.

Fildes, J. (2010) HP Outlines memory of the future. 8 April. Accessed on 5th April 2011 at www.news.bbc.co.uk/2/hi/8609885.stm

Fitzpatrick, M. (2010) Smart specs unite world and data. 8 October. Accessed on 5th April 2011 at www.bbc.com/news/technology-1149429

Flatters, P. (2009) *Demography: A Draft Report Trajectory Group*. London: Trajectory Group.

Flatters, P. and Wilmott, M. (2009) Understanding the post recession consumer. *Harvard Business Review*. July–August, 106–112.

Fraunhofer-Gesellschaft (2009) *Artificial skin manufactured in fully automated Process*, accessed 24th September 2009. http://www.sciencedaily.com/releases/2009/05/090518102959.htm

Freitas, R. (2010) The future of nanomedicine. *The Futurist* 44, 18–21.

Frost and Suillvan (2009) *Invest Frost automotive and transportation, January*, accessed 10 September 2010. http://www.frost.com

Fullerton, D., Leicester, A. and Smith, S. (2008) Environmental taxes. *NBER Working Paper* No. 14197. July, accessed 23 July 2009. http://www.nber.org/papers/w14197

Furedi, F. (1997) *The Culture of Fear*. London: Continuum Books.

Furedi, F. (2006) *Culture of Fear Revisited: Risk-taking and the Morality of Low Expectation*. London: Continuum.

Future Foundation (2007) *NVision Central Scenario UK*. London: Future Foundation.

Future Foundation (2011) *New middle classes*, accessed 11 October 2011. http://www.futurefoundation.net

Galli, C., Lagutina, I., Crotti, G., Colleoni, S., Turini, P., Ponderato, N., Duchi, R. and Giovanna, L. (2003) Pregnancy: A cloned horse born to its dam twin. *Nature* 424, accessed 7 June 2011. http://www.nature.com/nature/journal/v424/n6949/full/424635a.html

Gamboa, H. and Fred, A. (2004) A behavioural biometric system based on human computer interaction. *Proceedings of SPIE* 5404, 381–392.

Gavin, L. (2009) *BT futurologist: We're living in sci-fi*, accessed 20 March 2011. http://www.guardian.co.uk/media/pda/2009/jul/23/bt-futurologist-science-fiction

Gehrels, C., Munster, O., Pen, M., Prins, M. and Thevent, J. (2004) *Choosing Amsterdam*. Amsterdam: Visit Amsterdam.

Giddens, A. (1991) *Modernity and Self Identity: Self and Society in the Late Modern Age*. Cambridge: Polity Press.

Gilfoyle, T. (1994) *City of Eros: New York City, Prostitution, and the Commercialization of Sex, 1790–1920*. Bloomington: Norton & Co.

Goertzel, B. (2009) *Brain–Computer Interfacing: from Prosthetic Limbs to Telepathy Chips*, accessed 1 March 2011. http://hplusmagazine.com/2009/07/13/brain-computer-interfacing-prosthetic-limbs-telepathy-chips/

Goldenberg, S. (2009) *California poised to shut gates on great outdoors as parks struggle with budgets*. 12th July, accessed 11 August 2011. http://www.guardian.co.uk/world/2009/jul/12/california-parks-budget-deficit

Goldstein, S., Lee, P., Pillai, P. and Campbell, J. (2009) *A tale of two planners: Modular robotic planning with LDP*, accessed 7 December 2010. http://www.cs.cmu.edu/~claytronics/papers/derosa-iros09.pdf

Gomes, L. (2010) Google translate tangles with computer learning. *Forbes Magazine* July 22.

Gray, C. (1995) *The Cyborg Handbook*. London: Routledge.

Greenfield, A. (2006) *Everyware: The Dawning Age of Ubiquitous Computing*. New York: New Riders.

Grimm, B., Lohmann, M., Heinsohn, K., Richter, C. and Metzler, D. (2009) The impact of demographic change on tourism and conclusions for tourism policy. A study commissioned by the Federal Ministry of Economics and Technology. Accessed 1 July 2010. http://www.bmwi.de/BMWi/Redaktion/PDF/Publikationen/Studien/aus wirkungen-demographischer-wandel-tourismus-kurzfassung-englisch,property=pdf, bereich=bmwi,sprache=de,rwb=true.pdf

Guthrie, J., Lin, B-H. and Frazao, E. (2002) Role of food prepared away from home in the American diet, 1977–78 versus 1994–96: Changes and consequences. *Journal of Nutrition Education and Behaviour* 34, 140–150.

Guttentag, D. (2009) Virtual reality: Applications and implications for tourism. *Tourism Management* 31, 637–651.

Halfacree, G. (2010) *Intel claims optical computing "milestone"*. July 28.

Hall, K. (2009) *World cup a $1.25 boost*. *Dominion Post*, accessed 7 June 2009. http://www.stuff.co.nz/business/industries/2271271/World-Cup-a-1-25b-boo-s-t

Hall, C.M., Sharples, L., Mitchell, R., Macionis, N. and Cambourne, B. (2003) *Food Tourism around the World: Development, Management and Marketing*. Oxford: Butterworth-Heinemann.

Haraway, D. (1991) *A Cyborg Manifesto: Science, Technology and Socialst-Feminism in the Late Twentieth Century. Simians, Cyborgs and Women: The Reinvention of Nature*. New York: Routledge. First published in the *Socialist Review* 1985: 149–181.

Harcourt, C. and Donovan, B. (2005) The many faces of sex work. *Sexually Transmitted Diseases* 81, 201–206.

Harris, W. (2011) *How haptic technology works*, accessed 2 March 2011. http://electronics.howstuffworks.com/gadgets/other-gadgets/haptic-technology.htm

Harrison, M. (2006) Learning lessons for the future. In T. Hampson (ed.) *2025: What Next for the Make Poverty History Generation*. London: Fabian Society.

Haru (2010) *About Campaign*, accessed 2 March 2011. http://www.haru2010.com/eng/index.html#/about/

Hatton, C. (2009) The future of technology. *Tourism Futures Proceeding*. Goldcoast 18th August.

Hayhoe, K., Cayanc, S., Field, C., Frumhoffe, P., Maurerf, E., Miller, N., Moser, S., Schneideri, S., Cahild, N., Clelandd, E., Daleg, L., Drapek, R., Hanemann, M., Kalksteinl, L., Lenihan, J., Lunch, C., Neilsonj, R., Sheridan, S. and Verville, J. (2004) Emissions pathways, climate change and impacts on California. *Proceedings of the National Academy of Sciences, USA* 101, 12422–12427.

HCEA (2009) *Top healthcare meetings and destinations*, accessed 10 January 2010. http://www.hcea.org/

HCEA (2011) *Top healthcare meeting and destinations*, accessed 10 May 2011. http://hcea.org

Healy, K. (2002) *Minority report's vision of the future*, accessed 13 March 2011. http://www.kieranhealy.org/blog/archives/2002/06/30/minority-reports-vision-of-the-future/

Heinlein, R., Davenport, B., Kornbluth, A., Bester, A. and Bloch, R. (1959) *The Science Fiction Novel: Imagination and Social Criticism*. University of Chicago: Advent Publishers.

Helford, E. (2006) The Stepford Wives and the gaze. *Feminist Media Studies* 6, 145–156.

HKTDC (2010) *Shanghai Municipality*, accessed 10 February 2011. http://www.hktdc.com/info/mi/a/mpcn/en/1X06BVOR/1/Profiles-Of-China-Provinces-Cities-And-Ind ustrial-Parks/SHANGHAI-MUNICIPALITY.htm

Hillsley, C. (2004) *Haptics technology makes the impossible possible*. 27 May. Accessed on 10th May 2011 at www.reading.ac.uk/news-and-events/release/PR11.aspx

Hirsch, R., Bezdek, R. and Wendling, R. (2005) *Peaking of world oil production: Impacts, mitigation and risk management*, accessed 10 October 2011. http://www.netl.doe.gov/publications/others/pdf/oil_peaking_NETL.pdf

Hochberg, L.R., Serruya, M.D., Friehs, G.M., Mukand, J.A., Saleh, M., Caplan, A.H., Branner, A., Chen, D., Penn, R.D. and Donoghue, J.P. (2006) Neuronal ensemble control of prosthetic devices by a human with tetraplegia. *Nature* 442, 164–171.

Hodson, M. and Marvin, S. (2009) Urban ecological security: A new urban paradigm. *International Journal of Urban & Regional Research* 33, 193–215.

Hoffman, D. (2005) Freud's theories about sex as relevant as ever. *Psychiatric News* 40, 18.

Honda (2009) *AMISO*, accessed 24 September 2009. http://world.honda.com/ASIMO/technology/intelligence.html

Horn, M. and Docksai, R. (2010) *Roadmap to the electric car*, accessed 10 December 2010. http://findarticles.com/p/articles/mi_go2133/is_201003/ai_n52370706/

Horng, J.-S. and Tsai, C-T. (2009) Government websites for promoting East Asian culinary tourism: A cross national analysis. *Tourism Management* 31, 74–85.

Horwath (2010a) China hotel profitability slumps: Howarth HTL. July 1.

Horwath (2010b) Hotel Market Sentiment Report – China. *Horwath HTL Newsletter Edition* 4, 1–10.

Hosansky, T. (2009) Bay state bans gifts. *Medical Meeetings* 36, accessed 12 December 2009. http://meetingsnet.com/medicalmeetings/0601-massachusetts-marketing-code/

Howells, D. (2009) *Adam Greenfield on the Elements of a Networked Urbanism*, accessed 19 February 2011. http://archive.danielhowells.net/blog/view/adam-greenfield-on-the-elements-of-a-networked-urbanism/

Howell, S., Sear, J. and Young, J. (2004) Cardiovascular medicine and Moore's Law. *British Journal of Anaesthesia* 93, 1–2.

Human Productivity Labs (2010) *Telepresence consultancy*, accessed 5 September. http://www.humanproductivitylab.com/en/category/telepresence-consulting/

HVS (2011) *China Hotel Investment Watch 2010*. Beijing: HVS.

ICCA (2011) *The International Association Meetings Market 1998–2010*, accessed 10 October 2011. http://www.iccaworld.com

IEA (2005) *Energy Prices and Taxes*. Paris: International Energy Agency.

IEA (2007) *World Energy Outlook*. Paris: International Energy Agency.

IEA (2009) *World Energy Projections 2009*, accessed 5 December 2010. http://www.eia.doe.gov/oiaf/ieo/excel/figure_14data.xls

Inayatullah, S. (2002) Reductionism or layered complexity? The future of Futures Studies. *Futures* 34, 295–302.

Intel (2005) *Moore's Law 40th Anniversary: Excerpts from 'A Conversation with Gordon Moore: Moore's Law'*, accessed 20 February 2011. http://www.intel.com/pressroom/kits/events/moores_law_40th/

iPhoneTechZone (2009) *Youngest Apple iPhone developer: Lim Ding Wen*, accessed 26 February 2011. http://www.iphonetechzone.com/2009/02/youngest-apple-iphone-developer-lim-ding-wen/

IRB (2009) *2011 Rugby World Cup*, accessed 7 June 2009. http://www.rugbyworldcup.com/

Isabel, B. (2009) Online Travel: The Internet is the key sales channel for tour operators. *ITB Berlin Special Press Release* March, 1–9.

Jackson, S. and Hokowhiti, B. (2002) Sports, tribes and technology: The New Zealand all Blacks Haka and the politics of identity. *Journal of Sport and Social Issues* 26, 125–129.

Jain, A.K., Ross, A. and Prabhakar, S. (2004) An introduction to biometric recognition. *IEEE Transactions on Circuits and Systems for Video Technology, Special Issue on Image- and Video-Based Biometrics* 14, 1–29.

James, C. (2003) *Global Status of Commercialized Transgenic Crops*, accessed 10th November 2010. http://www.isaaa.org/Kc/Publications/pdfs/isaaabriefs/Briefs%2030.pdf

Jelliffe, D.B. (1967) Parallel food classifications in developing and industrialized countries. *The American Journal of Clinical Nutrition* 20, 279–281.

Jenkins, R. (2002) *Pierre Bourdieu*. London: Routlege.

June, L. (2009) *DARPA working on 'Silent Talk' telepathic communication for soldiers*. 14 May.

Juricich, R. (2008) *Scenarios. Department of Water Resources*, accessed 28 June 2011. http://www.waterplan.water.ca.gov/scenarios/index.cfm

Kaku, M. (2011) *Physics of the Future: How Science Will Shape Human Destiny and Our Daily Lives by the Year 2100*. London: Allen Lane.

Kavaratzis, M. and Ashworth, G. (2006) Changing the tide: The campaign to re-brand Amsterdam. *Working Paper, University of Groningen*, accessed 26 September 2011. http://www-sre.wu-wien.ac.at/ersa/ersaconfs/ersa06/papers/346.pdf

Keim, B. (2009) *Designer babies: A right to choose. Wired*, accessed 7 June. www.wired.com/wiredscience/2009/03/designerdebate

Keller, J. (2009) *An interdisciplinary incubator*, accessed 24 September 2009. http://gsas.tufts.edu/1176473084631/GSAS-Page-gsas2w_1215594031419.html

Kersey, J. (2008) *Companies worldwide rely on Polycom video and telepresence to cut carbon emissions for a greener planet*, accessed 5 September 2010. http://www.polycom.com/company/news_room/press_releases/2008/20080605_1.html

King, M. (2003) *The Penguin History of New Zealand*. Auckland: Penguin Books (NZ) Ltd.

Kinsey, A. (1998) *Sexual Behavior in the Human Male*. Bloomington: Indiana University Press.

Kirkpatrick, M. (2010) *Internet of things*, accessed 10 December 2010. http://www.readwriteweb.com/archives/internet_of_things_explained_video_intro.php#

Klein, R.A. (2011) The cruise sector and it's environmental impact. *Tourism and the Implications of Climate Change: Issues and Actions* 3, 113–130.

Koedijk, F., Vriend, H., Vennea and Van, M. (2009) HIV and sexually transmitted infections in the Netherlands. Epidemiology and surveillance, Centre for Infectious Disease Control. *The Hague*. Report – RIVM-report 210261005.

Koga, T., Suzuki, K., Hirokawa, J., Ogawa, H. and Matsuhira, N. (2007) ApriAlpha V3 – Sharp ear robot – And the omni-directional auditory process. *SICE-ICASE, 2006. International Joint Conference*, Corporate Res. & Dev. Center, TOSHIBA Corp, 18–21 October.

Korea Tourism Organisation (2010) *Yoo family*, accessed 5 November 2010. http://english.visitkorea.or.kr/enu/SI/SI_EN_3_1_1_1.jsp?cid=617194

Krautkraemer, J. (2005) *Economics of Natural Resource Scarcity: The State of the Debate*. Washington: Resources for the Future.

Kuoni (2008) *Kouni Long Haul Travel Report*, accessed 10 December 2010. http://www.kuoni.co.uk/en/services/about_kuoni/news/reports/pages/longhaulreport2007.aspx

Kurzweil, R. (2005) *The Singularity is Near*. New York: Penguin Books.

Laar, M. van de, Boer, I.M. de, Koedijk F. and Coul, E. (2005) *HIV and sexually transmitted infections in the Netherlands in 2004. An update: November 2005*, accessed 26 September 2009. http://www.rivm.nl/bibliotheek/rapporten/441100022.html

Large, H. and Meier, L. (2009) *The New Middle Classes: Globalizing Lifestyles, Consumption and Environmental Concern*. London: Springer.

Larsen, J., Axhausen, K. and Urry, J. (2006) Geographies of social networks: meetings, travel and communications. *Mobilities* 1, 261–283.

Lee, M.-J. Popkins, B. and Lim, S. (2002) The unique aspects of the nutrition transition in South Korea: The retention of healthful elements in their traditional diet. *Public Health Nutrition* 5, 197–203.

Leeb, R., Doron, F., Muller-Putz, G.R., Scherer, R., Salter, M. and Pfurtscheller, G. (2007) Self-packed asynchronous BCI control of a wheelchair in virtual environments: A case study with a tetraplegic. *Computational Intelligence and Neuroscience* April 2007, 1–8.

Levy, D. (2007) *Love+Sex with Robots*. New York: Harper Perennail.

Levy, D. (2009) *Robot prostitutes as alternatives to human sex workers*, accessed 29 September 2009. www.roboethics.org/.../LEVY%20Robot%20Prostitutes%20as%20Alternatives%20to%20Hu...

Lift Asia (2008) *The long here, the big now*, accessed 19 February 2011. http://liftconference.com/long-here-big-now

Lindgren, M. and Bandhold, H. (2009) *Scenario Planning: The Link between Future and Strategy*. New York: Palgrave Macmillan.

Lipschutz, R.L. (2006) Soylent Green . . . . . is . . . . PEOPLE!': Labour, bodies and capital in the global political economy. *Millennium – Journal of International Studies* 34, 573–578.

Lister, G. (1999) *Hopes and fears for the future of health: A European scenario for health and care in 2022*, accessed 2 October 2008. http://www.jbs.cam.ac.uk/research/health/polfutures/pdf/hopes.pdf

Lock, S. (2010) Are you smart phone savvy? *Victorian Tourism Conference 2010*, University of Ballarat.

Lohman, M. and Danielsson, J. (2004) How to get the future of tourism out of today's consumer survey. Prospects for senior and kids travel in Germany. *7th International Forum on Tourism Statistics*, Stockholm, Sweden. 9–11th June, accessed 10 October 2011. http://www.tourismforum.scb.se/Consumer_Surveys.asp

Lonely Planet (2011) *Mobile*, accessed 16 February 2011. http://www.lonelyplanet.com/mobile/

Lookotels (2011) *Home*, accessed 10 February 2011. http://www.lookotels.com/htmls/indexUK.html

Los Angeles Convention & Visitor Bureau (2008) *Research briefing*, accessed 12 July 2009. http://discoverlosangeles.com/business-services/research-and-reports/lastatspublic08.pdf

Lynn, R. (2004) *Ins and outs of teledildonics*, accessed 24 September 2009. http://www.wired.com/culture/lifestyle/commentary/sexdrive/2004/09/65064

Lynton, N. and Thogersen, K.H. (2010) *Reckoning with Chinese Gen Y*. 25 January. Accessed on 4th January 2011 at www.businessweek.com/globalbiz/content/jan2010/qb20100125-065225.htm

Mair, J. and Thompson, K. (2009) The UK association conference attendance decision-making process. *Tourism Management* 30, 400–409.

Malthus, T. and Gilbert, G. (2008) *An Essay on the Principle of Population*. Oxford: Oxford Press.

Mareli, Z. (2007) *Software learns when it pays to deceive. New Scientist 30th May*, accessed 7 June 2009. http://www.newscientist.com/article/mg19426066.600-software-learns-when-it-pays-to-deceive.html

Martin, C., Steege, F. and Gross, H. (2010) Estimation of pointing poses for visually instructing mobile robots under real world conditions. *Gross Robotics and Autonomous Systems* 15, 174–185.

Maslow, A. (1998) *Toward a Psychology of Being*. New York: Wiley.

Maslow, A.H. (1970) *Motivation and Personality* (2nd edn). New York: Harper & Row.

McCarthy, C. (2009) *Google powers new NYC information hub*. 21 January. Accessed 10th April 2011 at news.cnet.com/8301-13577_3-101474-36.html

McEwen, W., Fang, X., Zhang, C. and Burkholder, R. (2006) Inside the mind of the Chinese consumer. *Harvard Business Review* March, 1–9.

McKeough, T. (2009) Somnus-Neu: Grier Govorko's Multimedia Bed. 1 November. Accessed 16th May 2011 at www.fastcompany.com/magazine/140/the-multimedia-bed.html

McKinsey & Co. (2011) *What's the biggest limit on city growth? (Hint: it's not steel or cement)*, accessed 10 February 2011. http://whatmatters.mckinseydigital.com/cities/what-s-the-biggest-limit-on-city-growth-hint-it-s-not-steel-or-cement

Medelin, J., Harou, J., and Olivares, M. (2006) Climate warming and water supply management in California. A Report by the University of California for the California Energy Commission and California Environmental Protection Agency, accessed 22 July. http://www.energy.ca.gov/2005publications/CEC-500-2005-195/CEC-500-2005-195-SF.PDF

Meinhold, B. (2010a) *H2Otel: Water-Powered Hotel Planned for Amsterdam.* 7 December. Accessed on 10th June 2011 at www.inhabitat.com/hzotel-water-powered-hotel-rethinks-hospitality

Meinhold, B. (2010b) *Lookotels Seeks to Roll Out Prefabricated Capsule Hotels in Spain.* 11 May. Accessed on 10th June 2011 at www.inhabitat.com/lookabels-a-prefabricated-capsule-hotel-concept/

Mennell, S. (1997) On the civilizing of appetite. In C. Counihan and P. van Esterik (eds) *Food and Culture: A Reader* (pp. 315–337). New York: Routledge.

Menzel, P. and D'Aluisio, F. (2009) *Evolution of a New Species.* Cambridge: MIT Press.

Merola, N. and Peña, J. (2010) The effects of avatar appearance in virtual worlds. *Journal of Virtual Worlds Research* 2, accessed 25 November 2010. http://journals.tdl.org/jvwr/article/view/843/706

Meston, C. and Buss, D.M. (2007) Why humans have sex. *Archives of Sexual Behaviour* 36, 477–507.

Metro (2008) *I want a mobile future? Long term transportation plan*, accessed 22 July 2010. http://www.metro.net/projects_studies/images/2008_draft_lrtp.pdf

Miah, A. (2004) *Genetically Modified Athletes.* London: Routledge.

Miller, C.C. (2010) *E-Books Top Hardcovers at Amazon.* 19 July. Accessed on 21st November 2011 at www.nytimes.com/2010/07/20/technology/20kindle.html

Mishima, S. (2011) *Japanese capsule hotels*, accessed 10 February 2011. http://gojapan.about.com/cs/accommodation/a/tokyocapsule1.htm

Mollenhorst, H., Volker, B. and Flap, H. (2008) Social context and personal relationships: The effect of meeting opportunities on similarity for relationships of different strength. *Mobilities* 30, 60–68.

Morris, D. (1994) *The Human Animal.* London: BBC Books.

Moscardo, G. and Benckendorff, P. (2010) Mythbusting: Generation Y and travel. In P. Benckendorff, G. Moscardo and D. Pendergast (eds) *Tourism and Generation Y* (pp. 16–26). Wallingford, Oxfordshire: CAB International.

Moscardo, G., Murphy, L. and Benckendorff, P. (2011). Generation Y and travel futures. In I. Yeoman, C. Hsu, K. Smith and S. Watson (eds) *Tourism and Demography* (pp. 87–100). Oxford: Goodfellow.

Mueller, H. and Kaufmann, E.L. (2001) Wellness tourism: Market analysis of a special health tourism segment and implications for the hotel industry. *Journal of Vacation Marketing* 7, 5–17.

Muskat, M. and Quack, H. (2005) The demographic change in Germany: Implication on tourism and leisure activity in the year 2015. In K. Wiermair, H. Pechlaner and T. Bieger (eds) *Time Shift, Leisure and Tourism: Impacts of Time Allocation on Successful Products and Services* (pp. 305–324). Berlin: Eric Schidt Verlag.

Mulcahy, J.D. (2009) Making the case for a viable, sustainable, gastronomic tourism industry in Ireland. Dissertation submitted in partial fulfilment of the requirements of the Degree of Master of Arts (Gastronomy). School of History and Politics, University of Adelaide.

Nanotechnology Now (2010) *European effort to bring smart textile at industrial manufacturing level.* 3 November.

NRC Handelsbad (2009) *Police ignore trafficking in women*, accessed 24 September 2009. http://www.nrc.nl/

Nolan, W. and Johnson, G. (1967) *Logan's Run*. New York: Corgi Books.

Ockels, W. (2011) *Energie oplossingen voor parken*. Keynote presentation at Landal Bestuurdersbijeenkomst 2011. Duurzaam; Onderneem 't samen! 7 April 2011.

OECD (2007) *Pension at a Glance*. Paris: OECD, accessed 15 October. http://www.oecd.org/document/35/0,3343,en_2649_34757_38717411_1_1_1_1,00.html

Office of Shanghai Chronicles (2009) *Real estate*, accessed 10 February 2011. http://www.shtong.gov.cn/node2/node82288/node82501/node82516/userobject1ai113507.html

Opperman, M. (1999) Sex tourism. *Annals of Tourism Research* 26, 251–266.

Orange (2008) *Orange future of football report*, accessed 23 May 2009. http://www.orange.co.uk/sport/football/pics/3395_1.htm

Owen, P. and Weatherston, C. (2002) Professionalization of New Zealand Rugby Union: Historical background, structural changes and competitive balance. University of Otago Economics Discussion Papers. No 0214, accessed 22 May 2009. http://divcom.otago.ac.nz/econ/research/discussionpapers/DP0214.pdf

Page, S. and Connell, J. (2006) *Tourism: A Modern Synthesis*. London: Thomson.

Page, S., Yeoman, I. and Greenwood, C. (2009) Transport and tourism in Scotland. A case study of scenario planning at VisitScotland. In S. Gossling, M. Hall and D. Weaver (eds) *Sustainable Tourism Futures: Perspectives on Systems, Restructuring and Innovations*. London: Routledge.

Page, S., Yeoman, I., Connell, J. and Greenwood, C. (2010) Scenario planning as a tool to understand uncertainty in tourism: The example of transport and tourism in Scotland 2025. *Current Issues in Tourism*. 13, 99–137.

Parry, M., Canziani, J., Lindem, P. and Hanson, C. (2007) *Contribution of Working Group II to the Fourth Assessment Report of the Intergovernmental Panel on Climate Change, 2007*. Cambridge: Cambridge University Press.

Parviz, B.A. (2009) *Augmented Reality in a Contact Lens*, accessed 10 September 2011. http://spectrum.ieee.org

Patel, R. (2007) *Stuffed and Starved*. London: Portfolio Books.

Peeters, P. (2010) Tourism transport, technology, and carbon emissions. In C. Schott, (ed.) *Tourism and the Implications of Climate Change: Issues and Actions. Bridging Tourism Theory and Practice* (Vol. 3, pp. 67–90). London: Emerald.

Pimentel, D. and Hart, K. (2008) Population growth in California – A threat to land and food production. *Cornell University Working Paper Series*, accessed 21 July 2011. http://74.125.155.132/search?q=cache:YPuoQrVBgXgJ:www.populationmedia.org/wp-content/uploads/2008/10/david-pimentel-rapid-population-growth-in-california.doc+Rapid+Population+Growth+in+California+A+Threat+to+Land+and+Food+Production&cd=2&hl=en&ct=clnk&gl=nz

Plog, S.C. (1974) Why destination areas rise and fall in popularity. *Cornell Hotel and Restaurant Administration Quarterly* 14, 55–58.

Poon, T. (2006) *Digital Holography and Three-Dimensional Display: Principles and Applications*. London: Springer.

Pricewaterhouse Coopers (2007) *Pharma 2020: The vision. which path will take you?* accessed 12 December 2009. http://www.pwc.com/gx/en/pharma-life-sciences/pharma-2020/pharma-2020-vision-path.jhtml

Pritchard, A. and Morgan, N. (2006) Hotel Babylon? Exploring hotels as liminal sites of transition and transgression. *Tourism Management* 27, 762–772.

Putz-Willems, M. (2009) Hotel architecture: Less is more – Or: Natural sustainable. In R. Conrady and M. Buck (eds) *Trends and Issues in Global Tourism*. Berlin: Springerlink.

Qian, Y. (2009) *Shanghai tourism may shatter records*. 29 April. Acessed 29th April 2011 at www.chinatrainticket.net/china-train-news/090506.htm

Roco, M. and Bainbridge, W. (2001) *Converging Technologies for Improving Human Performance.* NSF/DOC sponsored report. Arlington.

Rozema, J. and Flowers, T. (2008) Crops for a salinized world. *Science* 322, 478–1480.

Rifkin, J. (1984) *The Age of Access: The New Culture of Hypercapitalism, Where all of Life is a Paid-For Experience.* London: Tarcher.

Rivard, D., Poitevin, J., Plasse, D., Carleton, M. and Currie, D.J. (2000) Changing species, richness and compostion of Canadian National Parks. *Conservation Biology* 14, 1099–1109.

Ruvinsky, J. (2003). *Haptic technology simulates the sense of touch – via computer tactile interface lets surgeons make 'incisions'; computer gamers feel their golf drives,* accessed 2 March 2011. http://news.stanford.edu/news/2003/april2/haptics-42.html

Sachs, A. (2010) *The travel gold rush 2020,* accessed 1 January 2010. www.oef.com/free/pdfs/travelgoldrush2020.pdf

Saenz, A. (2010) *Google puts artificial intelligence into the cloud with new API.* 25 August.

Salton, J. (2009) *Gestural interfaces make touch screens look so 'last year'.* 13 December.

Sanchez-Azofeifa, G.A., Daily, G., Pfaff, A. and Busch, C. (2002) Integrity and isolation of Costa Rica's National Parks and Biological reserves: Examining the dynamics of land cover change. *Biological Conservation* 109, 123–135.

Santich, B. (1996) *Looking for Flavour.* Kent Town: Wakefield Press.

Saunders, Y. (2008) *Paying for Pleasure: Men Who Buy Sex.* Cullompton: William Publishing.

Saunders, T. (2009) *Cisco Sets Sail for Teleconferencing,* accessed 5 September 2010. http://www.v3.co.uk/vnunet/news/2158699/cisco-sets-sail

Savills (2009) *Hospitality, Shanghai – China,* accessed 10 February 2011. http://www.savills.com.hk/research-pdfs/asian-city—sh-1h-2010.pdf

Scherer, J. (2006) Interview with Fraser Holland, Sponsorship and Marketing Manager, New Zealand Rugby Union. *International Journal of Sports Marketing & Sponsorship.* January, p. 98, accessed 7 June 2009. http://find.galegroup.com/itx/infomark.do?action=interpret&contentSet_IAC-Documents&type=retrieve&tabID=T002&prodId=AONE&docId=A143440351&source=gale&version=1.0&userGroupName=vuw&finalAuth=true

Schwartz, B. (2004) *Paradox of Choice.* New York: Harper Collins.

Scott, D., McBoyle, G. and Schwartzentruber, M. (2004) Climate change and the distribution of resources for tourism in North America. *Climate Research* 27, 105–117.

Shanghai Municipal Statistics Bureau (2006) *Shanghai basic facts,* accessed 29 January 2011. http://www.stats-sh.gov.cn/english/shgl/qjmb/qjmb.htm

Shanghai Municipal Statistics Bureau (2010) *Statistical Yearbook 2010,* accessed 29 January 2011. http://www.stats-sh.gov.cn/2004shtj/tjnj/tjnj2010.htm

Shanghai World Expo (2010) *Brief Introduction of World Expo Shanghai,* accessed 29 January 2011. http://en.expo2010.cn/a/20081116/000004.htm

Shankland, S. (2011) *Coming soon: Wave your hand to control your phone.* 17 February.

Shared Hope International (2007) *Demand,* accessed 24 September 2009. http://www.sharedhope.og/files/demand_us.pdf

Shoemaker, P. and Shoemaker, J. (2009) *Chips, Clones and Living Beyond 100.* London: Pearson Education.

Singapore Business Times (2009) *Becoming a biomedical hub,* 14th July, accessed 10 February 2012. http://www.biotechsingapore.com

Singapore Tourist Board (2009) *Tourism statistics,* accessed 10 April 2010. http://app.stb.gov.sq

Sikken, B., Davies, N., Hayashi, C. and Olkkonen, H. (2007) *The Future of Pensions and Healthcare in a Rapidly Ageing World: Scenarios to 2030.* Bern: World Economic Forum.

Sinn, H. (1999) The crisis in Germany's pension insurance systems and how it can be solved. *NBER Working Paper NI 7304*. Cambridge, MA: National Bureau of Economic Research.

SixthSense (2009) *About*, accessed 19 February 2011. http://www.pranavmistry.com/projects/sixthsense/

SmartAction (2011) *Artificial Intelligence*, accessed 27 February 2011. http://www.smartaction.com/our-difference/artificial-intelligence

Smith, C. (2010) *The next oil shock. Parliamentary library*, accessed 6 December 2011. http://www.parliament.nz/en-NZ/ParlSupport/ResearchPapers/4/6/a/00PLEco10041-The-next-oil-shock.htm

Social Security Administration (2002) *Social Security throughout the World*. Washington, DC: SAA.

SPARC (2009) *Sport, Recreation and Physical Activity Participation among New Zealand Adults*. Wellington: SPARC Publication.

Spire Research and Consulting (2010) Generation Y and Z: Is marketing to the young all about technology? Accessed 10 September 2011. http://jp.spireresearch.com

Stancil, B. and Dadush, U. (2010) *The world order in 2050*, accessed 30 December 2010. http://carnegieendowment.org/files/World_Order_in_2050.pdf

Statistics Singapore (2012) *Statistics tourism*, accessed at http://www.singstat.gov.sg/stats/themes/economy/tourism.htm#

Statistics New Zealand (2009) *Population projections*, accessed 25 May 2009. http://www.stats.govt.nz/analytical-reports/human-capital-statistics/part-1-demographics-and-health.htm

Stein, M. (1974) *Lovers, Friends, Slaves, Nine Male Sexual Types: Their Psychological Transactions with Call Girls*. New York: Berkeley Publishing.

Steigert, K. and Kim, D.H. (2009) *Structural Changes in Food Retailing: Six Country Case Studies*. FRSG Publications, accessed 10 November 2010. http://www.aae.wisc.edu/fsrg/publications/Monographs/!food_retailing2009.pdf

Stelarc, D. (2000) From psycho-body to cyber-systems: Images as post-human entities. In D. Bell and B. Kennedy (eds) *The Cybercultures Reader* (pp. 560–576). New York: Routledge.

Stern, N. (2006) *The Economics of Climate Change*. Cabinet Office, HM Treasury. Cambridge: Cambridge University Press.

Steynberg, A. and Dry, A. (2004) *Fischer–Tropsch Technology*. Amsterdam: Elsevier.

Stiehl, W.D. and Breazeal, C. (2005) Affective touch for robotic companions. *Proceedings of Affective Computing and Intelligent Interaction*, Bejing.

Strachan, S. and Murray-Smith, R. (2009) Bearing-based selection in mobile spatial interaction. *Pers Ubiquit Comput* 13, 265–280.

Strahen, D. (2008) *The Last Oil Shock: A Survival Guide to the Imminent Extinction of Petroleum Man*. London: John Murray Books.

Strand, S. (1999) Forecasting the future: Pitfalls in controlling for uncertainty. *Futures* 31, 333–350.

Sukhdev, P. (2010) *Mainstreaming the economics of nature*, accessed 10 December 2010. http://www.teebweb.org/Portals/25/TEEB%20Synthesis/TEEB_SynthReport_09_2010_online.pdf

Swartz, D. (1998) *Culture and Power: The Sociology of Pierre Bourieu*. Chicago: University of Chicago Press.

Syed, A. (2011) *Advanced Building Technologies for Sustainability*. Chichester: John Wiley & Son.

Talwar, R. (2009) *Interview with Futurist Rohit Talwar on the Future of the Meetings Industry*. 19th November.

Talwar, R. (2010a) *Hotels 2020: Beyond segmentation*, accessed 20 March 2011 http://www.amadeus.com/hotelit/beyond-segmentation.html

Talwar, R. (2010b) *Conventions 2020*, accessed 30 December 2010. http://convention2020.meetingsreview.com/

Tan, L. (2010) *Women who buy sex back corkey's brothel plan*, accessed on the 17 September 2010. http://www.nzherald.co.nz/nz/news/article.cfm?c_id=1&objectid=10664197

Tapscott, D. (2009) *Grown Up Digital*. New York: McGraw-Hill.

Techcast (2001) *Artificial Intelligence (AI)*, accessed 1 March 2011. http://techcast.org/BreakthroughAnalysis.aspx?ID=92

Techcast (2010) *Online technology forecasting survey*, accessed 23 February 2011. http://techcast.org/BreakthroughAnalysis.aspx?ID=54

Techcast (2011) *Biometrics*, accessed 23 February 2011.

The Economist (2010) Light without logic: Optical devices are finally going inside computers, but only in parts. 13 May.

The Wheelchair Guide (2008) *Wheelchair controls and BCI*, accessed 1 March 2011. http://www.wheelchairguide.net/wheelchair-controls-and-bci/

TNS Global (2008) *Digital life digital world*, accessed 15 February 2011. http://www.tnsglobal.com/_assets/files/TNS_Market_Research_Digital_World_Digital Life.pdf

Todras-Whitehill, E. (2006) *In 2014 You'll Never Have to Clean Your House Again*. 6 January.

Toshiba (2005) *Toshiba to showcase advances in sophisticated home life support Robot*, accessed 6 February 2011. http://www.toshiba.co.jp/about/press/2005_05/pr2001.htm

Tourism New Zealand (2010) *100% Web ready*, accessed 18 February 2011. http://www.tourismnewzealand.com/campaigns/consumer-marketing/100percent-web-ready-/

Travelmole (2007) *India – A Market of Incredible Opportunity*, accessed 10 December 2010. http://www.travelmole.com/stories/1116229.php?mpnlog=1

Travolution (2009) *Best Way to Book is Online, Says Children Survey*, accessed 1 February 2011. http://www.travolution.co.uk/articles/2009/08/20/2806/best-way-to-book-is-online-says-childrens-survey.html

Trend Hunter (2008) *Insperience Economcy*, accessed 16 September 2009. www.trendhunter.com

Trendwatching (2008) *Trendwatching Yearly Report 2008*, accessed 23 May 2008. www.trendwaching.com.

Tucker, P. (2008) AI chasers. *The Futurist* 42, 14–20.

Turkle, S. (2005) *Second Self: Computers and the Human Spirit*. Boston: MIT Press.

Turner, D., Giorno, C., De Serres, A., Vourch, A. and Richardson, P. (1998) The macroeconomic implications of ageing on a global context. *OECD Ageing Working Paper* AWP1-2, Paris. France: OECD.

UNODC (2009) *Global report on trafficking in persons*, accessed 26 September 2009. http://www.unodc.org/documents/human-trafficking/Global_Report_on_TIP.pdf

UN World Tourism Organization (2009) *Barometer 7*, 9–10.

United Nations (2009) *World Populations Prospects: The 2008 Revision*. New York: United Nations.

United Nations (2010) *State of Cities Report*, accessed 10 November 2011. http://www.unhabitat.org/content.asp?cid=8051&catid=7&typeid=46&subMenuId=0

United Nations (2011) *World population prospects*, accessed 2nd March 2011 at www. esa.un.org/unpd/wpp/Excel-Data/population.htm

United Nations Population Division (2011) *World Population Prospects: The 2010 Revision*. New York: United Nations.

United Nations World Tourism Organisation (2010) *Economics*, accessed 10 December 2010. http://www.unwto.org/facts/menu.html

United Nations World Tourism Organisation and European Travel Commission (2008) *The Indian Outbound Travel Market with a Special Insight into the Image of Europe as a Destination*. Madrid: World Tourism Organisation.

United Nations World Tourism Organisation and European Travel Commission (2009) *The China Outbound Travel Market with a Special Insight into the Image of Europe as a Destination*. Madrid: World Tourism Organisation.

University of California, Irvine (2008) *Scientists to Study Synthetic Telepathy*, accessed 1 March 2011. http://today.uci.edu/iframe.php?p=/news/release_detail_iframe.asp?key=1808

USA Today (2008) *Six get heavy sentences in Dutch human trafficking trial*, accessed 24 September 2009. http://www.usatoday.com/news/world/2008-07-11-Dutch-human-trafficking_N.htm

Utter, D. (2006) *Biometrics comes to Disney world*. 1 September.

Veen, M. (2003) When food is luxury. *World Archaeology* 34, 405–427.

Warde, A. and Hetherington, K. (1994). English households and routine food practices. *Sociological Review* 42, 758–778.

Warde, A. and Martens, L. (2000) *Eating Out: Social Differentiation, Consumption and Pleasure*. Cambridge: Cambridge University Press.

WATG (2011a) *Redefining the urban hotel experience*, accessed 10 February 2011. http://www.watg.com/?pageid=C2DB3073-1372-6883-16030E669C7CFB1F

WATG (2011b) *Bucket list lodging*, accessed 1 February 2011. http://www.watg.com/?pageid=E466F313-1372-6883-16946FE0F46F7F86

Watters, E. (2004) *Urban Tribes: Are Friends the New Family?* New York: Bloomsbury.

Watter, E. (2003) *Urban Tribes*. New York: Bloomsbury.

Watson, J. (2004) *DNA: The Secret Life*. London: Arrow Books.

Weiser, M. and Brown, J.S. (1996) *The coming age of calm technology*, accessed 5 February 2011. http://www.ubiq.com/hypertext/weiser/acmfuture2endnote.htm

Whitehead, G. (2005a) The Future of an Information Society. Lecture to VisitScotland Future Tourism Series. 17 March, Edinburgh.

Whitehead, G. (2005b) Where Are You Going? VisitScotland Futures Lecturers. Apex Hotel, Edinburgh, 13 September.

Willmott, M. and Nelson, W. (2005) *Complicated Lives: The Malaise of Modernity*. Chichester: Wiley.

Wolpaw, J.R., Birbaumer, N., McFarland, D.J., Pfurtscheller, G. and Vaughan, T.M. (2002) Brain–computer interfaces for communication and control. *Clinical Neurophysiology* 113, 767–791.

World Bank (2007) *World Economic Prospects*. New York: World Bank.

World Bank (2009) *Global economic prospects: Technology diffusion in the developing world*, accessed 30 December 2010. http://siteresources.worldbank.org/INTGEP2008/Resources/complete-report.pdf

World Economic Forum (2007) *Travel and Tourism Competitiveness Report*. Geneva: WEF.

Yang, S. (2004) *UC Berkeley researchers developing robotic exoskeleton that can enhance human strength and endurance*, accessed 14 June 2004. http://www.berkeley.edu/news/media/releases/2004/03/03_exo.shtml

YDreams (2010) *Visitors Centre, Ciudad Grupo Santander, Madrid*, accessed 25 February 2011. http://www.ydreams.com/#/en/projects/publicurbanexperiences/gruposantanderfinancialcityvisitorscenterydreams/

Yeoman, I. (2008) *Tomorrows Tourists: Scenarios & Trends*. Oxford: Elsevier.

Yeoman, I. (2010a) *The new food tourist: Gordon Ramsay eat your heart out*, accessed 10 November 2011. http://www.tomorrowstourist.com/food_tourist.php

Yeoman, I. (2010b) Demography trends. In I. Yeoman, C. Hsu, K. Smith and S. Watson (eds) *Tourism and Demography* (Chapter 1). Oxford: Goodfellows.

Yeoman, I. and McMahon-Beattie, U. (2006) Tomorrow's tourist and the information society. *Journal of Vacation Marketing* 12, 269–291.

Yeoman, I. and Butterfield, S. (2011) Tourism and demography: An overview. In I. Yeoman, C. Hsu, K. Smith and S. Watson (eds) *Tourism and Demography* (pp. 1–22). Oxford: Goodfellows.

Yeoman, I., Lennon, J., Blake, A., Galt, M., Greenwood, C. and McMahon-Beattie, U. (2007) Oil depletion: What does this mean for Scottish tourism. *Tourism Management* 25, 1354–1385.

Yeoman, I., Hsu, C., Smith, K. and Watson, S. (2010) *Tourism and Demography*. Oxford: Goodfellow.

Yeoman, I., Hsu, C., Smith, K. and Watson, S. (2011) *Tourism and Demography*. Oxford: Goodfellows

Ying, W. (2011) Land prices hit record highs in Shanghai area. *China Daily*, accessed 23 February 2011 at http://www.chinadaily.com.cn/usa/business/2011-02/15/content_12015940.htm

Yoshimi, T., Matsuhira, N., Suzuki, K., Tamamonto, D., Ozaki, F., Hirokawa, J. and Ogawa, H. (2004) Development of a concept model of a robotic information home appliance, ApriAlpha. *Proceedings of 2004 IEEE/RSJ International Conference on Intelligent Robots and Systems*, Sendai, Japan, 28 September–2 October.

Zhang, H.Q, Pine, R. and Lam, T. (2005) *Tourism and Hotel Development in China: From Political to Economic Success*. New York: Haworth Hospitality Press.

Zin, A. (1998) Leisure traveler choice models of Theme Hotels using psychographics. *Journal of Travel Research* 36, 3–15.

Index

Lightning Source UK Ltd.
Milton Keynes UK
UKHW020005110119

335361UK00003B/269/P